WITHDRAWN

A Theory of Socialism and Capitalism

The Ludwig von Mises Institute's Studies in Austrian Economics

306.3
H777t

A Theory of Socialism and Capitalism

Economics, Politics, and Ethics

Hans-Hermann Hoppe
Department of Economics
University of Nevada, Las Vegas

Kluwer Academic Publishers
Boston/Dordrecht/London

Distributors for North America:
Kluwer Academic Publishers
101 Philip Drive
Assinippi Park
Norwell, Massachusetts 02061 USA

Distributors for the UK and Ireland:
Kluwer Academic Publishers
Falcon House, Queen Square
Lancaster LA1 1RN, UNITED KINGDOM

Distributors for all other countries:
Kluwer Academic Publishers Group
Distribution Centre
Post Office Box 322
3300 AH Dordrecht, THE NETHERLANDS

Library of Congress Cataloging-in-Publication Data

Hoppe, Hans-Hermann.
A theory of socialism and capitalism : economics, politics, and ethics / by Hans-Hermann Hoppe.
p. cm.
Includes index.
ISBN 0-89838-279-3
1. Socialism. 2. Capitalism. 3. Property 4. Comparative economics. 5. Comparative government. I. Title.
HX73.H67 1988
306′.3--dc 19 88-14066
CIP

Copyright © 1989 by Kluwer Academic Publishers

All rights reserved. No part of this publication may be reproduced, stored in a retrieval system, or transmitted in any form or by any means, mechanical, photocopying, recording, or otherwise, without the prior written permission of the publisher, Kluwer Academic Publishers, 101 Philip Drive, Assinippi Park, Norwell, Massachusetts 02061.

Printed in the United States of America

Contents

88-8061

Contents

About the Author

Hans-Hermann Hoppe was born on September 2, 1949, in Peine, West Germany. He attended the Universitatet des Saarlandes, Saarbruecken, the Goethe-Universitaet, Frankfurt/M., and the University of Michigan, Ann Arbor, for studies in Philosophy, Sociology, History, and Economics. He earned his Ph.D. (Philosophy, 1974) and his "Habilitation" (Sociology and Economics, 1981), both from the Goethe-Universitaet, Frankfurt/M.

He taught at several German universities as well as at the Johns Hopkins University Bologna Center for Advanced International Studies, Bologna, Italy. He is presently a Professor of Economics at the University of Nevada, Las Vegas and a Senior Fellow of the Ludwig von Mises Institute.

Hoppe is the author of *Handeln und Erkennen* (Bern 1976); *Kritik der kausalwissenschaftlichen Sozialforschung* (Opladen 1983); *Eigentum, Anarchie und Staat* (Opladen 1987) and numerous articles on philosophy, economics and the social sciences.

Acknowledgements

Three institutions assisted me while I wrote this treatise. As a Heisenberg Scholar I enjoyed the most generous financial support from the German Science Foundation (DFG) from 1982 through 1986. The present study is the most recent work I completed during this period. Additional support came from the Johns Hopkins University Bologna Center for Advanced International Studies, where I spent the academic year 1984-1985 as a Visiting Professor. The lectures delivered there provided the core of what is presented here. Finally, during the academic year 1985/86, when my research took on its present form and which I spent in New York City, I received the most unbureaucratic and cordial help from the Center for Libertarian Studies.

My wife Margaret gave unflagging emotional support for my work. She also took on the task, often enough against my stubborn resistance, of editing my writing in a foreign language.

My deepest gratitude is to my teacher and friend Murray N. Rothbard. To his scholarly and personal example I owe more than I can properly express. He read an earlier draft of the study and provided me with invaluable comments. Innumerous discussions with him were a never ending source of inspiration and his enthusiasm was a constant encouragement.

To these people and institutions I owe a sincere "thank you."

A Theory of Socialism and Capitalism

1

INTRODUCTION

The following study on the economics, politics and morals of socialism and capitalism is a systematic treatise on political theory. Interdisciplinary in scope, it will discuss the central problems of political economy and political philosophy: how to organize society so as to promote the production of wealth and eradicate poverty, and how to arrange it so as to make it a just social order.

But in doing this I will also constantly touch upon and illuminate social and political problems in the narrower, more common sense of these terms. In fact, it is one of the major goals of this treatise to develop and explain the conceptual and argumentative tools, economic and moral, needed to analyze and evaluate any kind of empirical social or political system, to understand or appraise any process of social change, and to explain or interpret similarities as well as differences in the social structure of any two or more different societies.

At the end of the treatise it should be clear that only by means of a theory, economic or moral, which is not itself derived from experience but rather starts from a logically incontestable statement (which is something very different from an "arbitrarily postulated axiom") and proceeds in a purely deductive way (perhaps using some explicitly introduced empirical and empirically testable assumption, in addition) to results which are themselves logically unassailable (and thus require no empirical testing whatsoever), will it become possible to organize or interpret an otherwise chaotic, overly complex array of unconnected, isolated facts or opinions about social reality to form a true, coherent economic or moral conceptual system. Hopefully it will be demonstrated that without such a theory, political economy and philosophy can be considered nothing other than groping in the dark, producing, at best, arbitrary opinions on what might have caused this or that, or what is better or worse than something else: opinions, that is, whose opposites can generally be defended as easily as the original positions themselves (which is to say that they cannot be defended in any strict sense at all!).

Specifically, a theory of property and property rights will be developed. It will be demonstrated that socialism, by no means an invention of nineteenth century Marxism but much older, must be conceptualized as an institutionalized interference with or aggression against private property and private property claims. Capitalism, on the other hand, is a social system based on the explicit recognition of private property and of nonaggressive, contractual exchanges between private property owners. Implied in this remark, as will become clear in the course of this treatise, is the belief that there must then exist varying types and degrees of socialism and capitalism, i.e., varying degrees to which private property rights are respected or ignored. Societies are not simply capitalist or socialist. Indeed, all existing societies are socialist to some extent. (Even the United States, certainly a society that is relatively more capitalist than most others, is, as will become apparent, amazingly socialist and has gradually become more so over time.)

One goal then, is to demonstrate that the overall degree of socialism, i.e., the overall degree of interference with property rights that exists in a given country, explains its overall wealth. The more socialist a country, the more hampered will be the process of production of new and the upkeep of old, existing wealth, and the poorer the country will remain or become.[1] The fact that the United States is, by and large, richer than Western Europe, and West Germany much richer than East Germany can be explained by their lesser degree of socialism, as can the fact that Switzerland is more prosperous than Austria, or that England, in the nineteenth century the richest country in the world, has now fallen to what is aptly called an underdeveloping country.

But the concern here will not be exclusively with the overall wealth effects, nor with the economic side of the problem alone. For one thing, in analyzing different types of socialism for which there exist real, historical examples (examples which, to be sure, very often are not called socialism, but are given a more appealing name[2]), it is important to explain why, and in what way, *every* intervention anywhere, big or small, here or there, produces a particular disruptive effect on the social structure which a superficial, theoretically untrained observer, blinded by an immediate "positive" consequence of a particular intervention, might not perceive. Yet this negative effect nonetheless exists, and with some delay will cause problems at a different place in the social fabric more numerous or severe than the ones originally solved by the initial act of intervening. Thus, for instance, highly visible positive effects of socialist policies such as "cheap food prices," "low rents," "free" this and "free" that, are not just positive things hanging in mid-air, unconnected to everything else, but rather are phenomena that have to be paid for somehow: by less and lower quality food, by housing shortages, decay and slums, by queuing up and corruption, and, further, by lower living standards, reduced capital-formation, and/or increased capital consumption. And a much less conspicuous but almost always "positively" mentioned fact--a greater feeling of solidarity among the people, the greater value attached to things like family, relatives, or friends, which is found to exist between, for instance, the East Germans as compared to their more "individualistic," egoistic West/German counterparts--is again not a simple, isolated, unanalyzable fact. Such feelings are the result of a social system of constant shortages and of continually repressed opportunities to improve one's situation by one's own means. In East Germany, in order to accomplish the most simple routine tasks, such as a house repair which in other countries requires no more than a telephone call, you simply must rely more heavily on "personal" relations (as compared to impersonal business relations); and where someone's "public" life is under constant observation by "society," you simply have to go private.

Analyzed in some detail are the particular disruptive effects that are produced: (1) by a traditional Marxist policy of nationalizing or socializing the means of production, or rather, by the expropriation of private owners of means of production; (2) by a revisionist, social-democratic policy of egalitarian income redistribution; (3) by a conservatively minded policy of attempting to preserve the status quo through economic and behavioral regulations and price controls; and (4) by a technocratically minded system of pragmatic, piecemeal social and economic engineering and intervention.

These policy types, which will be analyzed sequentially, are not completely homogeneous and mutually exclusive. Each one can be carried through to varying degrees, there are different ways of doing things under each of these categories of policy and the different policy schemes can be combined to a certain extent. In fact, every given society is a mixture of all of them as it is the result of diverse political forces which have varied at different times in strength and influence. The reason for analyzing them separately (apart from the obvious one that not all problems can be discussed at once) is that they constitute policy schemes associated with clearly distinguishable social groups, movements, parties, etc., and that each policy scheme affects overall wealth in a somewhat different way.

And socialism will by no means be analyzed solely from an economic point of view. Of course, socialism, especially its Marxist or so-called "scientific" brand, has always pretended to be an economically superior organization of society (apart from all of its other alleged qualities) compared to the so-called "anarchy of production" of capitalism[3]. But socialism does not collapse once it is demonstrated that in fact the opposite is true and it brings impoverishment, not wealth. Certainly, socialism loses much of its attractiveness for most people once this is understood. However, it is definitely not at its argumentative end so long as it can claim--whatever its *economic* performance may be--that it represents a higher morality, that it is more just, that it has an ethically superior foundation.

Hopefully however, by a close analysis of the theory of property implicit in the different versions of socialism, this treatise will make clear that nothing could be farther from the truth. It will be demonstrated that the property theory implicit in socialism does not normally pass even the first decisive test (the necessary if not sufficient condition) required of rules of human conduct which claim to be morally justified or justifiable. This test, as formulated in the so-called golden rule or, similarly, in the Kantian categorical imperative, requires that in order to be just, a rule must be a *general* one applicable to every single person in the same way. The rule cannot specify different rights or obligations for different categories of people (one for the red- headed, and one for others, or one for women and a different one for men), as such a "particularistic" rule, naturally, could never, not even in principle, be accepted as a fair rule by everyone. Particularistic rules, however, of the type "I can hit you, but you are not allowed to hit me," are, as will become clear in the course of this treatise, at the very base of all practiced forms of socialism. Not only economically but in the field of morals, too, socialism turns out to be an ill-conceived system of social organization. Again, in spite of its bad public reputation, it is capitalism, a social system based squarely on the recognition of private property and of contractual relations between owners of private property, that wins outright. It will be demonstrated that the property theory implicit in capitalism not only passes the first test of "universalization" but it turns out to be the logical precondition (*die Bedingung der Moeglichkeit*) of any kind of argumentative justification: Whoever argues in favor of *anything*, and in particular in favor of certain norms as being fair, must, implicitly at least, presuppose the validity of the property norms implicit in capitalism. To deny their validity as norms of universal acceptability and argue in favor of socialism is thus self-contradictory.

The reconstruction of the morals of private property and its ethical justification then leads to a reevaluation of socialism and, as it turns out, the institution of the state, depending as it does for its very existence on taxation and forced membership (citizenship), as the very incorporation of socialist ideas on property. Without any solid economic or moral reasons for their existence, socialism and the state are then reduced to and will be explained as phenomena of merely socio-psychological relevance.

Led by such considerations, the discussion finally returns to economics. The concluding chapters deal with the constructive task of explaining the workings of a pure capitalist social order as the morally and economically required alternative to socialism. More specifically, they will be devoted to an analysis of how a social system based on a private property ethics would come to grips with the problem of monopoly and the production of so-called "public goods," and in particular with the production of security, i.e., of police and judicial services. It will be argued that, contrary to much that has been written in the economics literature on monopoly and public goods, neither problem exists or, if they did exist, would still not suffice in any meaningful sense to prove any economic deficiency in a pure market system. Rather, a capitalist order always, without exception and necessarily so, provides in the most efficient way for the most urgent wants of voluntary consumers, including the areas of police and the courts. With this constructive task completed, the argument will have been brought full circle, and the demolition of the intellectual credibility of socialism, morally and economically, should be complete.

2

PROPERTY, CONTRACT, AGGRESSION, CAPITALISM, SOCIALISM

Before advancing to the more exciting field of analyzing diverse policy schemes from the standpoint of economic theory and political philosophy, it is essential to introduce and explain the basic concepts used throughout the following study. Indeed, the concepts explained in this chapter--the concepts of property, contract, aggression, capitalism and socialism--are so basic, so fundamental, that one cannot even avoid making use of them, if at times only implicitly. Unfortunately, though, the very fact that in analyzing any kind of human action and/or any kind of interpersonal relationship one must make use of these concepts does not imply that everyone has a precise understanding of them. It seems instead to be the other way around. Because the concept of property, for instance, is so basic that everyone seems to have some immediate understanding of it, most people never think about it carefully and can, as a consequence, produce at best a very vague definition. But starting from imprecisely stated or assumed definitions and building a complex network of thought upon them can lead only to intellectual disaster. For the original imprecisions and loopholes will then pervade and distort everything derived from them. To avoid this the concept of property must first be clarified.

Next to the concept of action, *property* is the most basic category in the social sciences. As a matter of fact, all other concepts to be introduced in this chapter--aggression, contract, capitalism and socialism--are definable in terms of property: *aggression* being aggression against property, *contract* being a nonaggressive relationship between property owners, *socialism* being an institutionalized policy of aggression against property, and *capitalism* being an institutionalized policy of the recognition of property and contractualism.

Let us start with an elucidation of the precondition necessary for the concept of property to emerge.[1] For a concept of property to arise, there must be a scarcity of goods. Should there be no scarcity, and should all goods be so-called "free goods" whose use by any one person for any one purpose would not in any way exclude (or interfere with or restrict) its use by any other person or for any other purpose, then there would be no need for property. If, let us say, due to some paradisiac superabundance of bananas, my present consumption of bananas does not in any way reduce my own future supply (possible consumption) of bananas, nor the present or the future supply of bananas for any other person, then the assignment of property rights, here with respect to bananas, would be superfluous. To develop the concept of property, it is necessary for goods to be scarce, so that conflicts over the use of these goods can possibly arise. It is the function of property rights to avoid such possible clashes over the use of scarce resources by assigning rights of exclusive ownership. Property is thus a normative concept: a concept designed to make a conflict-free interaction possible by stipulating mutually binding rules of conduct (norms) regarding scarce resources.[2] It does not need much comment to see that there is indeed scarcity of goods, of all sorts of goods, everywhere, and the need for property rights is thus evident. As a matter of fact, even if we were to assume that we lived in the Garden of Eden, where there was a superabundance of everything needed not only to sustain one's life but to indulge in every possible comfort by simply stretching out one's hand, the concept of property would necessarily have to evolve. For even under these "ideal" circumstances, every person's physical body would still be a scarce resource and thus the need for the establishment of property rules, i.e., rules regarding people's bodies, would exist. One is not used to thinking of one's own body in terms of a scarce good, but in imagining the most ideal situation one could ever hope for, the Garden of Eden, it becomes possible to realize that one's body is indeed the *prototype* of a scarce good for the use of which property rights, i.e., rights of exclusive ownership, somehow have to be established, in order to avoid clashes.

As a matter of fact, as long as a person acts,[3] i.e., as long as a person intentionally tries to change a state of affairs that is subjectively perceived and evaluated as less satisfactory into a state that appears more rewarding, this action necessarily involves a choice regarding the use of this person's body. And choosing, preferring one thing or state over another, evidently implies that not everything, not all possible pleasures or satisfactions, can be had at one and the same time, but rather that something considered less valuable must be given up in order to attain something else considered to be more valuable.[4] Thus choosing always implies the incurrence of costs: foregoing possible enjoyments because the means needed to attain them are scarce and are bound up in some alternative use which promises returns valued more highly than the opportunities forfeited.[5] Even in the Garden of Eden I could not *simultaneously* eat an apple, smoke a cigarette, have a drink, climb up a tree, read a book, build a house, play with my cat, drive a car, etc. I would have to make choices and could do things only sequentially. And this would be so because there is only one body that I can use to do these things and enjoy the satisfaction derived from doing them. I do not have a superabundance of bodies which would allow me to enjoy all possible satisfactions simultaneously, in one single bliss. And I would be restrained by scarcity in another respect as well: as long as this scarce resource "body" is not indestructible and is not equipped with eternal health and energy, but rather is an organism with only a limited life span, time is scarce, too. The time used up in pursuing goal A reduces the time left to pursue other goals. And the longer it takes to reach a desired result, the higher the costs involved in waiting will be, and the higher the expected satisfaction must be in order to justify these costs.

Thus, because of the scarcity of body and time, even in the Garden of Eden property regulations would have to be established. Without them, and assuming now that more than one person exists, that their range of action overlaps, and that there is no preestablished harmony and synchronization of interests among these persons, conflicts over the use of one's own body would be unavoidable. I might, for instance, want to use my body to enjoy drinking a cup of tea, while someone else might want to start a love affair with it, thus preventing me from having my tea and also reducing the time left to pursue my own goals by means of this body. In order to avoid such possible clashes, rules of exclusive ownership must be formulated. In fact, so long as there is action, there is a necessity for the establishment of property norms.

To keep things simple and free of distracting details let us continue to assume, for another stretch of analysis, that we indeed inhabit a Garden of Eden, where exclusively one's body, its standing room, and time are scarce resources. What can the prototype of a scarce good, a person's body, tell us about property and its conceptual derivatives?

While even in a world with only one type of scarce resource all sorts of norms regulating exclusive ownership with respect to scarce means are conceivable in principle (for example, a rule such as "On Mondays I determine to which uses our bodies can be put, on Tuesdays you determine their use," etc.), it is certain that not all of them would in fact have the same chance of being proposed and accepted. It then seems to be best to start one's analysis with the property norm, which would most likely be accepted by the inhabitants of Eden as the "natural position" regarding the assignment of rights of exclusive ownership in bodies. To be sure, at this stage of the argument we are not yet concerned with ethics, with the problem of the moral justification of norms. Thus, while it can well be admitted from the very outset that I am indeed going to argue later on that the natural position is the only morally defendable one, and while I am also convinced that it is the natural one *because* it is morally defendable, at this stage, natural does not imply any moral connotation. It is simply meant to be a socio-psychological category used to indicate that this position would probably find the most support in public opinion.[6] Indeed, its naturalness is reflected by the very fact that in talking about bodies, it is almost impossible to avoid using possessive (possession-indicating) expressions as well. A body is normally referred to as a specific person's body: my body, yours, his, etc. (and, incidentally, the same is done whenever one speaks of actions!); and one does not have the slightest problem distinguishing what is mine, yours, etc.; clearly, in doing so, one is assigning property-titles and distinguishing between proper owners of scarce resources.

What, then, *is* the natural position regarding property implicit in one's natural way of speaking about bodies? Every person has the exclusive right of ownership of his body within the boundaries of its surface. Every person can put his body to those uses that he thinks best for his immediate or long-run interest, well-being, or satisfaction, as long as he does not interfere with another person's rights to control the use of his/her respective body. This "ownership" of one's own body implies one's right to invite (agree to) another person's doing something with (to) one's own body: my right to do with my body whatever I want, that is, includes the right to ask and let someone else use my body, love it, examine it, inject medicines or drugs into it, change its physical appearance and even beat, damage, or kill it, if that should be what I like and agree to. Interpersonal relationships of this sort are and will be called *contractual exchanges*. They are characterized by the fact that an agreement on the use of scarce resources is reached, which is based on mutual respect and recognition of each and all of the exchanging partners' domain of exclusive control over their respective bodies. By definition, such contractual exchanges, while not necessarily advantageous for each and all of the exchanging partners *in retrospect* (I might not like my looks afterwards, even though the surgeon did exactly what I told him to do to my face), are always, and necessarily so, mutually advantageous for every participant ex ante, otherwise the exchange simply would not take place.

If, on the other hand, an action is performed that uninvitedly invades or changes the physical integrity of another person's body and puts this body to a use that is not to this very person's own liking, this action, according to the natural position regarding property, is called *aggression*.[7] It would be aggression if a person tried to satisfy his sexual or sadistic desires by raping or beating another person's body without having this person's explicit consent. And it would be aggression as well, if a person were physically stopped from performing certain actions with his body which might not be to someone else's *liking*, such as wearing pink socks or curly hair, or getting drunk everyday, or first sleeping and then philosophizing instead of doing it the other way around, but which, if indeed performed, would not in itself cause a change in the physical integrity of any other person's body.[8] By definition, then, an aggressive act always and necessarily implies that a person, by performing it, increases his/her satisfaction at the expense of a decrease in the satisfaction of another person.

What is the underlying rationale of this natural position regarding property? At the bottom of the natural property theory lies the idea of basing the assignment of an exclusive ownership right on the existence of an objective, intersubjectively ascertainable link between owner and the property owned and, mutatis mutandis, of calling all property claims that can only invoke purely subjective evidence in their favor aggressive. While I can cite in favor of my property claim regarding my body the objective fact that I was the body's first occupant--its first user--anyone else who claims to have the right to control this body can cite nothing of the sort. No one could call my body a product of his will, as I could claim it to be the product of mine; such a claim to the right to determine the use of the scarce resource "my body" would be a claim of nonusers, of nonproducers, and would be based exclusively on subjective opinion, i.e., on a merely verbal declaration that things should be this or that way. Of course, such verbal claims could (and very likely always will) point to certain *facts*, too ("I am bigger, I am smarter, I am poorer or I am very special, etc.!"), and could thereby try to legitimize themselves. But facts such as these do not (and cannot) establish any objective link between a given scarce resource and any particular person(s). Everyone's ownership of every particular resource can equally well be established or excluded on such grounds. It is such property claims, derived from thin air, with purely verbal links between owners and things owned, which, according to the natural theory of property, are called aggressive. As compared with this, my property claim regarding my body can point to a determinate natural link; and it can do so because my body has been *produced*, and everything produced (as contrasted with things "given"), logically, has a determinate connection with some definite individual producer(s); it has been produced *by me*. To avoid any misunderstanding, "to produce" is not to say "to create out of nothing" (after all, my body is also a naturally given thing); it means to change a naturally given thing according to a plan, to transform nature. It is also not to say "to transform each and every part of it" (after all, my body has lots of parts with respect to which I never did anything!); it means instead to transform a thing within (including/excluding) borders, or, even more precisely, to produce borderlines for things. And finally, "to produce" also is not to say that the process of production must go on indefinitely (after all, I am sleeping sometimes, and my body is certainly not a product of my actions right then!), it simply means that it was produced in the past and can be recognized as such. It is such property claims, then, which can be derived from past, embordering productive efforts and which can be tied to specific individuals as producers, which are called "natural" or "nonaggressive."[9]

The ideas of capitalism and socialism should be almost clear at this point. But before leaving the Garden of Eden once and for all, a look at the *consequences* of the introduction of elements of aggressively founded ownership into paradise should be taken, as this will help elucidate, purely and simply, the central economic and social problem of every type of real socialism, i.e., of socialism in a world of all-around scarcity, the detailed analysis of which then is the concern of the following chapters.

Even in the land of milk and honey, people evidently could choose different lifestyles, set different goals for themselves, have different standards as to what kind of personality they want to develop and what achievements to strive for. True, one would not need to work in order to make a living as there would be a superabundance of everything. But, put drastically, one could still choose to become a drunk or a philosopher, which is to say, more technically, one could choose to put one's body to uses that would be more or less immediately rewarding from the point of view of the acting person, or one could put one's body to such uses which would only bear fruit in a more or less distant future. Decisions of the afore-mentioned type might be called "consumption decisions." Decisions, on the other hand, to put one's body to a use that only pays later, i.e., choices induced by some reward or satisfaction anticipated in a more or less distant future requiring the actor to overcome disutility of waiting (time is scarce!), might be called "investment" decisions--decisions, that is, to invest in "human capital," in the capital embodied in one's own physical body.[10] Now assume that aggressively founded ownership is introduced. Whereas before every person was the exclusive owner of his body and could decide on his own whether to become a drunk or a philosopher, now a system is established in which a person's right to determine how to use his body is curtailed or completely eliminated, and instead, this right is partly or fully delegated to another person who is not naturally linked to the respective body as its producer. What would be the consequence of this? The abolition of private ownership of one's body can be far-reaching: the nonproducers can have the right to determine all of the uses of "my" body all of the time, or their right to do so can be restricted with respect to time and/or domains, and these restrictions again can be flexible (with the nonproducers having the right to change the restrictive definitions according to their own taste) or fixed once and for all, and so the effects can, of course, be more or less drastic! But whatever the degree, socialization of ownership always, and necessarily so, produces two types of effects. The first effect, "economic" in the narrower sense of the term, is a reduction in the amount of investment in human capital as defined above. The natural owner of a body cannot help but make decisions regarding that body as long as he does not commit suicide and decides to stay alive, however restricted his ownership rights might be. But since he can no longer decide on his own, undisturbed by others, to what uses to put his body, the value attached to it by him is now lower; the want satisfaction, the psychic income, that is to say, which he can derive from his body by putting it to certain uses is reduced because the range of options available to him has been limited. But then, with every action necessarily implying costs (as explained above), and with a given inclination to overcome costs in exchange for expected rewards or profits, the natural owner is faced with a situation in which the costs of action must be reduced in order to bring them back in line with the reduced expected income. In the Garden of Eden, there is only one way left to do this: by shortening the waiting time, reducing the disutility of waiting, and choosing a course of action that promises earlier returns. Thus, the introduction of aggressively founded ownership leads to a tendency to reduce investment decisions and favors consumption decisions. Put drastically, it leads to a tendency to turn philosophers into drunks. This tendency is permanent and more

ALLEGHENY COLLEGE LIBRARY

pronounced when the threat of intervention with the natural owner's rights is permanent, and it is less so to the degree that the threat is restricted to certain times or domains. In any case, though, the rate of investment in human capital is lower than it would be with the right of exclusive control of natural owners over their bodies being untouched and absolute.

The second effect might be called social. The introduction of elements of aggressively founded ownership implies a change in the social structure, a change in the composition of society with respect to personality or character types. Abandoning the natural theory of property evidently implies a redistribution of income. The psychic income of persons in their capacity as users of their "own" natural body, as persons expressing themselves in this body and deriving satisfaction from doing so, is reduced *at the expense* of an increase in the psychic income of persons in their capacity as invaders of other peoples' bodies. It has become relatively more difficult and costly to derive satisfaction from using one's body without invading that of others, and relatively less difficult and costly to gain satisfaction by using other peoples' bodies for one's own purposes. This fact alone does not imply any social change, but once a single empirical assumption is made, it does: Assuming that the desire to gain satisfaction at the expense of a loss in satisfaction available to others by instrumentalizing another person's body exists as a human desire, that it may not be instilled in everybody and to the same extent, but that it exists in some people sometimes to some degree and so conceivably can be suppressed or encouraged and favored by some given institutional arrangement, consequences are imminent. And surely, this assumption is true. Then, the redistribution of chances for income acquisition must result in more people using aggression to gain personal satisfaction and/or more people becoming more aggressive, i.e., shifting increasingly from nonaggressive to aggressive roles, and slowly changing their personality as a consequence of this; and this change in the character structure, in the moral composition of society, in turn leads to another reduction in the level of investment in human capital.

In short, with these two effects we have already pinpointed the most fundamental reasons for socialism's being an economically inferior system of property arrangements. Indeed, both effects will reappear again and again in the course of the following analyses of socialist policy schemes. All that is left now is to explain the natural theory of property as regards the real world of all around scarcity, for this is the point of departure for all forms of real socialism.

Notwithstanding some evident differences between bodies and all other scarce resources, all conceptual distinctions can be made and applied again without difficulties: Unlike bodies, which are never "unowned" but always have a natural owner, all other scarce resources can indeed be unowned. This is the case as long as they remain in their natural state, unused by anyone. They only become someone's property once they are treated as scarce means, that is, as soon as they are occupied in some objective borders and put to some specific use by someone. This act of acquiring previously unowned resources is called "original appropriation."[11] Once unowned resources are appropriated it becomes an aggression to uninvitedly change their physical characteristics or to restrict the owner's range of uses to which he can put these resources, as long as a particular use does not affect the physical characteristics of anyone else's property--just as in the case of bodies. Only in the course of a contractual relationship, i.e., when the natural owner of a scarce means explicitly agrees, is it possible for someone else to utilize and change previously acquired things. And only if the original or previous owner deliberately transfers his property title to someone else, either in exchange for something or as a free gift, can this other person himself become the owner of such things. Unlike bodies, though, which for the same "natural" reason can never be *un*owned and also can never be parted with by the natural owner *completely* but only be "lent out" as long as the owners' agreement lasts, naturally all other scarce resources can be "alienated" and a property title for them can be relinquished once and for all.[12]

A social system based on this natural position regarding the assignment of property rights is, and will from now on be called *pure capitalist*. And since its ideas can also be discerned as the dominating ideas of private law, i.e., of the norms regulating relations between private persons, it might also be termed a pure private law system.[13] This system is based on the idea that to be nonaggressive, claims to property must be backed by the "objective" fact of an act of original appropriation, of previous ownership, or by a mutually beneficial contractual relationship. This relationship can either be a deliberate cooperation between property owners or the deliberate transfer of property titles from one owner to another. If this system is altered and instead a policy is instituted that assigns rights of exclusive control over scarce means, however partial, to persons or groups of persons that can point neither to an act of previous usership of the things concerned, nor to a contractual relation with some previous user- owner, then this will be called (partial) *socialism*.

It will be the task of the next four chapters to explain how different ways of deviating from a pure capitalist system, different ways of redistributing property titles away from natural owners of things (i.e., from people who have put some particular resources to a specific use and so are naturally linked to them, and onto people who have not yet done anything with the resources but who have simply made a verbal, declarative claim regarding them) lowers investment and increases consumption, and in addition causes a change in the composition of the population by favoring non-productive over productive people.

3

SOCIALISM RUSSIAN STYLE

We have defined socialism as an institutionalized policy of redistribution of property titles. More precisely, it is a transfer of property titles from people who have actually put scarce means to some use or who have acquired them contractually from persons who have done so previously onto persons who have neither done anything with the things in question nor acquired them contractually. For a highly unrealistic world--the Garden of Eden--I then pointed out the socio-economic consequences of such a system of assigning property rights were then pointed out: a reduction of investment in human capital and increased incentives for the evolution of nonproductive personality types.

I now want to enlarge and concretize this analysis of socialism and its socio-economic impact by looking at different though equally typical versions of socialism. In this chapter I will concentrate on the analysis of what most people have come to view as "socialism par excellence" (if not the only type of socialism there is), this probably being the most appropriate starting point for any discussion of socialism. This "socialism par excellence" is a social system in which the means of production, that is, the scarce resources used to produce consumption goods, are "nationalized" or "socialized."

Indeed, while Karl Marx, and like him most of our contemporary intellectuals of the left, was almost exclusively concerned with the analysis of the economic and social defects of capitalism, and in all of his writings made only a few general and vague remarks about the constructive problem of the organization of the process of production under socialism, capitalism's allegedly superior alternative, there can be no doubt that this is what he considered the cornerstone of a socialist policy and the key to a better and more prosperous future.[1] Accordingly, socialization of the means of production has been advocated by all socialists of orthodox Marxist persuasion ever since. It is not only what the communist parties of the West officially have in store for us, though they become increasingly reluctant to say so in order to seize power. In all of the Western socialist and social-democratic parties a more or less numerous, outspoken, and eloquent minority of some influence also exists, which arduously supports such a scheme and proposes socialization, if not of all means of production, then at least of those of big industry and big business. Most importantly, smaller or bigger sectors of nationalized industries have become part of social reality even in the so-called "most capitalist" countries; and of course an almost complete socialization of the means of production has been tried out in the Soviet Union and later in all of the Soviet-dominated countries of Eastern Europe, as well as in a number of other countries all over the world. The following analysis should thus enable us to understand the economic and social problems of societies, insofar as they are characterized by nationalized means of production. And in particular, it should help us to understand the central problems that plague Russia and its satellites, as these countries have carried a policy of socialization so far that it can justly be said to be their dominant structural feature. It is because of this fact that the type of socialism under investigation is called "Russian" style.[2]

As regards the motivational forces pushing socialization schemes, they are avowedly egalitarian. Once you allow private property in the means of production, you allow differences. If I own resource A, then you do not own it, and our relationship to this resource is thus different. By abolishing private ownership everyone's position vis a vis means of production is equalized with one stroke, or so it seems. Everyone becomes co-owner of everything, reflecting everyone's equal standing as human beings. And the economic rationale of such a scheme is that it is supposedly more efficient. To the untrained observer unfamiliar with the action-coordinating function of prices, capitalism as based on private ownership of means of production simply appears chaotic. It seems to be a wasteful system characterized by duplicating efforts, ruinous competition, and the absence of concerted, coordinated action. As Marxists call it depreciatively, it is an "anarchy of production." Only when collective ownership is substituted for private does it seemingly become possible to eliminate this waste by implementing a single, comprehensive, coordinated production plan.

More important, though, than motivation and promises is what a socialization of means of production really amounts to.[3] The property rules that are adopted under a socialization policy and which constitute the basic legal principles of countries like Russia are characterized by two complementary features. First, nobody owns the socialized means of production; they are "socially" owned, which is to say precisely: no person, or no group of persons, or all taken together is allowed to either acquire them or sell them and keep the receipts from their sale privately. Their use is determined by people not in the role of an owner but of a caretaker of things. And secondly, no person or group of persons or all taken together is allowed to engage newly in private investment and create new private means of production. They can neither invest by transforming the existing, nonproductively used resources into productive ones, by original saving, by pooling resources with other people, nor by a mixture of these techniques. Investment can only be done by caretakers of things, never for private profit, always on behalf of the community of caretakers with whom the possible profits from investments would have to be shared.[4]

What does it mean to have such a caretaker economy? What, in particular, does it imply to change from an economy built on the natural theory of property to a socialized one? In passing, two observations should be made, which will already throw some light on the above-mentioned socialist promises of equality and efficiency. Declaring everybody a co-owner of everything solves the problem of differences in ownership only nominally. It does not solve the real underlying problem: differences in the power to control. In an economy based on private ownership, the owner determines what should be done with the means of production. In a socialized economy this can no longer happen, as there is no such owner. Nonetheless, the problem of determining what should be done with the means of production still exists and must be solved somehow, provided there is no prestabilized and presynchronized harmony of interests among all of the people (in which case no problems whatsoever would exist anymore), but rather some degree of disagreement. Only one view as to what should be done can in fact prevail and others must mutatis mutandis be excluded. But then again there must be inequalities between people: someone's or some groups' opinion must win over that of others. The difference between a private property economy and a socialized one is only *how* whose will prevails in cases of disagreement is to be determined. In capitalism there must be somebody who controls, and others who do not, and hence real differences among people exist, but the issue of whose opinion prevails is resolved by original appropriation and contract. In socialism, too, real differences between controllers and noncontrollers must, of necessity, exist; only in the case of socialism, the position of those whose opinion wins is not determined by previous usership or contract, but by political means.[5] This difference is certainly a highly important one, and our discussion will return to it later in this chapter and again in later chapters, but here it suffices to say that--contrary to socialism's egalitarian promises--it is not a difference between a non-egalitarian and an egalitarian system as regards power of control.

The second observation is intimately connected with the first and concerns socialism's allegedly superior coordinating capabilities. Again closer inspection reveals that the difference is merely illusory, created only by semantics: to say that an economy of private owners is supplanted by a nationalized one creates the impression that instead of a multitude of decision-making units, all of a sudden there is only one such unit. In fact, nothing has changed at all. There are as many individuals with as many different interests as before. Just as much as capitalism then, socialism has to find a solution to the problem of determining how to coordinate the uses of different means of production, given the fact of differing views among people on how this should be accomplished. The difference between capitalism and socialism is again one of *how* coordination is achieved, and not between chaos and coordination, as the socialist semantic insinuates. Instead of simply letting individuals do what they want, capitalism coordinates actions by constraining people to respect previous user-ownership. Socialism, on the other hand, instead of letting people do whatever pleases them, coordinates individual plans by superimposing on one person's or group of persons' plan that of another disagreeing person or group *regardless* of prior ownership and mutual exchange agreements.[6] It hardly deserves comment that this difference, too, is of the utmost importance. But it is not, as Marxist socialism would like us to believe, a difference between social planning and no planning at all; on the contrary, as soon as the coordinating mechanisms of socialism and capitalism are brought into the open and reconstructed, socialism's claim to greater efficiency immediately begins to lose much of its credibility, and the opposite thesis appears to be more convincing.

How well-founded this thesis indeed is, and exactly why it is that capitalism's, and not socialism's, coordinating mechanism proves to be economically superior will become clear when one turns away from apparent differences and concentrates on real ones instead, and looks at the redistribution of property titles, and hence of income, which is implied in giving up capitalism in favor of a caretaker economy, as characterized above. From the standpoint of the natural theory of property--the foundation of capitalism--the adoption of the basic principles of a caretaker economy means that property titles are redistributed away from actual producers and users of means of production, and away from those who have acquired these means by mutual consent from previous users, to a community of caretakers in which, at the very best, every person remains the caretaker of the things he previously owned. But even in this case each previous user and each contractor would be hurt, as he could no longer sell the means of production and keep the receipt from the sale privately, nor could he privately appropriate the profit from using them the way they are used, and hence the value of the means of production *for him* would fall. Mutatis mutandis, every nonuser and noncontractor of these means of production would be favored by being promoted to the rank of caretaker of them, with at least partial say over resources which he had previously neither used nor contracted to use, and *his* income would rise.

In addition to this redistributive scheme there is another one, implied by the prohibition of newly created private capital or by the degree of hampering (dependent as it is on the size of the socialized part of the economy) under which this process must now take place: a redistribution away from people who have forgone possible consumption and instead saved up funds in order to employ them productively, i.e., for the purpose of producing future consumption goods, and who now can no longer do so or who now have fewer options available, toward nonsavers, who in adopting the redistribution scheme, gain a say, however partial, over the saver's funds.

The socio-economic consequences of a policy of socialization are essentially implied in these formulations. But before taking a more detailed look at them, it might be worthwhile to review and clarify the central features of the real world in which this socialization scheme would purportedly take place. It should be recalled that one is dealing with a changing world; that man, in addition, can learn with respect to this world and so does not necessarily know today what he will know at a later point in time; that there is a scarcity of a multitude of goods and that accordingly man is pressed by a multitude of needs, not all of which he can satisfy at the same time and/or without sacrificing the satisfaction of other needs; because of this, man must choose and order his needs in a scale of preferences according to the rank of urgency that they have for him; also, more specifically, that neither the process of original appropriation of resources perceived as scarce, nor the process of production of new and the upkeep of old means of production, nor the process of contracting, is costless for man; that all of these activities cost at the very least *time*, which could be spent otherwise, e.g., for leisure activities; and in addition one should not forget that one is dealing with a world characterized by the division of labor, which is to say that one is not talking about a world of self-sufficient producers, but one in which production is carried out for a market of independent consumers.

With this in mind, then, what are the effects of socializing the means of production? To begin with, what are the "economic" consequences, in the colloquial sense of the term? There are three intimately related effects.[7] First--and this is the immediate general effect of all types of socialism--there is a relative drop in the rate of investment, the rate of capital formation. Since "socialization" favors the nonuser, the nonproducer, and the noncontractor of means of production and, mutatis mutandis, raises the costs for users, producers, and contractors, there will be fewer people acting in the latter roles. There will be less original appropriation of natural resources whose scarcity is realized, there will be less production of new and less upkeep of old factors of production, and there will be less contracting. For all of these activities involve costs and the costs of performing them have been raised, and there are alternative courses of action, such as leisure-consumption activities, which at the same time have become relatively less costly, and thus more open and available to actors. Along the same line, because everyone's investment outlets have dried up as it is no longer permissible to convert private savings into private investment, or because the outlets have been limited to the extent to which the economy is socialized, there will therefore be less saving and more consuming, less work and more leisure. After all, you can not become a capitalist any longer, or your possibility of becoming one has been restricted, and so there is at least one reason less to save! Needless to say, the result of this will be a reduced output of exchangeable goods and a lowering of the living standard in terms of such goods. And since these lowered living standards are *forced* upon people and are not the natural choice of consumers who deliberately change their relative evaluation of leisure and exchangeable goods as the result of work, i.e., since it is experienced as an unwanted impoverishment, a tendency will evolve to compensate for such losses by going underground, by moonlighting and creating black markets.

Secondly, a policy of the socialization of means of production will result in a wasteful use of such means, i.e., in use which at best satisfies second-rate needs and at worst, satisfies no needs at all but exclusively increases costs.[8] The reason for this is the existence and unavoidability of change! Once it is admitted that there can be change in consumer demand, change in technological knowledge, and change in the natural environment in which the process of production has to take place--and all of this indeed takes place constantly and unceasingly--then it must also be admitted that there is a constant and never-ending need to reorganize and reshuffle the whole structure of social production. There is always a need to withdraw old investments from some lines of production and, together with new ones, pour them into other lines, thus making certain productive establishments, certain branches, or even certain sectors of the economy shrink and others expand. Now assume--and this is precisely what is done under a socialization scheme--that it is either completely illegal or extremely difficult to sell the collectively owned means of production into private hands. This process of reorganizing the structure of production will then--even if it does not stop altogether--at least be seriously hampered! The reason is basically a simple one, but still of the utmost importance. Because the means of production either cannot be sold, or selling them is made very difficult for the selling caretaker or the private buyer or both, no market prices for the means of production exist, or the formation of such prices is hindered and made more costly. But then the caretaker-producer of the socialized means of production can no longer correctly establish the actual monetary costs involved in using the resources or in making any changes in the production structure. Nor can he compare these costs with his expected monetary income from sales. In not being permitted to take any offers from other private individuals who might see an alternative way of using some given means of production, or in being restricted from taking such offers, the caretaker simply does not know what he is missing, what the foregone opportunities are, and is not able to correctly assess the monetary costs of withholding the resources. He cannot discover whether his way of using them or changing their use is worth the result in terms of monetary returns, or whether the costs involved are actually higher than the returns and so cause an absolute drop in the value of the output of consumer goods. Nor can he establish whether his way of producing for consumer demand is indeed the most efficient way (as compared with conceivable alternative ways) of satisfying the most urgent consumer needs, or if less urgent needs are being satisfied at the expense of neglecting more urgent ones, thus causing at least a relative drop in the value of the goods produced. Without being able to resort unrestrictedly to the means of economic calculation, there is simply no way of knowing. Of course one could go ahead and try to do one's best. That might even be successful sometimes, though one would have no way of assuring oneself that it is. But, in any case, the larger the consumer market is which one has to serve, and the more the knowledge regarding preferences of different groups of consumers, special circumstances of historical time and geographical space, and possibilities of technology is dispersed among different individuals, the more likely it is that one will go wrong. A misallocation of means of production, with wastes and shortages as the two sides of the same coin, must ensue. In hampering and of course even more so, in making it outright illegal for private entrepreneurs to bid away means of production from caretakers, a system of socialized production prevents opportunities for improvement from being taken up to the full extent they are perceived. Again, it hardly needs to be pointed out that this, too, contributes to impoverishment.[9]

Thirdly, socializing the means of production causes relative impoverishment, i.e., a drop in the general standard of living, by leading to an overutilization of the given factors of production. The reason for this, again, lies in the peculiar position of a caretaker as compared with that of a private owner. A private owner who has the right to sell the factors of production and keep the money receipts privately will, because of this, try to avoid any increase in production which occurs at the expense of the value of the capital employed. His objective is to maximize the value of the products produced *plus* that of the resources used in producing them because he owns both of them. Thus he will stop producing when the value of the marginal product produced is lower than the depreciation of the capital used to produce it. Accordingly, he will, for instance, reduce the depreciation costs involved in producing, and instead engage in increased conservation, if he anticipates future price rises for the products produced and vice versa. The situation of the caretaker, i.e., the incentive structure which he is facing, is quite different in this respect. Because he cannot sell the means of production, his incentive to not produce, and thereby utilize the capital employed, at the expense of an excessive reduction in capital value is, if not completely gone, then at least relatively reduced. True, since the caretaker in a socialized economy also cannot privately appropriate the receipts from the sale of products, but must hand them over to the community of caretakers at large to be used at their discretion, his incentive to produce and sell products *at all* is relatively weakened as well. It is precisely this fact that explains the lower rate of capital formation. But as long as the caretaker works and produces at all, his interest in gaining an income evidently exists, even if it cannot be used for purposes of private capital formation, but only for private consumption and/or the creation of private, nonproductively used wealth. The caretaker's inability to sell the means of production, then, implies that the incentive to increase his *private income* at the expense of capital value is raised. Accordingly, to the extent that he sees his income dependent on the output of products produced (the salary paid to him by the community of caretakers might be dependent on this!), his incentive will be raised to increase this output at the expense of capital. Furthermore, since the actual caretaker, insofar as he is not identical with the community of caretakers, can never be completely and permanently supervised and thus can derive income from using the means of production for private purposes (i.e., the production of privately used, non- or black-marketed goods) he will be encouraged to increase this output at the expense of capital value to the extent that he sees his income dependent on such private production. In any case, capital consumption and overuse of existing capital will occur; and increased capital consumption once more implies relative impoverishment, since the production of future exchange goods will, as a consequence, be reduced.

While implied in this analysis of the threefold economic consequences of socializing the means of production--reduced investment, misallocation, and overutilization, all of which lead to reduced living standards--in order to reach a full understanding of Russian-type societies it is interesting and indeed important to point out specifically that the above analysis also applies to the productive factor of labor. With respect to labor, too, socialization implies lowered investment, misallocation, and overutilization. First, since the owners of labor factors can no longer become self-employed, or since the opportunity to do so is restricted, on the whole there will be less investment in human capital. Second, since the owners of labor factors can no longer sell their labor services to the highest bidder (for to the extent to which the economy is socialized, separate bidders having independent control over specific complementary factors of production, including the money needed to pay labor, and who take up opportunities and risks independently, on their own account, are no longer allowed to exist!) the monetary cost of using a given labor factor, or of combining it with complementary factors, can no longer be established, and hence all sorts of misallocations of labor will ensue. And third, since the owners of labor factors in a socialized economy own at best only part of the proceeds from their labor while the remainder belongs to the community of caretakers, there will be an increased incentive for these caretakers to supplement their private income at the expense of losses in the capital value embodied in the laborers, so that an overutilization of labor will result.[10]

Last, but certainly not least, a policy of the socialization of the means of production affects the character structure of society, the importance of which can hardly be exaggerated. As has been pointed out repeatedly, adopting Russian-type socialism instead of capitalism based on the natural theory of property implies giving a relative advantage to nonusers, nonproducers, and noncontractors as regards property titles of the means of production and the income that can be derived from using of these means. If people have an interest in stabilizing and, if possible, increasing their income and they can shift relatively easily from the role of a user- producer or contractor into that of a nonuser, nonproducer, or noncontractor-assumptions, to be sure, whose validity can hardly be disputed--then, responding to the shift in the incentive structure affected by socialization, people will increasingly engage in nonproductive and noncontractual activities and, as time goes on, their personalities will be changed. A former ability to perceive and to anticipate situations of scarcity, to take up productive opportunities, to be aware of technological possibilities, to anticipate changes in demand, to develop marketing strategies and to detect chances for mutually advantageous exchanges, in short: the ability to initiate, to work and to respond to other people's needs, will be diminished, if not completely extinguished. People will have become different persons, with different skills, who, should the policy suddenly be changed and capitalism reintroduced, could not go back to their former selves immediately and rekindle their old productive spirit, even if they wanted to. They will simply have forgotten how to do it and will have to relearn, slowly, with high psychic costs involved, just as it involved high costs for them to suppress their productive skills in the first place. But this is only half the picture of the social consequences of socialization. It can be completed by recalling the above findings regarding capitalism's and socialism's apparent differences. This will bring out the other side of the personality change caused by socializing, complementing the just mentioned loss in productive capacity. The fact must be recalled that socialism, too, must solve the problem of who is to control and coordinate various means of production. Contrary to capitalism's solution to this problem, though, in socialism the assignment of different positions in the production structure to different people is a *political* matter, i.e., a matter accomplished irrespective of considerations of previous user-ownership and the existence of contractual, mutually agreeable exchange, but rather by superimposing one person's will upon that of another (disagreeing) one. Evidently, a person's position in the production structure has an immediate effect on his income, be it in terms of exchangeable goods, psychic income, status, and the like. Accordingly, as people want to improve their income and want to move into more highly evaluated positions in the hierarchy of caretakers, they increasingly have to use their political talents. It becomes irrelevant, or is at least of reduced importance, to be a more efficient producer or contractor in order to rise in the hierarchy of income recipients. Instead, it is increasingly important to have the peculiar skills of a politician, i.e., a person who through persuasion, demagoguery and intrigue, through promises, bribes, and threats, manages to assemble public support for his own position. Depending on the intensity of the desire for higher incomes, people will have to spend less time developing their productive skills and more time cultivating political talents. And since different people have differing degrees of productive and political talents, different people will rise to the top now, so that one finds increasing numbers of politicians everywhere in the hierarchical order of caretakers. All the way to the very top there will be people incompetent to do the job they are supposed to do. It is no hindrance in a caretaker's career for him to be dumb, indolent, inefficient, and uncaring, as long as he commands superior political skills, and accordingly people like this will be taking care of the means of production everywhere.[11]

A look at Russia and other East-bloc countries in which a policy of socialization of means of production has been carried out to a considerable degree can help illustrate the truth of the above conclusions. Even a superficial acquaintance with these countries suffices to see the validity of the first and main conclusion. The general standard of living in the East-bloc countries, though admittedly different from country to country (a difference that itself would have to be explained by the degree of strictness with which the socialization scheme was and presently is carried through in practice), is clearly much lower than that in the so-called capitalist countries of the West. (This is true even though the degree to which Western countries are socialized, though differing from country to country, is itself quite considerable and normally very much underestimated as will become clear in later chapters.) Though the theory does not and cannot make a precise prediction of how drastic the impoverishment effect of a socialization policy will be, except that it will be a noticeable one, it is certainly worth mentioning that when almost complete socialization was first put into effect in immediate post-World War I Russia, this experience cost literally millions of lives, and it required a marked change in policy, the New Economic Policy (NEP), merely a few years later in 1921, reintroducing elements of private ownership, to moderate these disastrous effects to levels that would prove tolerable.[12] Indeed, repeated changes in policy made Russia go through a similar experience more than once. Similar, though somewhat less drastic, results from a policy of socialization were experienced in all of the East European countries after World War II. There, too, moderate privatization of small farming, the crafts, or small businesses had to be permitted repeatedly in order to prevent outright economic breakdowns.[13] Nonetheless, in spite of such reforms, which incidentally prove the point that contrary to socialist propaganda it is private and not social ownership that improves economic performance, and in spite of the fact that moonlighting, illegal productive activities, bartering, and black market trade are ubiquitous phenomena in all of these countries, just as the theory would lead one to expect, and that this underground economy takes up part of the slack and helps to improve things, the standard of living in the East-bloc countries is lamentably low. All sorts of basic consumer goods are entirely lacking, in far too short supply or of extremely poor quality.[14]

The case of West and East Germany is particularly instructive. Here, history provides us with an example that comes as close to that of a controlled social experiment as one could probably hope to get. A quite homogeneous population, with very much the same history, culture, character structure, work ethics, divided after Hitler-Germany's defeat in World War II. In West Germany, more because of lucky circumstances than the pressure of public opinion, a remarkably free market economy was adopted, the previous system of all-around price controls abolished in one stroke, and almost complete freedom of movement, trade, and occupation introduced.[15] In East Germany, on the other hand, under Soviet Russian dominance, socialization of the means of production, i.e., an expropriation of the previous private owners, was implemented. Two different institutional frameworks, two different incentive structures have thus been applied to the same population. The difference in the results is impressive.[16] While both countries do well in their respective blocs, West Germany has the highest standard of living among the major West-European nations and East Germany prides itself in being the most well-off country in the East bloc, the standard of living in the West is so much higher and has become relatively more so over time, that despite the transfer of considerable amounts of money from West to East by government as well as private citizens and increasingly socialist policies in the West, the visitor going from West to East is simply stunned as he enters an almost completely different, impoverished world. As a matter of fact, while all of the East-European countries are plagued by the emigration problem of people wanting to leave for the more prosperous capitalist West with its increased opportunities, and while they all have gradually established tighter border controls, thus turning these countries into sort of gigantic prisoner camps in order to prevent this outflow, the case of Germany is a most striking one. With language differences, traditionally the most severe natural barrier for emigrants, nonexistent, the difference in living standards between the two Germanys proved to be so great and emigration from East to West took on such proportions, that in 1961 the socialist regime in East Germany, in a last desperate step, finally had to close its borders to the West completely. To keep the population in, it had to build a system the likes of which the world had never seen of walls, barbed wire, electrified fences, mine fields, automatic shooting devices, watchtowers, etc., almost 900 miles long, for the sole purpose of preventing its people from running away from the consequences of Russian-type socialism.

Besides exemplifying the main point, the case of the two Germanys, because of its experimental-like character, proves particularly helpful in illustrating the truth of the rest of the theoretically derived conclusions. Looking at comparable social positions, almost nowhere in West Germany will one find people working as little, as slowly, or as negligently (while the working *hours*, higher in the East, are of course regulated!) as their East German counterparts. Not, to be sure, because of any alleged differences in mentality or work ethics, as those are very much the same historically, but because the incentive to work is considerably reduced by a policy scheme that effectively closes all or most outlets for private investment. Effective work in East Germany is most likely to be found in the underground economy. And in response to the various disincentives to work, and in particular to work in the "officially" controlled economy, there is also a tendency among East Germans to withdraw from public life and to stress the importance of privacy, the family, relatives, and personal friends and connections, significantly exceeding what is seen in the West.[17]

There is also ample evidence of misallocation, just as the theory would lead one to expect. While the phenomenon of productive factors that are not used (at least not continuously) but are simply inactive because complementary factors are lacking can of course be observed in the West, in the East (and again, in the German case certainly not because of differences in organizational talents) it is observed everywhere as a permanent feature of life. And while it is normally quite difficult in the West, and requires special entrepreneurial talent to point out changes in the use of certain means of production that would result in an overall improvement in the output of consumer goods, this is relatively easy in the East-bloc countries. Almost everyone working in East Germany knows many ways to put the means of production to more urgent uses than ones that are currently being used, where they are evidently wasted and cause shortages of other, more heavily demanded goods. But since they are not able to bid them away and must instead go through tedious political procedures to initiate any changes, nothing much can be or indeed is done.

Experience also corroborates what has been said about the other side of the coin: the overutilization of publicly owned means of production. In West Germany such public goods also exist, and as would be expected, they are in relatively bad shape. But in East Germany, and no differently or in fact even worse in the other Soviet-dominated countries, where all factors of production are socially owned, insufficiently maintained, deteriorating, unrepaired, rusting, even simply vandalized production factors, machinery, and buildings are truly rampant. Further, the ecology crisis is much more dramatic in the East, in spite of the relatively underdeveloped state of the general economy, than in the West--and all this is not, as the case of Germany proves clearly enough, because there are differences in people's "natural" inclination to care and to be careful.

Finally, as regards the theoretically predicted changes in the social and personality structure, complaints about superiors are, of course, quite a common phenomenon everywhere. But in the countries of Russian-type socialism, where the assignment of positions in the hierarchy of caretakers is and must be entirely a *political* affair, such complaints about downright incompetent, unqualified, and ridiculous superiors are, even if not more loudly voiced, most frequent, most severe, and best-founded, and decent people are most often driven to despair or cynicism as a consequence. And since a few people from East Germany still go to West Germany at an age where they are still members of the labor force, some as escapees but more frequently because a sort of ransom has been paid for them, sufficient material also exists to illustrate the conclusion that in the long run a socialized economy will reduce people's productive capacities. Among those going to the West there is a significant number who led quite normal productive lives in the East but who, despite the absence of any linguistic and cultural barriers, prove to be incapable of, or have the greatest difficulties, adapting to Western society with its increased demand for productive and competitive skills and spirits.

4

SOCIALISM SOCIAL-DEMOCRATIC STYLE

In the last chapter I analyzed the orthodox marxist version of socialism--socialism Russian-style, as it was called--and explained its effects on the process of production and the social moral structure. I went on to point out that the theoretically foreseen consequences of relative impoverishment proved to be so powerful that in fact a policy of socializing the means of production could never actually be carried through to its logical end: the socialization of *all* production factors, without causing an immediate economic disaster. Indeed, sooner or later all actual realizations of Marxist socialism have had to reintroduce elements of private ownership in the means of production in order to overcome or prevent manifest bankruptcy. Even moderate "market" socialism, however, cannot prevent a relative impoverishment of the population, if the idea of socialized production is not abandoned entirely, once and for all.

Much more so than any theoretical argument, it has been the disappointing experience with Russian-type socialism which has led to a constant decline in the popularity of orthodox Marxist socialism and has spurred the emergence and development of modern social-democratic socialism, which will be the concern of this chapter. Both types of socialism, to be sure, derive from the same ideological sources.[1] Both are egalitarian in motivation, at least in theory,[2] and both have essentially the same ultimate goal: the abolishment of capitalism as a social system based on private ownership and the establishment of a new society, characterized by brotherly solidarity and the eradication of scarcity; a society in which everyone is paid "according to his needs." From the very beginnings of the socialist movement in the mid-nineteenth century, though, there have been conflicting ideas on the methods best suited for achieving these goals. While generally there was agreement on the necessity of socializing the means of production, there were always diverging opinions on how to proceed. On the one hand, within the socialist movement there were the advocates of a revolutionary course of action. They propagated the violent overthrow of the existing governments, the complete expropriation of all capitalists in one stroke, and the temporary (i.e., until scarcity would indeed, as promised, be eradicated) dictatorship of the proletariat, i.e., of those who were not capitalists but who had to sell their labor services, in order to stabilize the new order. On the other hand there were the reformists who advocated a gradualist approach. They reasoned that with the enlargement of the franchise, and ultimately with a system of universal suffrage, socialism's victory could be attained through democratic, parliamentary action. This would be so because capitalism, according to common socialist doctrine, would bring about a tendency towards the proletarization of society, i.e., a tendency for fewer people to be self-employed and more to become employees instead. And in accordance with common socialist beliefs, this tendency would in turn produce an increasingly uniform proletarian class consciousness which then would lead to a swelling voter turnout for the socialist party. And, so they reasoned, as this strategy was much more in line with public opinion (more appealing to the mostly peacefully-minded workers and at the same time less frightening to the capitalists), by adopting it, socialism's ultimate success would only become more assured.

Both of these forces co-existed within the socialist movement, though their relationship was at times quite strained, until the Bolshevik Revolution of October, 1917 in Russia. In practice, the socialist movement generally took the reformist path, while in the field of ideological debate the revolutionaries dominated.[3] The Russian events changed this. With Lenin in the lead, for the first time the revolutionary socialists realized their program and the socialist movement as a whole had to take a stand vis à vis the Russian experiment. As a consequence, the socialist movement split into two branches with two separate parties: a communist party either more or less in favor of the Russian events, and a socialist or social-democratic party with reservations, or against them. Still, the split was not over the issue of socialization; both were in favor of that. It was an open split over the issue of revolutionary vs. democratic parliamentary change. Faced with the actual experience of the Russian revolution--the violence, the bloodshed, the practice of uncontrolled expropriation, the fact that thousands of new leaders, very often of questionable reputation or simply shady, inferior characters, were being swept to the political helm--the social democrats, in their attempt to gain public support, felt they had to abandon their revolutionary image and become, not only in practice but in theory as well, a decidedly reformist, democratic party. And even some of the communist parties of the West, dedicated as they were to a theory of revolutionary change, but just as much in need of public support, felt they had to find some fault, at least, with the peculiar Bolshevik way of implementing the revolution. They, too, increasingly thought it necessary to play the reformist, democratic game, if only in practice.

However, this was only the first step in the transformation of the socialist movement effected by the experience of the Russian revolution. The next step, as indicated, was forced upon it by the dim experience with Soviet Russia's economic performance. Regardless of their differing views on the desirability of revolutionary changes and equally unfamiliar with or unable or unwilling to grasp abstract economic reasoning, socialists and communists alike could still, during a sort of honeymoon period which they felt the new experiment deserved, entertain the most illusory hopes about the economic achievements of a policy of socialization. But this period could not last forever, and the facts had to be faced and the results evaluated after some time had elapsed. For every decently neutral observer of things, and later for every alert visitor and traveler, it became evident that socialism Russian-style did not mean more but rather *less* wealth and that it was a system above all, that in having to allow even small niches of private capital formation, had in fact already admitted its own economic inferiority, if only implicitly. As this experience became more widely known, and in particular when after World War II the Soviet experiment was repeated in the East European countries, producing the very same dim results and thus disproving the thesis that the Soviet mess was only due to a special Asian mentality of the people, in their race for public support the socialist, i.e., the social-democratic and communist, parties of the West were forced to modify their programs further. The communists now saw various flaws in the Russian implementation of the socialization program as well, and increasingly toyed with the idea of more decentralized planning and decision-making and of partial socialization, i.e., socialization only of major firms and industries, although they never entirely abandoned the idea of socialized production.[4] The socialist or social-democratic parties, on the other hand, less sympathetic from the beginning towards the Russian model of socialism and through their decidedly reformist-democratic policy already inclined to accept compromises such as partial socialization, had to make a further adaptive move. These parties, in response to the Russian and East European experiences, increasingly gave up the notion of socialized production altogether and instead put more and more emphasis on the idea of income taxation and equalization, and, in another move, on equalization of opportunity, as being the true cornerstones of socialism.

While this shift from Russian-type socialism towards a social-democratic one took place, and still is taking place in all Western societies, it was not equally strong everywhere. Roughly speaking and only looking at Europe, the displacement of the old by the new kind of socialism has been more pronounced, the more immediate and direct the experience with Russian-type socialism for the population in which the socialist and/or communist parties had to find supporters and voters. Of all the major countries, in West Germany, where the contact with this type of socialism is the most direct, where millions of people still have ample opportunities to see with their own eyes the mischief that has been done to the people in East Germany, this displacement was the most complete. Here, in 1959, the social democrats adopted (or rather were forced by public opinion to adopt) a new party program in which all obvious traces of a Marxist past were conspicuously absent, that rather explicitly mentioned the importance of private ownership and markets, that talked about socialization only as a mere possibility, and that instead heavily stressed the importance of redistributive measures. Here, the protagonists of a policy of socialization of the means of production within the social-democratic party have been considerably outnumbered ever since; and here the communist parties, even when they are only in favor of peaceful and partial socialization, have been reduced to insignificance.[5] In countries further removed from the iron curtain, like France, Italy, Spain, and also Great Britain, this change has been less dramatic. Nonetheless, it is safe to say that today only social-democratic socialism, as represented most typically by the German social-democrats, can claim widespread popularity in the West. As a matter of fact, due partly to the influence of the Socialist International--the association of socialist and social-democratic parties--social-democratic socialism can now be said to be one of the most widespread ideologies of our age, increasingly shaping the political programs and actual policies not only of explicitly socialist parties, and to a lesser degree those of the western communists, but also of groups and parties who would not even in their most far-fetched dreams *call* themselves socialists, like the east coast "liberal" Democrats in the United States.[6] And in the field of international politics the ideas of social-democratic socialism, in particular of a redistributive approach towards the so-called North-South conflict, have almost become something like the official position among all "well-informed" and "well-intentioned" men; a consensus extending far beyond those who think of themselves as socialists.[7]

What are the central features of socialism social-democratic-style? There are basically two characteristics. First, in positive contradistinction to the traditional Marxist-style socialism, social-democratic socialism does not outlaw private ownership in the means of production and it even accepts the idea of *all* means of production being privately owned--with the exception only of education, traffic and communication, central banking, and the police and courts. In principle, everyone has the right to privately appropriate and own means of production, to sell, buy, or newly produce them, to give them away as a present, or to rent them out to someone else under a contractual arrangement. But secondly, no owner of means of production rightfully owns *all* of the income that can be derived from the usage of his means of production and no owner is left to decide how much of the *total* income from production to allocate to consumption and investment. Instead, part of the income from production rightfully belongs to society, has to be handed over to it, and is then, according to ideas of egalitarianism or distributive justice, redistributed to its individual members. Furthermore, though the respective income-shares that go to the producer and to society might be fixed at any given point in time, the share that rightfully belongs to the producer is in principle flexible and the determination of its size, as well as that of society's share, is not up to the producer, but rightfully belongs to society.[8]

Seen from the point of view of the natural theory of property--the theory underlying capitalism--the adoption of these rules implies that the rights of the natural owner have been aggressively invaded. According to this theory of property, it should be recalled, the user-owner of the means of production can do whatever he wants with them; and whatever the outcome of his usage, it is his own private income, which he can use again as he pleases, as long as he does not change the physical integrity of someone else's property and exclusively relies on contractual exchanges. From the standpoint of the natural theory of property, there are not two separate processes--the production of income and then, after income is produced, its distribution. There is only one process: in producing income it is automatically distributed; the producer is the owner. As compared with this, socialism social-democratic style advocates the partial expropriation of the natural owner by redistributing part of the income from production to people who, whatever their merits otherwise, definitely did *not* produce the income in question and definitely did *not* have any contractual claims to it, and who, in addition, have the right to determine unilaterally, i.e., without having to wait for the affected producer's consent, how far this partial expropriation can go.

It should be clear from this description that, contrary to the impression which socialism social-democratic style is intended to generate among the public, the difference between both types of socialism is not of a categorical nature. Rather, it is only a matter of degree. Certainly, the first mentioned rule seems to inaugurate a fundamental difference in that it allows private ownership. But then the second rule in principle allows the expropriation of all of the producer's income from production and thus reduces his ownership right to a purely nominal one. Of course, social-democratic socialism does not *have* to go as far as reducing private ownership to one in name only. And admittedly, as the income-share that the producer is forced to hand over to society can in fact be quite moderate, this, in practice, can make a tremendous difference as regards economic performance. But still, it must be realized that from the standpoint of the nonproducing fellowmen, the degree of expropriation of private producers' income is a matter of expediency, which suffices to reduce the difference between both types of socialism--Russian and social-democratic style--once and for all to a difference only of degree. It should be apparent what this important fact implies for a producer. It means that however low the presently fixed degree of expropriation might be, his productive efforts take place under the ever-present threat that in the future the income-share which must be handed over to society will be raised unilaterally. It does not need much comment to see how this increases the risk, or the cost of producing, and hence lowers the rate of investment.

With this statement a first step in the analysis that follows has already been taken. What are the economic, in the colloquial sense of the term, consequences of adopting a system of social-democratic socialism? After what has just been said, it is probably no longer altogether surprising to hear that at least as regards the general direction of the effects, they are quite similar to those of traditional Marxist-type socialism. Still, to the extent that social-democratic socialism settles for partial expropriation and the redistribution of producer incomes, some of the impoverishment effects that result from a policy of fully socializing means of production can be circumvented. Since these resources can still be bought and sold, the problem most typical of a caretaker economy--that no market prices for means of production exist and hence neither monetary calculation nor accounting are possible, with ensuing misallocations and the waste of scarce resources in usages that are at best of only secondary importance--is avoided. In addition, the problem of overutilization is at least reduced. Also, since private investment and capital formation is still possible to the extent that some portion of income from production is left with the producer to use at his discretion, under socialism social-democratic style there is a relatively higher incentive to work, to save, and to invest.

Nonetheless, by no means can all impoverishment effects be avoided. Socialism social-democratic style, however good it might look in comparison with Russian-type socialism, still necessarily leads to a reduction in investment and thus in future wealth as compared with that under capitalism.[9] By taking part of the income from production away from the owner-producer, however small that part may be, and giving it to people who did not produce the income in question, the costs of production (which are never zero, as producing, appropriating, contractings always imply at least the use of time, which could be used otherwise, for leisure, consumption, or underground work, for instance) rise, and, mutatis mutandis, the costs of nonproducing and/or underground production fall, however slightly. As a consequence there will be relatively less production and investment, even though, for reasons to be discussed shortly, the absolute level of production and wealth might still rise. There will be relatively more leisure, more consumption, and more moonlighting, and hence, all in all, relative impoverishment. And this tendency will be more pronounced the higher the income from production that is redistributed, and the more imminent the likelihood that it will be raised in the future by unilateral, noncontractual societal decision.

For a long time by far the most popular idea for implementing the general policy goal of social-democratic socialism was to redistribute monetary income by means of income taxation or a general sales tax levied on producers. A look at this particular technique shall further clarify our point and avoid some frequently encountered misunderstandings and misconceptions about the general effect of relative impoverishment. What is the economic effect of introducing income or sales taxation where there has been none before, or of raising an existing level of taxation to a new height?[10] In answering this, I will further ignore the complications that result from the different possible ways of redistributing tax money to different individuals or groups of individuals--these shall be discussed later in this chapter. Here we will only take into account the general fact, true by definition for all redistributive systems, that any redistribution of tax money is a transfer from monetary income producers and contractual money recipients to people in their capacity as nonproducers and nonrecipients of contractual money incomes. Introducing or raising taxation thus implies that monetary income flowing from production is reduced for the producer and increased for people in their roles as nonproducers and noncontractors. This changes the relative costs of production for monetary return versus nonproduction and production for nonmonetary returns. Accordingly, insofar as this change is perceived by people, they will increasingly resort to leisurely consumption and/or production for the purpose of barter, simultaneously reducing their productive efforts undertaken for monetary rewards. In any case, the output of goods to be purchased with money will fall, which is to say the purchasing power of money decreases, and hence the general standard of living will decline.

Against this reasoning it is sometimes argued that it has been frequently observed empirically that a rise in the level of taxation was actually accompanied by a rise (not a fall) in the gross national product (GNP), and that the above reasoning, however plausible, must thus be considered empirically invalid. This alleged counter-argument exhibits a simple misunderstanding: a confusion between absolute and relative reduction. In the above analysis the conclusion is reached that the effect of higher taxes is a relative reduction in production for monetary returns; a reduction, that is, as compared with the level of production that would have been attained had the degree of taxation not been altered. It does not say or imply anything with respect to the absolute level of output produced. As a matter of fact, absolute growth of GNP is not only compatible with our analysis but can be seen as a perfectly normal phenomenon to the extent that advances in productivity are possible and actually take place. If it has become possible, through improvement in the technology of production, to produce a higher output with an identical input (in terms of costs), or a physically identical output with a reduced input, then the coincidence of increased taxation and increased output is anything but surprising. But, to be sure, this does not at all affect the validity of what has been stated about *relative* impoverishment resulting from taxation.

Another objection that enjoys some popularity is that raising taxes leads to a reduction in monetary income, and that this reduction raises the marginal utility of money as compared with other forms of income (like leisure) and thus, instead of lowering it, actually helps to increase the tendency to work for monetary return. This observation, to be sure, is perfectly true. But it is a misconception to believe that it does anything to invalidate the relative impoverishment thesis. First of all, in order to get the full picture it should be noted that through taxation, not only the monetary income for some people (the producers) is reduced but simultaneously monetary income for other people (nonproducers) is increased, and for these people the marginal utility of money and hence their inclination to work for monetary return would be reduced. But this is by no means all that need be said, as this might still leave the impression that taxation simply does not affect the output of exchangeable goods at all--since it will reduce the marginal utility of money income for some and increase it for others, with both effects cancelling each other out. But this impression would be wrong. As a matter of fact, this would be a denial of what has been assumed at the outset: that a tax hike, i.e., a higher monetary contribution forced upon disapproving income producers, has actually taken place and has been perceived as such--and would hence involve a logical contradiction. Intuitively, the flaw in the belief that taxation is "neutral" as regards output becomes apparent as soon as the argument is carried to its ultimate extreme. It would then amount to the statement that even complete expropriation of all of the producers' monetary income and the transfer of it to a group of nonproducers would not make any difference, since the increased laziness of the nonproducers resulting from this redistribution would be fully compensated by an increased workaholism on the part of the producers (which is certainly absurd). What is overlooked in this sort of reasoning is that the introduction of taxation or the rise in any given level of taxation does not only imply favoring nonproducers at the expense of producers, it also simultaneously changes, for producers and nonproducers of monetary income alike, the cost attached to different methods of achieving an (increasing) monetary income. For it is now relatively less costly to attain additional monetary income *through nonproductive means*, i.e., not through actually *producing* more goods but by participating in the process of noncontractual acquisitions of goods *already produced*. Even if producers are indeed more intent upon attaining additional money as a consequence of a higher tax, they will increasingly do so not by intensifying their productive efforts but rather through exploitative methods. This explains why taxation is not, and never can be, neutral. With (increased) taxation a different legal incentive structure is institutionalized: one that changes the relative costs of *production* for monetary income versus nonproduction, including nonproduction for leisurely purposes and nonproduction for monetary return, and also versus production for nonmonetary return (barter). And if such a different incentive structure is applied to one and the same population, then, and necessarily so, a decrease in the output of goods produced for monetary return must result.[11]

While income and sales taxation are the most common techniques, they do not exhaust social-democratic socialism's repertoire of redistributive methods. No matter how the taxes are redistributed to the individuals composing a given society, no matter, for instance, to what extent monetary income is equalized, since these individuals can and do lead different lifestyles and since they allocate different portions of the monetary income assigned to them to consumption or to the formation of nonproductively used private wealth, sooner or later significant differences between people will again emerge, if not with respect to their monetary income, then with respect to private wealth. And not surprisingly, these differences will steadily become more pronounced if a purely contractual inheritance law exists. Hence, social-democratic socialism, motivated as it is by egalitarian zeal, includes private wealth in its policy schemes and imposes a tax on it, too, and in particular imposes an inheritance tax in order to satisfy the popular outcry over "unearned riches" falling upon heirs.

Economically, these measures immediately reduce the amount of private wealth formation. As the enjoyment of private wealth is made relatively more costly by the tax, less wealth will be newly created, increased consumption will ensue--including that of existing stocks of nonproductively used riches--and the overall standard of living, which of course also depends on the comforts derived from private wealth, will sink.

Similar conclusions about impoverishment effects are reached when the third major field of tax policies--that of "natural assets"--is analyzed. For reasons to be discussed below, this field, next to the two traditional fields of monetary income and private wealth taxation, has gained more prominence over time under the heading of opportunity equalization. It did not take much to discover that a person's position in life does not depend exclusively on monetary income or the wealth of nonproductively used goods. There are other things that are important in life and which bring additional income, even though it may not be in the form of money or other exchange goods: a nice family, an education, health, good looks, etc. I will call these nonexchangeable goods from which (psychic) income can be derived "natural assets." Redistributive socialism, led by egalitarian ideals, is also irritated by existing differences in such assets, and tries, if not to eradicate, then at least to moderate them. But these assets, being nonexchangeable goods, cannot be easily expropriated and the proceeds then redistributed. It is also not very practical, to say the least, to achieve this goal by directly reducing the nonmonetary income from natural assets of higher income people to the level of lower income people by, for instance, ruining the health of the healthy and so making them equal to the sick, or by smashing the good-looking people's faces to make them look like their less fortunate bad-looking fellows.[12] Thus, the common method social-democratic socialism advocates in order to create "equality of opportunity" is taxation of natural assets. Those people who are thought to receive a relatively higher nonmonetary income from some asset, like health, are subject to an additional tax, to be paid in money. This tax is then redistributed to those people whose respective income is relatively low to help compensate them for this fact. An additional tax, for instance, is levied on the healthy to help the unhealthy pay their doctor bills, or on the good-looking to help the ugly pay for plastic surgery or to buy themselves a drink so that they can forget about their lot. The economic consequences of such redistributive schemes should be clear. Insofar as the psychic income, represented by health, for instance, requires some productive, time and cost-consuming effort, and as people can, in principle, shift from productive roles into nonproductive ones, or channel their productive efforts into different, non- or less heavily taxed lines of nonexchangeable or exchangeable goods production, they will do so because of the increased costs involved in the production of personal health. The overall production of the wealth in question will fall, the general standard of health, that is, will be reduced. And even with truly natural assets, like intelligence, about which people can admittedly do little or nothing, consequences of the same kind will result, though only with a time lag of one generation. Realizing that it has become relatively more costly to be intelligent and less so to be nonintelligent, and wanting as much income (of all sorts) as possible for one's offspring, the incentive for intelligent people to produce offspring has been lowered and for nonintelligent ones raised. Given the laws of genetics, the result will be a population that is all in all less intelligent. And besides, in any case of taxation of natural assets, true for the example of health as well as for that of intelligence, because monetary income is taxed, a tendency similar to the one resulting from income taxation will set in, i.e., a tendency to reduce one's efforts for monetary return and instead increasingly engage in productive activity for nonmonetary return or in all sorts of nonproductive enterprises. And, of course, all this once again reduces the general standard of living.

But this is still not all that has to be said about the consequences of socialism social-democratic-style, as it will also have remote yet nonetheless highly important effects on the social-moral structure of society, which will become visible when one considers the long-term effects of introducing redistributive policies. It probably no longer comes as a surprise that in this regard, too, the difference between Russian-type socialism and socialism social-democratic style, while highly interesting in some details, is not of a principal kind.

As should be recalled, the effect of the former on the formation of personality types was twofold, reducing the incentive to develop productive skills, and favoring at the same time the development of political talents. This precisely is also the overall consequence of social-democratic socialism. As social-democratic socialism favors nonproductive roles as well as productive ones that escape public notice and so cannot be reached by taxation, the character of the population changes accordingly. This process might be slow, but as long as the peculiar incentive structure established by redistributive policies lasts, it is constantly operative. Less investment in the development and improvement of one's productive skills will take place and, as a consequence, people will become increasingly unable to secure their income on their own, by producing or contracting. And as the degree of taxation rises and the circle of taxed income widens, people will increasingly develop personalities as inconspicuous, as uniform, and as mediocre as is possible--at least as far as public appearance is concerned. At the same time, as a person's income simultaneously becomes dependent on politics, i.e., on society's decision on how to redistribute taxes (which is reached, to be sure, not by contracting, but rather by superimposing one person's will on another's recalcitrant one!), the more dependent it becomes, the more people will have to politicalize, i.e., the more time and energy they will have to invest in the development of their special talents for achieving personal advantages at the expense (i.e., in a noncontractual way) of others or of preventing such exploitation from occurring.

The *difference* between both types of socialism lies (only) in the following: under Russian-type socialism society's control over the means of production, and hence over the income produced with them, is complete, and so far there seems to be no more room to engage in political debate about the proper degree of politicalization of society. The issue is settled--just as it is settled at the other end of the spectrum, under pure capitalism, where there is no room for politics at all and all relations are exclusively contractual. Under social-democratic socialism, on the other hand, social control over income produced privately is actually only partial, and increased or full control exists only as society's not yet actualized right, making only for a potential threat hanging over the heads of private producers. But living with the threat of being fully taxed rather than actually being so taxed explains an interesting feature of social-democratic socialism as regards the general development toward increasingly politicalized characters. It explains why under a system of social-democratic socialism the sort of politicalization is different from that under Russian-type socialism. Under the latter, time and effort is spent nonproductively, discussing how to distribute the socially owned income; under the former, to be sure, this is also done, but time and effort are also used for political quarrels over the issue of how large or small the socially administered income-shares should actually be. Under a system of socialized means of production where this issue is settled once and for all, there is then relatively more withdrawal from public life, resignation, and cynicism to be observed. Social-democratic socialism, on the other hand, where the question is still open, and where producers and nonproducers alike can still entertain some hope of improving their position by decreasing or increasing taxation, has less of such privatization and, instead, more often has people actively engaged in political agitation either in favor of increasing society's control of privately produced incomes, or against it.[13]

With the general similarity as well as this specific difference between both types of socialism explained, the task remains of presenting a brief analysis of some modifying forces influencing the general development toward unproductive politicalized personalities. These are effected by differing approaches to the desirable pattern of income distribution. Russian and social-democratic socialism alike are faced with the question of how to distribute income that happens to be socially controlled. For Russian-type socialism it is a matter of what salaries to pay to individuals who have been assigned to various positions in the caretaker economy. For redistributive socialism it is the question of how much tax to allocate to whom. While there are in principle innumerable ways to do this, the egalitarian philosophy of both kinds of socialism effectively reduces the available options to three general types.[14] The first one is the method of more or less equalizing everybody's monetary income (and possibly also private, nonproductively used wealth). Teachers, doctors, construction workers and miners, factory managers and cleaning ladies all earn pretty much the same salary, or the difference between them is at least considerably reduced.[15] It does not need much comment to realize that this approach reduces the incentive to work most drastically, for it no longer makes much difference--salary-wise--if one works diligently all day or fools around most of the time. Hence, disutility of labor being a fact of life, people will increasingly fool around, with the average income that everyone seems to be guaranteed constantly falling, in relative terms. Thus, this approach relatively strengthens the tendency toward withdrawal, disillusionment, cynicism, and mutatis mutandis, contributes to a relative reduction in the general atmosphere of politicization. The second approach has the more moderate aim of guaranteeing a minimum income which, though normally somehow linked to average income, falls well below it.[16] This, too, reduces the incentive to work, since, to the extent that they are only marginal income producers with incomes from production only slightly above the minimum, people will now be more inclined to reduce or even stop their work, enjoy leisure instead, and settle for the minimum income. Thus more people than otherwise will fall below the minimum line, or more people than otherwise will keep or acquire those characteristics on whose existence payment of minimum salaries is bound, and as a consequence, again, the average income to which the minimum salary is linked will fall below the level that it otherwise would have reached. But, of course, the incentive to work is reduced to a smaller degree under the second than the first scheme. On the other hand, the second approach will lead to a relatively higher degree of active politicization (and less of resigned withdrawal), because, unlike average income, which can be objectively ascertained, the level at which the minimum income is fixed is a completely subjective, arbitrary affair, which is thus particularly prone to becoming a permanent political issue.

Undoubtedly, the highest degree of active politicization is reached when the third distributional approach is chosen. Its goal, gaining more and more prominence for social democracy, is to achieve equality of opportunity.[17] The idea is to create, through redistributional measures, a situation in which everyone's chance of achieving any possible (income) position in life is equal--very much as in a lottery where each ticket has the same chance of being a winner or a loser--and, in addition, to have a corrective mechanism which helps rectify situations of "undeserved bad luck" (whatever that may be) which might occur in the course of the ongoing game of chance. Taken literally, of course, this idea is absurd: there is no way of equalizing the opportunity of someone living in the Alps and someone residing at the seaside. In addition, it seems quite clear that the idea of a corrective mechanism is simply incompatible with the lottery idea. Yet it is precisely this high degree of vagueness and confusion which contributes to the popular appeal of this concept. What constitutes an opportunity, what makes an opportunity different or the same, worse or better, how much and what kind of compensation is needed to equalize opportunities which admittedly cannot be equalized in physical terms (as in the Alps-seaside example), what is undeserved bad luck and what a rectification, are all completely subjective matters. They are dependent on subjective evaluations, changing as they do, and there is then--if one indeed applies the equality of opportunity concept-- an unlimited reservoir of all sorts of distributional demands, for all sorts of reasons and for all sorts of people. This is so, in particular, because equalizing opportunity is compatible with demands for *differences* in monetary income or private wealth. A and B might have the same income and might both be equally rich, but A might be black, or a woman, or have bad eyesight, or be a resident of Texas, or may have ten children, or no husband, or be over 65, whereas B might be none of these but something else, and hence A might argue that his opportunities to attain everything possible in life are different, or rather worse, than B's, and that he should somehow be compensated for this, thus making their monetary incomes, which were the same before, now different. And B, of course, could argue in exactly the same way by simply reversing the implied evaluation of opportunities. As a consequence, an unheard of degree of politicalization will ensue. Everything seems fair now, and producers and nonproducers alike, the former for defensive and the latter for aggressive purposes, will be driven into spending more and more time in the role of raising, destroying, and countering distributional demands. And to be sure, this activity, like the engagement in leisurely activities, is not only nonproductive but in clear contrast to the role of enjoying leisure, implies spending time for the very purpose of actually disrupting the undisturbed enjoyment of wealth produced, as well as its new production.

But not only is increased politicalization stimulated (above and beyond the level implied by socialism generally) by promoting the idea of equalizing opportunity. There is once more, and this is perhaps one of the most interesting features of new social-democratic-socialism as compared with its traditional Marxist form, a new and different character to the kind of politicalization implied by it. Under any policy of distribution, there must be people who support and promote it. And normally, though not exclusively so, this is done by those who profit most from it. Thus, under a system of income and wealth-equalization and also under that of a minimum income policy, it is mainly the "have-nots" who are the supporters of the politicalization of social life. Given the fact that on the average they happen to be those with relatively lower intellectual, in particular verbal capabilities, this makes for politics which appears to lack much intellectual sophistication, to say the least. Put more bluntly, politics tends to be outright dull, dumb, and appalling, even to a considerable number of the have-nots themselves. On the other hand, in adopting the idea of equalizing opportunity, differences in monetary income and wealth are not only allowed to exist but even become quite pronounced, provided that this is justifiable by some underlying discrepancies in the opportunity structure for which the former differences help compensate. Now in this sort of politics the haves can participate, too. As a matter of fact, being the ones who on the average command superior verbal skills, and the task of defining opportunities as better or worse being essentially one of persuasive rhetorical powers, this is exactly their sort of game. Thus the haves will now become the dominant force in sustaining the process of politicalization. Increasingly it will be people from their ranks that move to the top of the socialist party organization, and accordingly the appearance and rhetoric of socialist politics will take on a different shape, becoming more and more intellectualized, changing its appeal and attracting a new class of supporters.

With this I have reached the stage in the analysis of social-democratic socialism where only a few remarks and observations are needed which will help *illustrate* the validity of the above theoretical considerations. Though it does not at all affect the validity of the conclusions reached above, depending as they do exclusively on the truth of the premises and the correctness of the deductions, there unfortunately exists no nearly perfect, quasi-experimental case to illustrate the workings of social-democratic socialism as compared with capitalism, as there was in the case of East and West Germany regarding Russian-type socialism. Illustrating the point would involve a comparison of manifestly different societies where the ceteris are clearly not paribus, and thus it would no longer be possible to neatly match certain causes with certain effects. Often, experiments in social-democratic socialism simply have not lasted long enough, or have been interrupted repeatedly by policies that could not definitely be classified as social-democratic socialism. Or else from the very beginning, they have been mixed with such different--and even inconsistent--policies as a result of political compromising, that in reality different causes and effects are so entangled that no striking illustrative evidence can be produced for *any* thesis of some degree of specificity. The task of disentangling causes and effects then becomes a genuinely theoretical one again, lacking the peculiar persuasiveness that characterizes experimentally produced evidence.

Nonetheless some evidence exists, if only of a more dubious quality. First, on the level of highly global observations, the general thesis about relative impoverishment brought about by redistributive socialism is illustrated by the fact that the standard of living is relatively higher and has become more so over time in the United States of America than in Western Europe, or, more specifically, than in the countries of the European Community (EC). Both regions are roughly comparable with respect to population size, ethnic and cultural diversity, tradition and heritage, and also with respect to natural endowments, but the United States is comparatively more capitalist and Europe more socialist. Every neutral observer will hardly fail to notice this point, as indicated also by such global measures as state expenditure as percent of GNP, which is roughly 35 percent in the United States as compared to about 50 percent or more in Western Europe. It also fits into the picture that the European countries (in particular Great Britain) exhibited more impressive rates of economic growth in the nineteenth century, which has been described repeatedly by historians as the period of classical liberalism, than in the twentieth, which, in contrast, has been termed that of socialism and statism. In the same way the validity of the theory is illustrated by the fact that Western Europe has been increasingly surpassed in rates of economic growth by some of the Pacific countries, such as Japan, Hong Kong, Singapore, and Malaysia; and that the latter, in adopting a relatively more capitalist course, have meanwhile achieved a much higher standard of living than socialistically inclined countries which started at about the same time with roughly the same basis of economic development, such as India.

Coming then to more specific observations, there are the recent experiences of Portugal, where in 1974 the autocratic Salazar regime of conservative socialism (on this type of socialism see the following chapter), which had kept Portugal one of the poorest countries in Europe, was supplanted in an upheaval by redistributive socialism (with elements of nationalization) and where since then the standard of living has fallen even further, literally turning the country into a third world region. There is also the socialist experiment of Mitterand's France, which produced an immediate deterioration of the economic situation, so noticeable--most conspicuous being a drastic rise in unemployment and repeated currency devaluations--that after less than two years, sharply reduced public support for the government forced a reversal in policy, which was almost comic in that it amounted to a complete denial of what only a few weeks before had been advocated as its dearest convictions.

The most instructive case, though, might again be provided by Germany and, this time, West Germany.[18] From 1949 to 1966 a liberal-conservative government which showed a remarkable commitment to the principles of a market economy existed, even though from the very beginning there was a considerable degree of conservative-socialist elements mixed in and these elements gained more importance over time. In any case, of all the major European nations, during this period West Germany was, in relative terms, definitely the most capitalist country, and the result of this was that it became Europe's most prosperous society, with growth rates that surpassed those of all its neighbors. Until 1961, millions of German refugees, and afterwards millions of foreign workers from southern European countries became integrated into its expanding economy, and unemployment and inflation were almost unknown. Then, after a brief transition period, from 1969 to 1982 (almost an equal time span) a social-democratically led socialist-liberal government took over. It raised taxes and social security contributions considerably, increased the number of public employees, poured additional tax funds into existing social programs and created new ones, and significantly increased spending on all sorts of so-called "public goods, "thereby allegedly equalizing opportunities and enhancing the overall "quality of life." By resorting to a Keynesian policy of deficit spending and unanticipated inflation, the effects of raising the socially guaranteed minimum provisions for nonproducers at the expense of more heavily taxed producers could be delayed for a few years (the motto of the economic policy of former West German Chancellor Helmut Schmidt was "rather 5% inflation than 5% unemployment"). They were only to become more drastic somewhat later, however, as unanticipated inflation and credit expansion had created and prolonged the over- or rather malinvestment typical of a boom. As a result, not only was there much more than 5 percent inflation, but unemployment also rose steadily and approached 10 percent; the growth of GNP became slower and slower until it actually fell in absolute terms during the last few years of the period. Instead of being an expanding economy, the absolute number of people employed decreased; more and more pressure was generated on foreign workers to leave the country and the immigration barriers were simultaneously raised to ever higher levels. All of this happened while the importance of the underground economy grew steadily.

But these were only the more evident effects of a narrowly defined economic kind. There were other effects of a different sort, which were actually of more lasting importance. With the new socialist-liberal government the idea of equalizing opportunity came to the ideological forefront. And as has been predicted theoretically, it was in particular the official spreading of the idea *mehr Demokratie wagen* ("risk more Democracy")--initially one of the most popular slogans of the new (Willy Brandt) era--that led to a degree of politicalization unheard of before. All sorts of demands were raised in the name of equality of opportunity; and there was hardly any sphere of life, from childhood to old age, from leisure to work conditions, that was not examined intensely for possible differences that it offered to different people with regard to opportunities defined as relevant. Not surprisingly, such opportunities and such differences were found constantly,[19] and, accordingly, the realm of politics seemed to expand almost daily. "There is no question that is not a political one" could be heard more and more often. In order to stay ahead of this development the parties in power had to change, too. In particular the Social Democrats, traditionally a blue-collar workers' party, had to develop a new image. With the idea of equalizing opportunity gaining ground, it increasingly became, as could be predicted, the party of the (verbal) intelligentsia, of social scientists and of teachers. And this "new" party, almost as if to prove the point that a process of politicalization will be sustained mainly by those who can profit from its distributional schemes and that the job of defining opportunities is essentially arbitrary and a matter of rhetorical power, then made it one of its central concerns to channel the most diverse political energies set in motion into the field of equalizing, above all, educational opportunities. In particular, they "equalized" the opportunities for a high school and university education, by offering the respective services not only free of charge but by literally *paying* large groups of students to take advantage of them. This not only increased the demand for educators, teachers, and social scientists, whose payment naturally had to come from taxes. It also amounted, somewhat ironically for a socialist party which argued that equalizing educational opportunities would imply an income transfer from the rich to the poor, in effect to a subsidy paid to the more intelligent at the expense of a complementary income reduction for the less intelligent, and, to the extent that there are higher numbers of intelligent people among the middle and upper social classes than among the lower, a subsidy to the haves paid by the have-nots.[20] As a result of this process of politicalization led by increased numbers of tax-paid educators gaining influence over increased numbers of students, there emerged (as could be predicted) a change in the mentality of the people. It was increasingly considered completely normal to satisfy all sorts of demands through political means, and to claim all sorts of alleged rights against other supposedly better-situated people and their property; and for a whole generation of people raised during this period, it became less and less natural to think of improving one's lot by productive effort or by contracting. Thus, when the actual economic crisis, necessitated by the redistributionist policy, arose, the people were less equipped than ever to overcome it, because over time the same policy had weakened precisely those skills and talents which were now most urgently required. Revealingly enough, when the socialist-liberal government was ousted in 1982, mainly because of its obviously miserable economic performance, it was still the prevalent opinion that the crisis should be resolved not by eliminating the causes, i.e., the swollen minimum provisions for nonproducers or noncontractors, but rather by another redistributive measure: by forcibly equalizing the available worktime for employed and unemployed people. And in line with this spirit the new conservative-liberal government in fact did no more than slow down the rate of growth of taxation.

5

THE SOCIALISM OF CONSERVATISM

In the two preceding chapters the forms of socialism most commonly known and identified as such, and that are indeed derived from basically the same ideological sources were discussed: socialism Russian-style, as most conspicuously represented by the communist countries of the East bloc; and social-democratic socialism, with its most typical representatives in the socialist and social-democratic parties of Western Europe, and to a lesser extent in the "liberals" of the United States. The property rules underlying their policy schemes were analyzed, and the idea presented that one can apply the property principles of Russian or social-democratic socialism in varying degrees: one can socialize all means of production or just a few, and one can tax away and redistribute almost all income, and almost all types of income, or one can do this with just a small portion of only a few types of income. But, as was demonstrated by theoretical means and, less stringently, through some illustrative empirical evidence, as long as one adheres to these principles *at all* and does not once and for all abandon the notion of ownership rights belonging to nonproducers (nonusers) and noncontractors, relative impoverishment must be the result.

This chapter will show that the same is true of conservatism, because it, too, is a form of socialism. Conservatism also produces impoverishment, and all the more so, the more resolutely it is applied. But before going into a systematic and detailed economic analysis of the peculiar ways in which conservatism produces this effect, it would be appropriate to take a short look at history, in order to better understand why conservatism indeed is socialism, and how it is related to the two egalitarian forms of socialism discussed previously.

Roughly speaking, before the eighteenth century in Europe and throughout the world, a social system of "feudalism" or "absolutism," which was in fact feudalism on a grander scale, existed.[1] In abstract terms, the social order of feudalism was characterized by a regional overlord who claimed ownership of some territory, including all of its resources and goods, and quite often also of all of the men placed upon it, without having originally appropriated them himself through use or work, and without having a contractual claim to them. On the contrary, the territory, or better, the various parts of it and the goods standing on it, had been actively occupied, used, and produced by different people before (the "natural owners"). The ownership claims of the feudal lords were thus derived from thin air. Hence, the practice, based on these alleged ownership rights, of renting land and other production factors out to the natural owners in return for goods and services unilaterally fixed by the overlord, had to be enforced against the will of these natural owners, by brutal force and armed violence, with the help of a noble caste of military men who were rewarded by the overlord for their services by being allowed to participate and share in his exploitative methods and proceeds. For the common man subject to this order, life meant tyranny, exploitation, economic stagnation, poverty, starvation, and despair.[2]

As might be expected, there was resistance to this system. Interestingly enough though (from a present-day perspective), it was not the peasant population who suffered most from the existing order, but the merchants and traders who became the leading opponents of the feudal system. Buying at a lower price in one place and traveling and selling at a higher price in a different place, as they did, made their subordination to any one feudal lord relatively weak. They were essentially a class of "international" men, crossing the borders of various feudal territories constantly. As such, in order to do business they required a stable, internationally valid legal system: a system of rules, valid regardless of time and place, defining property and contract, which would facilitate the evolution of the institutions of credit, banking and insurance essential to any large-scale trading business. Naturally, this caused friction between the merchants and the feudal lords as representatives of various arbitrary, regional, legal systems. The merchants became feudalism's outcasts, permanently threatened and harassed by the noble military caste attempting to bring them under their control.[3]

In order to escape this threat the merchants were forced to organize themselves and help establish small fortified trading places at the very fringes of the centers of feudal power. As places of partial exterritoriality and at least partial freedom, they soon attracted growing numbers of the peasantry running away from feudal exploitation and economic misery, and they grew into small towns, fostering the development of crafts and productive enterprises which could not have emerged in the surroundings of exploitation and legal instability characteristic of the feudal order itself. This process was more pronounced where the feudal powers were relatively weak and where power was dispersed among a great number of often very minor, rival feudal lords. It was in the cities of northern Italy, the cities of the Hanseatic league, and those of Flanders that the spirit of capitalism first blossomed, and commerce and production reached their highest levels.[4]

But this partial emancipation from the restrictions and the stagnation of feudalism was only temporary, and was followed by reaction and decline. This was due in part to internal weaknesses in the movement of the new merchant class itself. Still too much ingrained in the minds of men was the feudal way of thinking in terms of different ranks assigned to people, of subordination and power, and of order having to be imposed upon men through coercion. Hence, in the newly emerging commercial centers a new set of noncontractual regulations and restrictions--now of "bourgeois" origin--was soon established, guilds that restrained free competition were formed, and a new merchant oligarchy arose.[5] More important, though, for this reactionary process was yet another fact. In their endeavor to free themselves from the exploitative interventions of the various feudal lords, the merchants had to look for natural allies. Understandably enough, they found such allies among those from the class of feudal lords who, though comparatively more powerful than their noble fellows, had the centers of their power at a relatively greater distance from the commercial towns seeking assistance. In aligning themselves with the merchant class, they sought to extend their power beyond its present range at the expense of other, minor lords.[6] In order to achieve this goal they first granted certain exemptions from the "normal" obligations falling upon the subjects of feudal rule to the rising urban centers, thus assuring their existence as places of partial freedom, and offered protection from the neighboring feudal powers. But as soon as the coalition had succeeded in its joint attempt to weaken the local lords and the merchant towns' "foreign" feudal ally had thereby become established as a real power outside of its own traditional territory, it moved ahead and established itself as a feudal super power, i.e., as a monarchy, with a king who superimposed his own exploitative rules onto those of the already existing feudal system. Absolutism had been born; and as this was nothing but feudalism on a larger scale, economic decline again set in, the towns disintegrated, and stagnation and misery returned.[7]

It was not until the late seventeenth and early eighteenth centuries, then, that feudalism came under truly heavy attack. This time the attack was more severe, because it was no longer simply the attempt of practical men--the merchants--to secure spheres of relative freedom in order to do their practical business. It was increasingly an ideological battle fought against feudalism. Intellectual reflection on the causes of the rise and decline of commerce and industry that had been experienced, and a more intensive study of Roman and in particular of Natural Law, which had both been rediscovered in the course of the merchants' struggle to develop an international merchant law and justify it against the competing claims of feudal law, had led to a sounder understanding of the concept of liberty, and of liberty as a prerequisite to economic prosperity.[8] As these ideas, culminating in such works as J. Locke's "Two Treatises on Government," 1688, and A. Smith's "Wealth of Nations," 1776, spread and occupied the minds of a steadily expanding circle of people, the old order lost its legitimacy. The old way of thinking in terms of feudal bonds gradually gave way to the idea of a contractual society. Finally, as outward expressions of this changed state of affairs in public opinion, the Glorious Revolution of 1688 in England, the American Revolution of 1776, and the French Revolution of 1789 came along; and nothing was the same after these revolutions had occurred. They proved, once and for all, that the old order was not invincible, and they sparked new hope for further progress on the road toward freedom and prosperity.

Liberalism, as the ideological movement that had brought about these earth-shattering events came to be called, emerged from these revolutions stronger than ever and became for somewhat more than half a century the dominating ideological force in Western Europe. It was the party of freedom and of private property acquired through occupation and contract, assigning to the state merely the role of enforcer of these natural rules.[9] With remnants of the feudal system still in effect everywhere, however shaken in their ideological foundation, it was the party representing an increasingly liberalized, deregulated, contractualized society, internally and externally, i.e., regarding domestic as well as foreign affairs and relations. And as under the pressure of liberal ideas the European societies became increasingly free of feudal restrictions, it also became the party of the Industrial Revolution, which was caused and stimulated by this very process of liberalization. Economic development set in at a pace never before experienced by mankind. Industry and commerce flourished, and capital formation and accumulation reached new heights. While the standard of living did not rise immediately for everyone, it became possible to support a growing number of people--people, that is, who only a few years before, under feudalism, would have died of starvation because of the lack of economic wealth, and who could now survive. In addition, with population growth leveling off below the growth rate of capital, now everyone could realistically entertain the hope of rising living standards being just around the corner.[10]

It is against this background of history (somewhat streamlined, of course, as it has just been presented) that the phenomenon of conservatism as a form of socialism and its relation to the two versions of socialism originating in Marxism must be seen and understood. All forms of socialism are ideological responses to the challenge posed by the advance of liberalism; but their stand taken against liberalism and feudalism--the old order that liberalism had helped to destroy--differs considerably. The advance of liberalism had stimulated social change at a pace, to an extent, and in variations unheard of before. The liberalization of society meant that increasingly only those people could keep a given social position once acquired who could do so by producing most efficiently for the most urgent wants of voluntary consumers with as little cost as possible, and by relying exclusively on contractual relationships with respect to the hiring of factors of production and, in particular, of labor. Empires upheld solely by force were crumbling under this pressure. And as consumer demand to which the production structure now increasingly had to adapt (and not vice versa) was changing constantly, and the upspring of new enterprises became increasingly less regulated (insofar as it was the result of original appropriation and/or contract), no one's relative position in the hierarchy of income and wealth was secure anymore. Instead, upward and downward social mobility increased significantly, for neither particular factor-owners nor owners of particular labor services were any longer immune to respective changes in demand. They were no longer guaranteed stable prices or a stable income.[11]

Old Marxist and new social-democratic socialism are the egalitarian, progressive answers to this challenge of change, uncertainty, and mobility. Like liberalism, they hail the destruction of feudalism and the advance of capitalism. They realize that it was capitalism that freed people from exploitative feudal bonds and produced enormous improvements in the economy; and they understand that capitalism, and the development of the productive forces brought about by it, was a necessary and positive evolutionary step on the way toward socialism. Socialism, as they conceive it, shares the same goals with liberalism: freedom and prosperity. But socialism supposedly improves on the achievements of liberalism by supplanting capitalism--the anarchy of production of private competitors which causes the just-mentioned change, mobility, uncertainty, and unrest in the social fabric--at its highest stage of development by a rationally planned and coordinated economy which prevents insecurities derived from this change from being felt at an individual level. Unfortunately, of course, as the last two chapters have sufficiently demonstrated, this is a rather confused idea. It is precisely by making individuals insensitive to change through redistributional measures that the incentive to adapt quickly to any future change is taken away, and hence the value, in terms of consumer evaluations, of the output produced will fall. And it is precisely because one plan is substituted for many seemingly uncoordinated ones that individual freedom is reduced and, mutatis mutandis, government by one man over another increased.

Conservatism, on the other hand, is the anti-egalitarian, reactionary answer to the dynamic changes set in motion by a liberalized society: It is anti-liberal and, rather than recognizing the achievements of liberalism, tends to idealize and glorify the old system of feudalism as orderly and stable.[12] As a postrevolutionary phenomenon, it does not necessarily and outrightly advocate a return to the prerevolutionary status quo ante and accepts certain changes, however regretfully, as irreversible. But it is hardly ruffled when old feudal powers that had lost all or parts of their estates to the natural owners in the course of the liberalization process are restored to their old position, and it definitely and openly propagates the conservation of the status quo, i.e., the given highly unequal distribution of property, wealth, and income. Its idea is to stop or slow down the permanent changes and mobility processes brought about by liberalism and capitalism as completely as possible and, instead, to recreate an orderly and stable social system in which everyone remains securely in the position that the past had assigned to him.[13]

In order to do so, conservatism must, and indeed does, advocate the legitimacy of noncontractual means in the acquisition and retention of property and income derived from it, since it was precisely the exclusive reliance on contractual relations that *caused* the very permanence of changes in the relative distribution of income and wealth. Just as feudalism allowed the acquisition and upholding of property and wealth by force, so conservatism ignores whether or not people have acquired or retain their given income-and wealth-position through original appropriation and contract. Instead, conservatism deems it appropriate and legitimate for a class of once-established owners to have the right to stop any social change that it considers a threat to their relative position in the social hierarchy of income and wealth, even if the various individual owner-users of various production factors did not contract into any such agreement. Conservatism, then, must be addressed as the ideological heir of feudalism. And as feudalism must be described as aristocratic socialism (which should be clear enough from its above characterization), so must conservatism be considered as the socialism of the bourgeois establishment. Liberalism, to which both the egalitarian and the conservative versions of socialism are ideological responses, reached the height of its influence around the mid-nineteenth century. Probably its very last glorious achievements were the repeal of the Corn Laws in England in 1846, accomplished by R. Cobden, J. Bright and the anti-corn law league, and the 1848 revolutions of continental Europe. Then, because of internal weaknesses and inconsistencies in the ideology of liberalism,[14] the diversions and the divisiveness which the various nation states' imperialist adventures had brought about, and last but not least because of the appeal that the different versions of socialism with their various promises of security and stability had and still have for the public's widespread distaste for dynamic change and mobility,[15] liberalism's decline set in. Socialism increasingly supplanted it as a dominating ideological force, thereby reversing the process of liberalization and once again imposing more and more noncontractual elements on society.[16] At different times and places, different types of socialism found support in public opinion to varying degrees, so that today traces of all of them can be found to coexist in different degrees everywhere and to compound their respective impoverishment effects on the process of production, the upkeep of wealth and the formation of character. But it is the influence of conservative socialism, in particular, that must be stressed, especially because it is very often overlooked or underestimated. If today the societies of Western Europe can be described as socialist, this is due much more to the influence of the socialism of conservatism than to that of egalitarian ideas. It is the peculiar way in which conservatism exerts its influence, though, that explains why this is often not recognized. Conservatism not only shapes the social structure by enacting policy; especially in societies like the European ones where the feudal past has never been completely shaken off but where a great number of feudal remnants survived even the peak of liberalism. An ideology such as conservatism also exerts its influence, very inconspicuously, by simply maintaining the status quo and letting things continue to be done according to age-old traditions. What then are the specifically conservative elements in present-day societies, and how do they produce relative impoverishment? With this question, we turn to the systematic analysis of conservatism and its economic and socio-economic effects. An abstract characterization of the property rules underlying conservatism and a description of these rules in terms of the natural theory of property shall again be the starting point. There are two such rules. First, conservative socialism, like social-democratic socialism, does not outlaw private property. Quite to the contrary: everything--all factors of production and all of the nonproductively used wealth--can in principle be privately owned, sold, bought, rented out, with the exception again only of such areas as education, traffic and communication, central banking, and security production. But then secondly, no owner owns *all* of his property and all of the income that can be derived from its utilization. Rather, part of this belongs to the society of present owners and income recipients, and society has the right to allocate present and future produced income and wealth to its individual members in such a way that the old, relative distribution of income and wealth is preserved. And it is also society's right to determine how large or small the income and wealth-share that is so administered should be, and what exactly is needed to preserve a given income and wealth-distribution.[17]

From the perspective of the natural theory of property, the property arrangement of conservatism again implies an aggression against the rights of natural owners. Natural owners of things can do whatever they wish with them, as long as they do not uninvitedly change the physical integrity of someone else's property. This implies, in particular, their right to change their property or to put it to different uses in order to adapt to anticipated changes in demand and so preserve or possibly enhance its value; and it also gives them the right to reap privately the benefits of increased property values that stem from unanticipated changes in demand--from changes, that is, that were lucky for them, but which they did not foresee or effectuate. But at the same time, since according to the principles of the natural theory of property every natural owner is only protected against physical invasion and the noncontractual acquisition and transfer of property titles, it also implies that everyone constantly and permanently runs the risk that through changes in demand or actions which other owners perform with their property, property values will fall below their given level. According to this theory, however, no one owns the *value* of his property and hence no one, at any time, has the right to preserve and restore his property *values*. As compared with this, conservatism aims precisely at such a preservation or restoration of values and their relative distribution. But this is only possible, of course, if a redistribution in the assignment of property titles takes place. Since no one's property values depend exclusively on one's own actions performed with one's own property, but also, and inescapably so, on other peoples' actions performed with scarce means under their own control (and beyond that of another's), in order to preserve given property values someone--some single person or some group of persons--would have to rightfully own all scarce means (far beyond those that are actually controlled or used by this person or group of persons). Furthermore, this group must literally own all persons' bodies, since the use that a person makes of his body can also influence (increase or decrease) existing property values. Thus, in order to realize the goal of conservatism, a redistribution of property titles must occur away from people as user-owners of scarce resources onto people who, whatever their merits as past producers, did not presently use or contractually acquire those things whose utilization had led to the change in the given distribution of values.

With this understood, the first conclusion regarding the general economic effect of conservatism lies at hand: with the natural owners of things fully or partially expropriated to the advantage of nonusers, nonproducers and noncontractors, conservatism eliminates or reduces the former's incentive to do something about the value of existing property and to adapt to changes in demand. The incentives to be aware of and to anticipate changes in demand, to quickly adjust existing property and to use it in a manner consistent with such changed circumstances, to increase productive efforts, and to save and invest are reduced, as the possible gains from such behavior can no longer be privately appropriated but will be socialized. Mutatis mutandis, the incentive is increased to do nothing in order to avoid the permanent risk of one's property values falling below their present level, as the possible losses from such behavior no longer have to be privately appropriated, but will also be socialized. Thus, since all these activities--the avoidance of risk, awareness, adaptability, work, and saving--are costly and require the use of time and possibly other scarce resources which at the same time could be used in alternative ways (for leisure and consumption, for instance), there will be fewer of the former activities and more of the latter, and as a consequence the general standard of living will fall. Hence, one would have to conclude that the conservative goal of preserving existing values and existing distributions of values among different individuals can only be accomplished at the expense of a general, relative drop in the overall value of newly produced and old, maintained goods, i.e., reduced social wealth.

It has probably become apparent by now that from the point of view of economic analysis, there is a striking similarity between the socialism of conservatism and social-democratic socialism. Both forms of socialism involve a redistribution of property titles away from producers/contractors onto non-producers/noncontractors, and both thereby separate the processes of producing and contracting from that of the actual acquisition of income and wealth. In doing this, both make the acquisition of income and wealth a political affair--an affair, that is, in the course of which one (group of) person(s) imposes its will regarding the use of scarce means onto the will of other, recalcitrant people; both versions of socialism, though in principle claiming full ownership of all of the income and wealth produced on behalf of nonproducers, allow their programs to be implemented in a gradual fashion and carried through to varying degrees; and both, as a consequence of all this, must, to the extent that the respective policy is indeed enacted, lead to relative impoverishment.

The difference between conservatism and what has been termed social-democratic socialism lies exclusively in the fact that they appeal to different people or to different sentiments in the same people in that they prefer a different way in which the income and wealth extracted noncontractually from producers is then redistributed to nonproducers. Redistributive socialism assigns income and wealth to nonproducers regardless of their past achievements as owners of wealth and income recipients, or even tries to eradicate existing differences. Conservatism, on the other hand, allocates income to nonproducers in accordance with their past, unequal income and wealth-position and aims at stabilizing the existing income distribution and existing income differentials.[18] The difference is thus merely one of social-psychology: in favoring different patterns of distribution, they grant privileges to different groups of nonproducers. Redistributive socialism particularly favors the have-nots among nonproducers, and especially disadvantages the haves among the producers; and, accordingly, it tends to find its supporters mostly among the former and its enemies among the latter. Conservatism grants special advantages to the haves among the group of nonproducers and particularly damages the interests of the have-nots among productive people; and so it tends to find its supporters mainly in the ranks of the former and spreads despair, hopelessness, and resentment among the latter group of people.

But although it is true that both systems of socialism are very much alike from an economic point of view, the difference between them with respect to their socio-psychological basis still has an impact on their respective economics. To be sure, this impact does not affect the general impoverishment effects resulting from the expropriation of producers (as explained above), which they both have in common. Instead, it influences the choices that social-democratic socialism on the one hand and conservatism on the other make among the specific instruments or techniques available for reaching their respective distributional goals. Social-democratic socialism's favorite technique is that of taxation, as described and analyzed in the preceding chapter. Conservatism can use this instrument, too, of course; and indeed it must make use of it to some extent, if only to finance the enforcement of its policies. But taxation is not its preferred technique, and the explanation for this is to be found in the social-psychology of conservatism. Dedicated to the preservation of a status quo of unequal positions of income, wealth, and status, taxation is simply too progressive an instrument for reaching conservative goals. To resort to taxation means that one lets changes in the distribution of wealth and income happen first, and only then, after they have come into existence, does one rectify things again and restore the old order. However, to proceed in this way not only causes bad feelings, particularly among those who through their own efforts have actually improved their relative position first and are then cut back again. But also, by letting progress occur and then trying to undo it, conservatism weakens its own justification, i.e., its reasoning that a given distribution of income and wealth is legitimate because it is the one which has always been in effect. Hence, conservatism prefers that changes do not occur in the first place, and it prefers to use policy measures that promise to do just this, or rather, promise to help make such changes less apparent.

There are three such general types of policy measures: price- controls, regulations, and behavior controls, all of which, to be sure, are socialistic measures, as is taxation, but all of which, interestingly enough, have generally been as neglected in attempts to assess the overall degree of socialism in different societies, as the importance of taxation in this regard has been overrated.[19] I will discuss these specific conservative policy schemes in turn.

Any change in (relative) prices evidently causes changes in the relative position of the people supplying the respective goods or services. Hence, in order to fix their position it would seem that all that need be done is fix prices--this is the conservative rationale for introducing price controls. To check the validity of this conclusion the economic effects of price-fixings need to be examined.[20] To begin with, it is assumed that a selective price control for one product or one group of products has been enacted and that the current market price has been decreed as the price above or below which the product may not to be sold. Now, as long as the fixed price is identical to the market price, the price control will simply be ineffective. The peculiar effects of price-fixing can only come about once this identity no longer exists. And as any price-fixing does not eliminate the causes that would have brought about price changes, but simply decrees that no attention be paid to them, this occurs as soon as there are any changes in demand, for whatever reason, for the product in question. If the demand increases (and prices, not being controlled, would go up as well) then the fixed price turns into an effective *maximum price*, i.e., a price above which it is illegal to sell. If the demand decreases (and prices, without controls, would fall), then the fixed price becomes an effective minimum price, i.e., a price below which it becomes illegal to sell.[21]

The consequence of imposing of a maximum price is an excess demand for the goods supplied. Not everyone willing to buy at the fixed price can do so. And this shortage will last as long as prices are not allowed to rise with the increased demand, and hence, no possibility exists for the producers (who assumedly had already been producing up to the point at which marginal costs, i.e., the cost of producing the last unit of the product concerned, equaled marginal revenue) to direct additional resources into the specific line of production, thus increasing output without incurring losses. Queues, rationing, favoritism, under-the-table payments, and black markets will become permanent features of life. And the shortages and other side effects which they bring along will even increase, as excess demand for the price-controlled goods will spill over to all other noncontrolled goods (in particular, of course, to substitutes), increase their (relative) prices, and thereby create an additional incentive to shift resources from controlled into noncontrolled lines of production.

Imposing a minimum price, i.e., a price above the potential market price below which sales become illegal, mutatis mutandis produces an excess of supply over demand. There will be a surplus of goods produced that simply cannot find buyers. And again: this surplus will continue as long as prices are not allowed to drop along with the reduced demand for the product in question. Milk and wine lakes, butter and grain mountains, to cite just a few examples, will develop and grow; and as the storage bins fill up it will become necessary to repeatedly destroy the surplus production (or, as an alternative, to pay the producers *not* to produce the surplus anymore). Surplus production will even become aggravated as the artificially high price attracts an even higher investment of resources in this particular field, which then will be lacking in other production lines where there is actually a greater need for them (in terms of consumer demand), and where, as a consequence, product prices will rise.

Maximum or minimum prices--in either case price controls will result in relative impoverishment. In any event they will lead to a situation in which there are too many (in terms of consumer demand) resources bound up in production lines of reduced importance and not enough are available in lines of increased relevance. Production factors can no longer be allocated so that the most urgent wants are satisfied first, the next urgent ones second, etc., or, more precisely, so that the production of any one product is not extended above (or reduced below) the level at which the utility of the marginal product falls below (or remains above) the marginal utility of any other product. Rather, the imposition of price controls means that less urgent wants are satisfied at the expense of reduced satisfaction of more urgent wants. And this is to say nothing else than that the standard of living will be reduced. That people waste their time scrambling for goods because they are in artificially low supply or that goods are thrown away because they are held in artificially high supply are only the two most conspicuous symptoms of this reduced social wealth.

But this is not all. The preceding analysis also reveals that conservatism cannot even reach its goal of distributional stability by means of partial price control. With only partially controlled prices, disruptions in the existing income and wealth position still must occur, as producers in uncontrolled lines of production, or in lines of production with minimum product prices are favored at the expense of those in controlled lines, or lines with maximum product prices. Hence there will continue to be an incentive for individual producers to shift from one line of production into a different, more profitable one, with the consequence that differences in the entrepreneurial alertness and ability to foresee and implement such profitable shifts will arise and result in disruptions of the established order. Conservatism then, if it is indeed uncompromising in its commitment to the preservation of the status quo, is driven to constantly enlargening the circle of goods subject to price controls and actually cannot stop short of complete price controls or price-freezing.[22] Only if the prices of all goods and services, of capital and of consumer goods alike, are frozen at some given level, and the production process is thus completely separated from demand--instead of disconnecting production and demand at only a few points or sectors as under partial price control--does it seem possible to preserve an existing distributional order in full. Not surprisingly, though, the price that has to be paid for such full-blown conservatism is even higher than that of only partial price controls.[23] With all-around price control, private ownership of means of production is in fact abolished. There can still be private owners in name, but the right to determine the use of their property and to engage in any contractual exchange that is deemed beneficial is lost completely. The immediate consequence of this silent expropriation of producers then will be a reduction in saving and investing and, mutatis mutandis, an increase in consumption. As one can no longer charge for the fruits of one's labor what the market will bear, there is simply less of a reason to work. And in addition, as prices are fixed--independent of the value that consumers attach to the products in question--there is also less of a reason to be concerned about the quality of the particular type of work or product that one still happens to perform or produce, and hence the quality of each and every product will fall.

But even more important than this is the impoverishment that results from the allocational chaos created by universal price controls. While all product prices, including those of all cost factors and, in particular, of labor are frozen, the demand for the various products still changes constantly. Without price controls, prices would follow the direction of this change and thereby create an incentive to constantly move out of less valued lines of production into more valued ones. Under universal price controls this mechanism is completely destroyed. Should the demand for a product increase, a shortage will develop as prices are not allowed to rise, and hence, because the profitability of producing the particular product has not been altered, no additional production factors will be attracted. As a consequence, excess demand, left unsatisfied, will spill over to other products, increasing the demand for them above the level that otherwise would have been established. But here again, prices are not allowed to rise with the increased demand, and again a shortage will develop. And so the process of shifting demand from most urgently wanted products to products of secondary importance, and from there to products of still lesser relevance, since again not everyone's attempt to buy at the controlled price can be satisfied, must go on and on. Finally, since there are no alternatives available and the paper money that people still have to spend has a lower intrinsic value than even the least valuable product available for sale, excess demand will spill over to products for which demand had originally declined. Hence, even in those lines of production where a surplus had emerged as the consequence of declining demand but where prices had not been allowed to fall accordingly, sales again will pick up as a consequence of unsatisfied demand elsewhere in the economy; in spite of the artificially high fixed price surpluses will become saleable; and, with profitability thus restored, an outflow of capital will be prevented even here.

The imposition of all-around price controls means that the system of production has become completely independent of the preferences of consumers for whose satisfaction production is actually undertaken. The producers can produce anything and the consumers have no choice but to buy it, whatever it is. Accordingly, any change in the production structure that is made or ordered to be made without the help offered by freely floating prices is nothing but a groping in the dark, replacing one arbitrary array of goods offered by another equally arbitrary one. There is simply no connection anymore between the production structure and the structure of demand. On the level of consumer experience this means, as has been described by G. Reisman, "... flooding people with shirts, while making them go barefoot, or inundating them with shoes while making them go shirtless; of giving them enormous quantities of writing paper, but no pens or ink, or vice versa; ... indeed of giving them any absurd combination of goods." But, of course, "... merely giving consumers unbalanced combinations of goods is itself equivalent to a major decline in production, for it represents just as much of a loss in human well-being."[24] The standard of living does not simply depend on some total physical output of production; it depends much more on the proper distribution or proportioning of the various specific production factors in producing a well-balanced composition of a variety of consumer goods. Universal price controls, as the 'ultima ratio' of conservatism, prevent such a well-proportioned composition from being brought about. Order and stability are only seemingly created; in truth they are a means of creating allocational chaos and arbitrariness, and thereby drastically reduce the general standard of living.

In addition, and this leads to the discussion of the second specifically conservative policy instrument, i.e., regulations, even if prices are controlled all-around this can only safeguard an existing order of income and wealth distribution if it is unrealistically assumed that products as well as their producers are "stationary." Changes in the existing order cannot be ruled out, though, if there are new and different products produced, new technologies for producing products are developed, or additional producers spring up. All of this would lead to disruptions in the existing order, as the old products, technologies, and producers, subject as they are to price controls, would then have to compete with new and different products and services (which, since they are new, *cannot* have been price-controlled), and they would probably lose some of their established income-share to the newcomers in the course of this competition. To compensate for such disruptions, conservatism could once again make use of the instrument of taxation, and indeed to some extent it does. But to let innovations occur first without hindrance and to then tax the gains away from the innovators and restore the old order is, as was explained, too progressive an instrument for a policy of conservatism. Conservatism prefers *regulations* as a means of preventing or slowing down innovations and the social changes that they bring about.

The most drastic way of regulating the system of production would be simply to outlaw any innovation. Such a policy, it should be noted, has its adherents among those who complain about others' consumerism, i.e., about the fact that today there are already "all too many" goods and services on the market, and who wish to freeze or even reduce this present diversity; and also, for slightly different reasons, among those who want to freeze present production technology out of the fear that technological innovations, as labor- saving devices, would "destroy" (existing) jobs. Nonetheless, an outright prohibition of all innovative change has hardly ever been seriously attempted--perhaps with the recent exception of the Pol Pot regime--because of a lack of support in public opinion which could not be convinced that such a policy would not be extremely costly in terms of welfare losses. Quite popular, though, has been an only slightly more moderate approach: While no change is ruled out in principle, any innovation must be officially approved (approved, that is, by people other than the innovator himself) before it can be implemented. This way, conservatism argues, it is assured that innovations are indeed socially acceptable, that progress is gradual, that it can be introduced simultaneously by all producers, and that everyone can share in its advantages. Compulsory, i.e., government-enforced, cartels are the most popular means for achieving this effect. By requiring all producers, or all producers of one industry, to become members of one supervisory organization--the cartel--it becomes possible to avoid the all-too-visible excess supply brought about by minimum price controls--through the imposition of production quotas. Moreover, the disruptions caused by any innovative measure can then be centrally monitored and moderated. But while this approach has been gaining ground constantly in

Europe and to a somewhat lesser degree in the United States, and while certain sectors of the economy are indeed already subject to very similar controls, the most popular and most frequently used conservative-socialist regulatory instrument is still that of establishing predefined standards for predefined categories of products or producers to which all innovations must conform. These regulations lay down the kind of qualifications a person must fulfill (other than the "normal" ones of being the rightful owner of things and of not damaging the physical integrity of other peoples' property through one's own actions) in order to have the right to establish himself as a producer of some sort; or they stipulate the kinds of tests (as regards, for instance, materials, appearance, or measurements) a product of a given type must undergo before being newly allowed on the market; or they prescribe definite checks that any technological improvement must pass in order to become a newly approbated method of production. With such regulatory means innovations can neither be completely ruled out, nor can it be altogether avoided that some changes might even be quite surprising. But as the predefined standards to which changes have to conform must of necessity be "conservative," i.e., formulated in terms of existing products, producers, or technologies, they serve the purpose of conservatism in that they will indeed at least slow down the speed of innovative changes and the range of possible surprises.

In any case, all these types of regulations, the first mentioned ones more and the latter less, will lead to a reduction in the general standard of living.[25] An innovation, to be sure, can only be successful, and thus allow the innovator to disrupt the existing order of income and wealth distribution, if it is indeed more highly valued by the consumers than the competing old products. The imposition of regulations, however, implies a redistribution of property titles away from the innovators and onto the established producers, products, and technologies. Hence, in fully or partially socializing possible income and wealth gains stemming from innovative changes in the process of production and mutatis mutandis by fully or partially socializing the possible losses from not innovating, the process of innovation will be slowed down, there will be fewer innovators and innovations, and instead, a strengthened tendency will emerge to settle for the way things are. This means nothing else than that the process of increasing consumer satisfaction by producing more highly evaluated goods and services in more efficient, cost-saving ways is brought to a standstill, or is at least hampered. Thus, even if in a somewhat different way than price controls, regulations will make the production structure fall out of line with demand, too. And while this might help safeguard an existing distribution of wealth, it must once again be paid for by a general decline in the overall wealth that is incorporated in this very same production structure.

Finally, the third specifically conservative policy instrument is behavioral controls. Price controls and regulations freeze the supply side of an economic system and thereby separate it from demand. But this does not preclude changes in demand from coming into existence; it only makes the supply side irresponsive to it. And so it can still happen that discrepancies not only emerge, but that they also become appallingly apparent as such. Behavioral controls are policy measures designed to control the demand side. They aim at the prevention or retardation of changes in demand in order to make the irresponsiveness of the supply side less visible, thereby completing the task of conservatism: the preservation of an existing order from disruptive changes of any kind.

Price controls and regulations on one side, and behavioral controls on the other are thus the two complementary parts of a conservative policy. And of these two complementary sides of conservatism, it might well be argued that it is the side of behavioral controls that is the most distinctive feature of a conservative policy. Though the different forms of socialism favor different categories of nonproductive and noninnovative people at the expense of different categories of potential producers and innovators, just as much as any other variant of socialism conservatism tends to produce less productive, less innovative people, forcing them to increase consumption or channel their productive and innovative energies into black markets. But of all the forms of socialism, it is only conservatism which as part of its program interferes directly with consumption and noncommercial exchanges. (All other forms, to be sure, have their effect on consumption, too, insofar as they lead to a reduction in the standard of living; but unlike conservatism, they leave the consumer pretty much alone with whatever is left for him to consume.) Conservatism not only cripples the development of one's productive talents; under the name "paternalism" it also wants to freeze the behavior of people in their roles as isolated consumers or as exchange partners in noncommercial forms of exchanges, thereby stifling or suppressing one's talent to develop a consumer lifestyle that best satisfies one's recreational needs, too.

Any change in the pattern of consumer behavior has its economic side effects. (If I let my hair grow longer this affects the barbers and the scissors industry; if more people divorce this affects lawyers and the housing market; if I start smoking marijuana this has consequences not only for the use of agricultural land but also for the ice cream industry, etc.; and above all, all such behavior disequilibrates the existing value system of whoever happens to feel affected by it.) Any change could thus appear to be a disruptive element vis à vis a conservative production structure, conservatism, in principle, would have to consider *all* actions--the whole lifestyle of people in their roles as individual consumers or noncommercial exchangers as proper objects of behavioral controls. Full-blown conservatism would amount to the establishment of a social system in which everything except the traditional way of behaving (which is explicitly allowed) is outlawed. In practice, conservatism could never go quite this far, as there are costs connected with controls and as it would normally have to reckon with rising resistance in the public opinion. "Normal" conservatism, then, is characterized instead by smaller or greater numbers of specific laws and prohibitions which outlaw and punish various forms of nonaggressive behavior of isolated consumers, or of people engaging in noncommercial exchanges--of actions, that is to say, which if indeed performed, would neither change the physical integrity of anyone else's property, nor violate anyone's right to refuse any exchange that does not seem advantageous, but which would rather (only) disrupt the established "paternal" order of social values.

Once again the effect of such a policy of behavioral controls is, in any case, relative impoverishment. Through the imposition of such controls not only is one group of people hurt by the fact that they are no longer allowed to perform certain nonaggressive forms of behavior but another group benefits from these controls in that they no longer have to tolerate such disliked forms of behavior. More specifically, the losers in this redistribution of property rights are the user-producers of the things whose consumption is now hampered, and those who gain are nonusers/nonproducers of the consumer goods in question. Thus, a new and different incentive structure regarding production or nonproduction is established and applied to a given population. The production of consumer goods has been made more costly since their value has fallen as a consequence of the imposition of controls regarding their use, and, mutatis mutandis, the acquisition of consumer satisfaction through nonproductive, noncontractual means has been made relatively less costly. As a consequence, there will be less production, less saving and investing, and a greater tendency instead to gain satisfaction at the expense of others through political, i.e., aggressive, methods. And, in particular, insofar as the restrictions imposed by behavioral controls concern the use that a person can make of his own body, the consequence will be a lowered value attached to it and, accordingly, a reduced investment in human capital.

With this we have reached the end of the theoretical analysis of conservatism as a special form of socialism. Once again, in order to round out the discussion a few remarks which might help illustrate the validity of the above conclusions shall be made. As in the discussion of social-democratic socialism, these illustrative observations should be read with some precautions: first, the validity of the conclusions reached in this chapter has been, can, and must be established independent of experience. And second, as far as experience and empirical evidence are concerned, there are unfortunately no examples of societies that could be studied for the effects of conservatism as compared to the other variants of socialism and capitalism. There is no quasi-experimental case study which alone could provide one with what is normally considered "striking" evidence. Reality is rather such that all sorts of policy measures--conservative, social-democratic, Marxist-socialist, and also capitalist-liberal--are so mixed and combined, that their respective effects cannot usually be neatly matched with definite causes, but must be disentangled and matched once more by purely theoretical means.

With this in mind, though, something might well be said about the actual performance of conservatism in history. Once more, the difference in the living standards between the United States and the countries of Western Europe (taken together) permits an observation that fits the theoretical picture. Surely, as mentioned in the previous chapter, Europe has more redistributive socialism--as indicated roughly by the overall degree of taxation--than the United States, and is poorer because of this. But more striking still is the difference that exists between the two with respect to the degree of conservatism.[26] Europe has a feudal past that is noticeable to this very day, in particular in the form of numerous regulations that restrict trade and hamper entry and prohibitions of nonaggressive actions, whereas the United States is remarkably free of this past. Connected with this is the fact that for long periods during the nineteenth and twentieth centuries, Europe had been shaped by policies of more or less explicitly conservative parties rather than by any other political ideology, whereas a genuinely conservative party never existed in the United States. Indeed, even the socialist parties of Western Europe were infected to a notable extent by conservatism, in particular under the influence of the labor unions, and imposed numerous conservative-socialist elements (regulations and price controls, that is) on the European societies during their periods of influence (while they admittedly helped abolish some of the conservative behavioral controls). In any case then, given that Europe is more socialist than the United States and its living standards are relatively lower, this is due less to the greater influence of social-democratic socialism in Europe and more to the influence of the socialism of conservatism--as indicated not so much by its higher overall degrees of taxation, but rather by the significantly higher numbers of price controls, regulations, and behavioral controls in Europe. I should hasten to add that the United States is not richer than it actually is and no longer exhibits its nineteenth century economic vigor not only because they adopted more and more of redistributive socialism's policies over time, but more so because they, too, increasingly fell prey to the conservative ideology of wanting to protect a status quo of income and wealth distribution from competition, and in particular the position of the haves among existing producers, by means of regulations and price controls.[27]

On even a more global level, another observation fits the theoretically derived picture of conservatism causing impoverishment. For outside the so-called Western world, the only countries that match the miserable economic performance of the outrightly Marxist-socialist regimes are precisely those societies in Latin America and Asia that have never seriously broken with their feudal past. In these societies, vast parts of the economy are even now almost completely exempt from the sphere and the pressure of freedom and competition and are instead locked in their traditional position by regulatory means, enforced, as it were, by outright aggression.

On the level of more specific observations the data also clearly indicate what the theory would lead one to expect. Returning to Western Europe, there can be little doubt that of the major European countries, Italy and France are the most conservative, especially if compared with the northern nations which, as far as socialism is concerned, have been leaning more toward its redistributive version.[28] While the level of taxation in Italy and France (state expenditure as part of GNP) is not higher than elsewhere in Europe, these two countries clearly exhibit more conservative-socialist elements than can be found anywhere else. Both Italy and France are studded with literally thousands of price controls and regulations, making it highly doubtful that there is any sector in their economies that can be called "free" with some justification. As a consequence (and as could have been predicted), the standard of living in both countries is significantly lower than that of northern Europe, as anyone who is not traveling exclusively in resort towns cannot fail to notice. In both countries, to be sure, one objective of conservatism seems to have been reached: the differences between the haves and the have-nots have been well-preserved--one will hardly find as extreme income and wealth differentials in West Germany or the United States as in Italy or France--but the price is a relative drop in social wealth. As a matter of fact, this drop is so significant that the standard of living for the lower and lower-middle class in both countries is at best only a bit higher than that in the more liberalized countries of the East bloc. And the southern provinces of Italy, in particular, where even more regulations have been piled on top of those valid everywhere in the country, have just barely left the camp of the third world nations.

Finally, as a last example that illustrates the impoverishment caused by conservative policies, the experience with national-socialism in Germany and to a lesser degree with Italian fascism should be mentioned. It is often not understood that both were conservative-socialist movements.[29] It is as such, i.e., as movements directed against the change and the social disruptions brought about by the dynamic forces of a free economy, that they--other than Marxist-socialist movements--could find support among the class of established proprietors, shop owners, farmers and entrepreneurs. But to derive from this the conclusion that it must have been a pro-capitalist movement or even the highest stage in the development of capitalism before its final demise, as Marxists normally do, is entirely wrong. Indeed, fascism's and Nazism's most fervently abhorred enemy was not socialism as such, but liberalism. Of course, both also despised the socialism of the Marxists and Bolshevists, because at least ideologically they were internationalists and pacifists (relying on the forces of history that would lead to a destruction of capitalism from within), while fascism and Nazism were nationalist movements devoted to war and conquest; and, probably even more important regarding its public support, because Marxism implied that the haves would be expropriated by the have-nots and the social order thus would be turned upside-down, while fascism and Nazism promised to preserve the given order.[30] But, and this is decisive for their classification as socialist (rather than capitalist) movements, to pursue this goal implies--as has been explained in detail above--just as much a denial of the rights of the individual user-owner of things to do with them whatever seems best (provided one does not physically damage another's property or engage in noncontractual exchanges), and just as much an expropriation of natural owners by "society" (that is, by people who neither produced nor contractually acquired the things in question) as does the policy of Marxism. And indeed, in order to reach this goal both fascism and Nazism did exactly what their classification as conservative-socialist would have led one to expect: they established highly controlled and regulated economies in which private ownership was still existent in name, but had in fact become meaningless, since the right to determine the use of the things owned had been almost completely lost to political institutions. The Nazis, in particular, imposed a system of almost complete price controls (including wage controls), devised the institution of four-year plans (almost like in Russia, where the plans spanned the period of five years) and established economic planning and supervising boards which had to approve all significant changes in the production structure. An "owner" could no longer decide what to produce or how to produce it, from whom to buy or to whom to sell, what prices to pay or to charge, or how to implement any changes. All this, to be sure, created a feeling of security. Everyone was assigned a fixed position, and wage-earners as well as owners of capital received a guaranteed, and in nominal terms, stable or even growing income. In addition, giant forced labor programs, the reintroduction of conscription, and finally the implementation of a war economy strengthened the illusion of economic expansion and prosperity.[31] But as would have to be expected from an economic system that destroys a producer's incentive to adjust to demand and avoid not adjusting to it, and that thereby separates demand from production, this feeling of prosperity proved to be nothing but an illusion. In reality, in terms of the goods that people could buy for their money the standard of living fell, not only in relative but even in absolute terms.[32] And in any case, even disregarding here all of the destruction that was caused by the war, Germany and to a lesser extent Italy were severely impoverished after the defeat of the Nazis and fascists.

6

THE SOCIALISM OF SOCIAL ENGINEERING and THE FOUNDATIONS OF ECONOMIC ANALYSIS

In light of the theoretical arguments presented in the preceding chapters it appears that there is no economic justification for socialism. Socialism promised to bring more economic prosperity to the people than capitalism, and much of its popularity is based on this promise. The arguments brought forward, though, have proved that the opposite is true. It has been shown that Russian-type socialism, characterized by nationalized or socialized means of production, necessarily involves economic waste since no prices for factors of production would exist (because means of production would not be allowed to be bought or sold), and hence no cost-accounting (which is the means for directing scarce resources with alternative uses into the most value-productive lines of production) could be accomplished. And as regards social-democratic and conservative socialism, it has been demonstrated that in any event, both imply a rise in the costs of production and, mutatis mutandis, a decline in the costs of its alternative, i.e., non-production or black-market production, and so would lead to a relative reduction in the production of wealth, since both versions of socialism establish an incentive structure that (compared to a capitalist system) relatively favors nonproducers and noncontractors over producers and contractors of goods, products and services.

Experience, too, supports this. By and large, living standards in the East European countries are significantly lower than in Western Europe, where the degree to which the socialization of means of production that has taken place, though certainly remarkable, is relatively much lower. Also, wherever one extends the degree of redistributive measures and the proportion of produced wealth that is redistributed is increased, as, for instance, in West Germany during the 1970s under social-democratic liberal government coalitions, there is a retardation in the social production of wealth or even an absolute reduction in the general standard of living. And wherever a society wants to preserve the status quo, that is, a given income and wealth distribution, by means of price controls, regulations, and behavioral controls--as, for instance, in Hitler's Germany or present-day Italy and France--the living standards will constantly fall further behind those of more liberal (capitalist) societies.

Nonetheless, socialism is very much alive and well, even in the West where social-democratic socialism and conservatism have remained powerful ideologies. How could this come about? One important factor is that its adherents abandoned the original idea of socialism's economic superiority and instead, resorted to a completely different argument: that socialism might not be economically superior but is morally preferable. This claim will be considered in Chapter 7. But that is certainly not the end of the story. Socialism has even regained strength in the field of economics. This became possible because socialism combined its forces with the ideology of empiricism, which traditionally has been strong in the Anglo-Saxon world and which, in particular through the influence of the so-called Vienna-circle of positivist philosophers, became the dominant philosophy-epistemology-methodology of the twentieth century, not only in the field of the natural sciences but also in the social sciences and economics. This applies not only to the philosophers and methodologists of these sciences (who, incidentally, have since freed themselves from the spell of empiricism and positivism) but probably even more so to the practitioners (who are still very much under its influence). Combining its force with empiricism or positivism, which includes for our purposes the so-called critical rationalism of K. R. Popper and his followers, socialism developed into what will henceforth be called the "socialism of social engineering."[1] It is a form of socialism very different in its style of reasoning from traditional Marxism, which was much more rationalistic and deductive--one that Marx had adopted from the classical economist D. Ricardo, the most important source for Marx's own economic writings. But it seems to be precisely because of this difference in style that the socialism of social-engineering has been able to win more and more support from the traditional camps of social-democratic and conservative socialists. In West Germany, for instance, the ideology of "piecemeal social engineering," as K. R. Popper has called his social philosophy,[2] has now become something like the common ground of "moderates" in all political parties, and only doctrinaires, so it seems, of either side do not subscribe to it. The former SPD-chancellor Helmut Schmidt even publicly endorsed Popperianism as his own philosophy.[3] However, it is in the United States that this philosophy is probably more deeply rooted, as it is almost custom-tailored to the American way of thinking in terms of practical problems and pragmatic methods and solutions.

How *could* empiricism-positivism help save socialism? On a highly abstract level the answer should be clear. Empiricism-positivism must be able to provide reasons why all the arguments given so far have failed to be decisive; it must try to prove how one can avoid drawing the conclusions that I have drawn and still claim to be rational and to operate in accordance with the rules of scientific inquiry. But how, in detail, can this be accomplished? On this the philosophy of empiricism and positivism offers two seemingly plausible arguments. The first and indeed the most central of its tenets is this:[4] knowledge regarding reality, which is called empirical knowledge, must be verifiable or at least falsifiable by experience; and experience is always of such a type that it could, in principle, have been other than it actually was so that no one could ever know in advance, i.e., before actually having had some particular experience, if the outcome would be one way or another. If, mutatis mutandis, knowledge is not verifiable or falsifiable by experience, then it is not knowledge about anything real--*empirical* knowledge, that is--but simply knowledge about words, about the use of terms, about signs and transformational rules for them--or *analytical* knowledge. And it is highly doubtful that analytical knowledge should be ranked as "knowledge" at all.

If one assumes this position, as I will do for the moment, it is not difficult to see how the above arguments could be severely rebuffed. The arguments regarding the impossibility of economic calculation and the cost-raising character of social-democratic or conservative measures necessarily leading to a decline in the production of goods and services and hence to reduced standards of living evidently claimed to be valid a priori, i.e., not falsifiable by any kind of experience, but rather known to be true prior to any later experiences. Now if this were indeed true, then according to the first and central tenet of empiricism-positivism, this argument could not contain any information about reality, but instead would have to be considered idle verbal quibbling--an exercise in tautological transformations of words such as "cost," "production," "output of production," "consumption"--which do not say anything about reality. Hence, empiricism concludes that insofar as reality, i.e., the *real* consequences of *real* socialism, is concerned, the arguments presented thus far carry no weight whatsoever. Rather, in order to say anything convincing about socialism, experience and experience alone would have to be the decisive thing to consider.

If this were indeed true (as I will still assume), it would at once dispose of all of the economic arguments against socialism which I have presented as being of a categorical nature. There simply could not be anything categorical about reality. But even then, wouldn't empiricism-positivism still have to face up to the real experiences with real socialism and wouldn't the result of this be just as decisive? In the preceding chapters, much more emphasis was placed on logical, principle, categorical (all used synonomously here) reasons directed against socialism's claims of offering a more promising way to economic prosperity than through capitalism; and experience was cited only loosely in order to illustrate a thesis whose validity could ultimately have been known independent of illustrative experience. Nonetheless, wouldn't even the somewhat unsystematically cited experience be sufficient to make a case against socialism?

The answer to these questions is a decisive "no." The second tenet of empiricism-positivism explains why. It formulates the extension or rather the application of the first tenet to the problem of causality and causal explanation or prediction. To causally explain or predict a real phenomenon is to formulate a statement of either the type "if A, then B" or, should the variables allow quantitative measurement, "if an increase (or decrease) of A, then an increase (or decrease) of B." As a statement referring to reality (with A and B being real phenomena), its validity can never be established with certainty, i.e., by examination of the proposition alone or of any other proposition from which the one in question could in turn be logically deduced, but will always be and remain hypothetical, depending on the outcome of future experiences which cannot be known in advance. Should experience confirm a hypothetical causal explanation, i.e., should one observe an instance where B indeed followed A, as predicted, this would not prove that the hypothesis is true, since A and B are general, abstract terms ("universals," as opposed to "proper names") which refer to events or processes of which there are (or, at least *might*, in principle, be) an indefinite number of instances, and hence later experiences could still possibly falsify it. And if an experience falsified a hypothesis, i.e., if one observed an instance of A that was not followed by B, this would not be decisive either, as it would still be possible that the hypothetically related phenomena were indeed causally linked and that some other previously neglected and uncontrolled circumstance ("variable") had simply prevented the hypothesized relationship from being actually observed. A falsification would only prove that the particular hypothesis under investigation was not completely correct as it stood, but rather needed some refinement, i.e., some specification of additional variables which one would have to watch out for and control in order to be able to observe the hypothesized relationship between A and B. But to be sure, a falsification would never prove once and for all that a relationship between some given phenomena did not exist.

Given that this empiricist-positivist position on causal explanation is correct, it is easy to see how socialism could be rescued from empirically justified criticism. Of course, a socialist-empiricist would not deny the facts. He would not argue that there indeed is a lower standard of living in Eastern than in Western Europe, and that increased taxation or a conservative policy of regulations and controls have indeed been found to correlate with a retardation or shrinking in the production of economic wealth. But within the boundaries of his methodology he could perfectly well deny that based on such experiences a principled case against socialism and its claim of offering a more promising path toward prosperity could be formulated. He could, that is to say, play down the (seemingly) falsifying experiences, and any other that might be cited, as merely accidental; as experiences that had been produced by some unfortunately neglected and uncontrolled circumstances which would disappear and indeed turn into its very opposite, revealing the true relationship between socialism and an increased production of social wealth, as soon as these circumstances had been controlled. Even the striking differences in the standard of living between East and West Germany--the example that I stressed so heavily because it most closely resembles that of a controlled social experiment--could thus be explained away: in arguing, for instance, that the higher living standards in the West must be explained not by its more capitalist mode of production, but by the fact that Marshall aid had streamed into West Germany while East Germany had to pay reparations to the Soviet Union; or by the fact that from the very beginning, East Germany encompassed Germany's less developed, rural, agricultural provinces and so had never had the same starting point; or that in the eastern provinces the tradition of serfdom had been discarded much later than in the western ones and so the mentality of the people was indeed different in both East and West Germany, etc.

In fact, whatever empirical evidence one brings forward against socialism, as soon as one adopts the empiricist-positivist philosophy, i.e., as soon as the idea of formulating a *principled* case either in favor of or against socialism is dropped as in vain and ill-conceived, and it is instead only admitted that one can, of course, err with respect to the *details* of some socialist policy plan but would then be flexible enough to amend certain points in one's policy whenever the outcome was not satisfactory, socialism is made immune to any decisive criticism, because any failure can always be ascribed to some as yet uncontrolled intervening variable. Not even the most perfectly conducted, controlled experiment, it should be noted, could change this situation a bit. It would never be possible to control all variables that might conceivably have some influence on the variable to be explained--for the practical reason that this would involve controlling literally all of the universe, and for the theoretical reason that no one at any point in time could possibly know what all the variables *are* which make up this universe. This is a question whose answer must permanently remain open to newly discovered and discerned experiences. Hence, the above characterized immunization strategy would work without exception and unfailingly. And since, as we know from the writings of the empiricists themselves, and in particular those of D. Hume, there exists no "band" that one could observe to connect visibly certain variables as causes and effects,[5] it should be noted that there would be no way whatsoever to exclude any variable as a possible disturbing influence from the outset without indeed trying it out and controlling it. Not even the seemingly most absurd and ridiculous variables, such as, for instance, differences in weather, or a fly passing by in one case but not in the other, could be ruled out in advance; all that could be done would be to point to experience again. ("Flies passing or not passing by never made a difference for the outcome of an experiment.") But according to the empiricist doctrine itself, this experience, referring as it does only to past instances, would once again not help decide the matter definitively, and a reference to it would only amount to a begging of the question.

No matter what the charges brought against socialism are, then, as long as they are based on empirical evidence the empiricist-socialist could argue that there is no way of knowing in advance what the results of a certain policy scheme will be without actually enacting it and letting experience speak for itself. And whatever the observable results are, the original socialist idea--the "hard-core" of one's "research programme" as the neo-Popperian philosopher Lakatos would have called it[6]--can always be rescued easily by pointing out some previously neglected, more or less plausible variable, whose noncontrol is hypothesized to be responsible for the negative result, with the newly revised hypothesis again needing to be tried out indefinitely, ad infinitum.[7] Experience only tells us that a particular socialist policy scheme did not reach the goal of producing more wealth; but it can never tell us if a slightly different one will produce any different results, or if it is possible to reach the goal of improving the production of wealth by any socialist policy at all.

I have now reached the point in my argument where I shall challenge the validity of these two central tenets of empiricism-positivism. What is wrong with them, and why cannot even empiricism help save socialism? The answer will be given in three stages. First, I will demonstrate that the empiricist position proves to be self-defeating at closer analysis because it itself must at least implicitly assume and presuppose the existence of non-empirical knowledge as knowledge about reality. This being mainly a destructive task, I will then have to address the question of how it is possible to have or conceive of knowledge that informs about reality, but which is not itself subject to confirmation or falsification by experience. And thirdly, I will show that such knowledge not only is conceivable and must be presupposed but that there are positive instances of it which serve as the firm epistemological foundation on which the economic case against socialism can be and indeed all along has been built.

In spite of the apparent plausibility of empiricism's central ideas, it might be noted at the very outset that even on the level of intuition things do not seem to be exactly the way empiricism would want them to be. It certainly is not evident that logic, mathematics, geometry, and also certain statements of pure economics, like the law of supply and demand or the quantity theory of money, because they do not allow any falsification by experience, or rather because their validity is independent of experience, do not give us any information about reality but are merely verbal quibble. The opposite seems much more plausible: that the propositions advanced by these disciplines--for instance, a statement of geometry such as "If a straight line S and a circle C have more than one point in common then S has exactly two points in common with C," or a statement more closely related to the field of action with which I am concerned here, such as "One cannot have his cake and eat it, too"--do in fact inform about reality and inform about what cannot possibly be different in reality at pain of contradiction.[8] If I had a cake and ate it, it can be concluded that I do not have it anymore--and this clearly is a conclusion that informs about reality without being falsifiable by experience.

But much more important than intuition, of course, is reflexive analysis, and this will prove the empiricist position to be simply self-defeating. If it were true that empirical knowledge must be falsifiable by experience and that analytical knowledge, which is not so falsifiable, thus cannot contain any empirical knowledge, then what kind of statement is this fundamental statement of empiricism *itself?* It must again be either analytical or empirical. If analytical, then according to its own doctrine this proposition is nothing but some scribbling on paper, hot air, entirely void of any meaningful content. It is only because the terms used in the statement such as "knowledge," "experience," "falsifiable," etc., have already been given some meaningful interpretation that this might at first be overlooked. But the entire meaninglessness of analytical statements follows conclusively from the empiricist-positivist ideology. Of course, and this is the first self-defeating trap, if this were true, then empiricism could not even say and mean what it seems to say and mean; it would be no more than a rustling of leaves in the wind. To mean anything at all, an interpretation must be given to the terms used, and an interpretation of terms, to be sure, is always (as long as one expression cannot be explained in terms of another one) a practical affair; an affair, that is, in which the usage of a term is practiced and learned with real instances of the concept designated by the term, and by which a term is thus tied to reality.[9] However, not just any arbitrary interpretation would do: "falsifiable," for instance, does not mean what one means by "red" or "green." In order to say what empiricism-positivism evidently wants to say when formulating its basic tenets, the terms must be given the meaning that they actually have for the empiricist as well as for those whom he wants to convince of the appropriateness of his methodology. But if the statement indeed means what we thought it did all along, then it evidently contains information about reality. As a matter of fact it informs us about the fundamental structure of reality: that there is nothing in it that can be known to be true in advance of future confirming or falsifying experiences. And if *this* proposition now is taken to be *analytical*, i.e., as a statement that does not allow falsification but whose truth can be established by an analysis of the meanings of the terms used alone, as has been assumed for the moment, then one has no less than a glaring contradiction at hand and empiricism once again proves to be self-defeating.[10]

Hence, it seems that empiricism-positivism would have to choose the other available option and declare its central creed itself to be an *empirical* statement. But then, clearly, the empiricist position would no longer carry any weight whatsoever: after all, the fundamental proposition of empiricism serving as the basis from which all sorts of rules of correct scientific inquiry are derived could be wrong, and no one could ever be sure if it was or was not so. One could equally well claim the exact opposite and within the confines of empiricism there would be no way of deciding which position was right or wrong. Indeed, if its central tenet were declared an empirical proposition, empiricism would cease to be a methodo-*logy*--a *logic* of science--altogether, and would be no more than a completely arbitrary verbal convention for calling certain (arbitrary) ways of dealing with certain statements certain (arbitrary) names. It would be a position void of any justification of why it, rather than any other one, should be adopted.[11]

However, this is not all that can be mustered against empiricism, even if the second available alternative is chosen. Upon closer inspection this escape route leads to another trap of self-defeat. Even if this route were chosen, it can be shown that the empiricist-positivist position must tacitly presuppose the existence of nonempirical knowledge as "real" knowledge. In order to realize this, let it be assumed that a causal explanation relating two or more events has been found to fit one particular instance of experiences regarding such events, and is then applied to a second instance, presumably to undergo some further empirical testing. Now, one should ask oneself what is the presupposition which must be made in order to relate the second instance of experience to the first as either confirming or falsifying it? At first it might seem almost self-evident that if in the second instance of experience the observations of the first were repeated, this would be a confirmation, and if not, a falsification--and clearly, the empiricist methodology assumes this to be evident, too, and does not require further explanation. But this is not true.[12] Experience, it should be noted, only reveals that two or more observations regarding the temporal sequence of two or more types of events can be "neutrally" classified as "repetition" or "nonrepetition." A neutral repetition only becomes a "positive" confirmation and a nonrepetition a "negative" falsification if, independent of what can actually be discovered by experience, it is assumed that there are constant causes which operate in time-invariant ways. If, contrary to this, it is assumed that causes in the course of time might operate sometimes this way and sometimes that way, then these repetitive or nonrepetitive occurrences simply are and remain neutrally registered experiences, completely independent of one another, and are not in any way logically related to each other as confirming or falsifying one another. There is one experience and then there is another, they are the same or they are differ ent, but that is all there is to it; nothing else follows.

Thus, the prerequisite of being able to say "falsify" or "confirm" is the constancy principle: the conviction that observable phenomena are in principle determined by causes that are constant and time-invariant in the way they operate, and that in principle contingency plays no part in the way causes operate. Only if the constancy principle is assumed to be valid does it follow from any failure to reproduce a result that there is something wrong with an original hypothesis; and only then can a successful reproduction indeed be interpreted as a confirmation. For only if two (or more) events are indeed cause and effect *and* causes operate in a time-invariant way must it be concluded that the functional relationship to be observed between causally related variables *must* be the same in all actual instances, and that if this is not indeed the case, something *must* be at fault with the particular specification of causes.

Obviously now, this constancy principle is not itself based on or derived from experience. There is not only no observable link connecting events. Even if such a link existed, experience could not reveal whether or not it was time-invariant. The principle cannot be disproved by experience either, since any event which might appear to disprove it (such as a failure to duplicate some experience) could be interpreted from the outset as if experience had shown here that merely one *particular* type of event was not the cause of another (otherwise the experience would have been successfully repeated). However, to the extent that experience cannot exclude the possibility that *another* set of events might actually be found which would turn out to be time-invariant in its way of operating, the validity of the constancy principle cannot be disproved.

Nonetheless, although neither derived from nor disprovable by experience, the constancy principle is nothing less than the logically necessary presupposition for there being experiences which can be regarded as either confirming or falsifying each other (in contrast to isolated, logically unconnected experiences). And hence, since empiricism-positivism assumes the existence of such logically related experiences, it must be concluded that it also implicitly assumes the existence of nonempirical knowledge about reality. It must assume that there are indeed time-invariantly operating causes, and it must assume that this is the case although experience could never possibly prove nor disprove it. Once again, then, empiricism turns out to be an inconsistent, contradictory philosophy.

By now it should be sufficiently clear that aprioristic knowledge must exist, or at least, that empiricism-positivism--the philosophy which is the most skeptical about its possibility--must in fact presuppose its existence.

Admittedly, though, the very idea of knowledge as knowledge about real things whose validity can be ascertained independent of experience is a difficult one to grasp--otherwise the overwhelming success of the philosophy of empiricism-positivism in the scientific community and in the opinion of the "educated public" could hardly be explained. Hence, before proceeding to the more concrete task of elucidating the specific aprioristic foundations on which the economic case against socialism rests, it would seem appropriate to make a few rather general comments which should help make it more plausible that there is indeed something like aprioristic knowledge.

It seems to be of great importance to first rid oneself of the notion that aprioristic knowledge has anything to do with "innate ideas" or with "intuitive" knowledge which would not have to be discovered somehow or learned. Innate or not, intuitive or not: these are questions that concern the *psychology* of knowledge. In comparison, epistemology is concerned exclusively with the question of the *validity* of knowledge and of how to ascertain validity--and, to be sure, the problem of aprioristic knowledge is solely an epistemological one. Aprioristic knowledge can be, and in fact quite often is, very similar to empirical knowledge from a psychological point of view, in that both types of knowledge must be acquired, discovered, learned. The process of discovering aprioristic knowledge might and very often indeed seems to be even more difficult and painstaking than that of acquiring empirical knowledge, which frequently enough simply seems to press itself onto us without our having done much about it; and also, it might well be the case genetically that the acquisition of aprioristic knowledge requires one's having previously had some sort of experience. But all this, it should be repeated, does not affect the question of the validation of knowledge, and it is precisely and exclusively in this regard that aprioristic and empirical knowledge differ categorically.[13]

On the positive side, the most important notion for understanding the possibility of a priori knowledge, I submit, is that there are not only nature-given things which one has to learn about through experience, but that there are also artificial, man-made things which may require the existence or use of natural materials, but which to the very extent that they are constructs can nonetheless not only be fully understood in terms of their structure and implications, but which also can be analyzed for the question of whether or not their method of construction can conceivably be altered.[14]

There are three major fields of constructs: language and thought, actions, and fabricated objects, all of which are man-made things. We shall not deal here with fabricated objects but will only mention in passing that Euclidean geometry, for instance, can be conceived of as ideal norms we cannot avoid using in constructing measurement instruments that make empirical measurements of space possible. (In so far, then, Euclidean geometry cannot be said to have been falsified by the theory of relativity; rather, this theory presupposes its validity through the use of its instruments of measuring.)[15] The field of action, as our area of main concern, will be analyzed when the aprioristic foundations of economics are discussed. The first explanation of aprioristic knowledge, then, as knowledge of rules of construction which cannot conceivably be altered, shall be given using the example of language and thought. This is chosen as the starting point, because it is language and thought which one uses in doing what is being done here, that is, in communicating, discussing, and arguing.

As empiricists see it, language is a conventionally accepted system of signs and sign-combinations, which, again by convention, are given some meaning, ultimately by means of ostensive definitions. According to this view, it may seem that although language is an artificial, man-made product, nothing can be known about it a priori. And indeed, there are lots of different languages, all using different signs, and the meaning of the terms used can be assigned and changed arbitrarily, so that everything there is to know about language must, or so it seems, be learned from experience. But this view is incorrect, or at best is only half of the truth. True, any language is a conventional sign system, but what is a convention? Evidently, it cannot be suggested that "convention" in turn be defined conventionally, as that would simply be begging the question. Everything can be *called* a convention (and, for that matter, a language), but surely not everything that can be called one *is* in fact a conventional agreement. Saying and being understood in saying "convention is used in such and such a way" presupposes that one already knows what a convention is, as this statement would already have to make use of language as a means of communication. Hence, one is forced to conclude that language is a conventional sign system and as such knowledge about it can only be empirical knowledge. But in order for there to be such a system it must be assumed that every speaker of a language already knows what a convention is, and he must know this not simply in the way he knows that "dog" means dog, but he must know the real, true meaning of convention. As such his knowledge of what a language is must be considered a priori. This insight can be repeated for more particular levels. There are all sorts of specific statements that can be made in a language, and surely experience plays a role here. However, knowing what it means to make a proposition can definitely not be learned from experience, but rather must be presupposed of any speaker of a language. What a proposition is cannot be explained to a speaker by just another statement unless he already knows how to interpret this as a proposition. And the same is true with definitions: it would not do to define "definition" ostensively by pointing to someone who is just pointing out some definition, because just as in the case in which the word "dog" is defined by pointing to a dog, an understanding of the meaning of ostensive definitions must already be presupposed when it is understood that pointing to a dog, accompanied by the sound [dog] means that "dog" means dog, so in the case of "definition." To define definition ostensively would be entirely meaningless, unless one already knew that the particular sound made was supposed to signify something whose identification should be assisted by pointing, and how then to identify particular objects as instances of general, abstract properties. In short, in order to define any term by convention, a speaker must be assumed to have a priori knowledge of the real meaning--the real definition--of "definition."[16]

The knowledge about language, then, that must be considered a priori in that it must be presupposed of any speaker speaking any language, is that of how to make real conventions, how to make a proposition by making a statement (i.e., how to mean something by saying something) and how to make a real definition and identify particular instances of general properties. Any denial of this would be self-refuting, as it would have to be made in a language, making propositions and using definitions. And as any experience is conceptual experience, i.e., experience in terms of some language--and to say that this is not so and mean it would only prove the point as it would have to be cast in a language, too--by *knowing* this to be true of a language a priori, one would also know an a priori truth about reality: that it is made of particular objects that have abstract properties, i.e., properties of which it is possible to find other instances; that any one object either does or does not have some definite property and so there are facts that can be said to be the case, true or wrong; and also that it cannot be known a priori what all the facts are, except that they indeed also must be facts, i.e., instances of particular abstract properties. And once again, one does not know all this from experience, as experience is only what can appear in the forms just described.[17]

With this in mind we can turn to the field of action in order to prove the specific point that one also has positive, aprioristic knowledge of actions and consequences of actions because actions, too, are man-made constructs which can be fully understood regarding their rules of construction; and that empiricism-positivism cannot--at pain of contradiction--possibly be thought to be weakening or even seriously challenging the economic case against socialism, as this case ultimately rests on such foundations, whereas the empiricist philosophy stands in contradiction to it.

In the first argumentative step I shall demonstrate that the empiricist methodology, contrary to its own claim, cannot possibly apply to actions and thereby reveal a first, albeit rather negative, instance of aprioristic knowledge about actions. Empiricism claims that actions, just as any other phenomenon, can and must be explained by means of causal hypotheses which can be confirmed or refuted by experience. Now if this were the case, then empiricism would be forced to assume (contrary to its own doctrine that there is no a priori knowledge as knowledge about reality) that time-invariantly operating causes with respect to actions exist. One would not know in advance which particular event might be the cause of a particular action--*experience* would have to reveal this. But in order to proceed the way that empiricism wants us to proceed--to relate different experiences regarding sequences of events as either confirming or falsifying each other, and if falsifying, then responding with a reformulation of the original causal hypothesis--a constancy over time in the operation of causes must be presupposed. However, if this were true, and actions could indeed be conceived as governed by time-invariantly operating causes, what about explaining the explainers, i.e., the persons who carry on the very process of hypothesis creation, of verification and falsification;--all of us, that is, who act the way the empiricists tell us to act? Evidently, to do all this--to assimilate confirming or falsifying experiences, to replace old hypotheses with new ones--one must assumedly be able to learn. However, if one is able to learn from experience, and the empiricist is compelled to admit this, then one cannot know at any given time what one will know at later time and how one will act on the basis of this knowledge. Rather, one can only reconstruct the causes of one's actions after the event, as one can only explain one's knowledge after one already possesses it. Thus, the empiricist methodology applied to the field of knowledge and action, which contains knowledge as its necessary ingredient, is simply contradictory--a logical absurdity.[18] The constancy principle may be correctly assumed within the sphere of natural objects and as such the methodology of empiricism may be applicable there, but with respect to actions, any attempt at causal empirical explanation is logically impossible, and this, which is definitely knowledge about something *real*, can be known with certainty. Nothing can be known a priori about any particular action; but a priori knowledge exists regarding actions insofar as they are actions at all. It can be known a priori that no action can be conceived of as predictable on the basis of constantly operating causes.

The second insight regarding action is of the same type. I will demonstrate that while actions themselves cannot be conceived of as caused, anything that is an action must presuppose the existence of causality in the physical world in which actions are performed. Causality--which the empiricist-positivist philosophy somehow had to assume existed in order to make its own methodological procedures logically feasible, even though its assumption definitely could not be said to be derived from experience and justified in terms of it--is a category of action, i.e., it is produced or constructed by us in following some procedural rule; and this rule, as it turns out, proves to be necessary in order to act at all. In other words, this rule is such that it cannot conceivably be falsified, as even the attempt to falsify it would have to presuppose it.

After what has been said about causality, it should indeed be easy to see that it is a produced rather than a given feature of reality. One does not experience and learn that there are causes which always operate in the same way and on the basis of which predictions about the future can be made. Rather, one establishes that phenomena have such causes by following a particular type of investigative procedure, by refusing on principle to allow any exceptions, i.e., instances of inconstancy, and by being prepared to deal with them by producing a new causal hypothesis each time any such an apparent inconstancy occurs. But what makes this way of proceeding necessary? Why does one *have* to act this way? Because behaving this way is what performing intentional actions is; and as long as one acts intentionally, presupposing constantly operating causes is precisely what one does. Intentional acts are characterized by the fact that an actor interferes in his environment and changes certain things, or prevents them from changing, and so diverts the "natural" course of events in order to achieve a preferred result or state of affairs; or should an active interference prove impossible, that he prepares himself for a result he cannot do anything about except anticipate in time, by watching out for temporally prior events which indicate the later result. In any case, in order to produce a result that otherwise would not have happened, or to be able to adapt to an inevitable result that otherwise would have come as a complete surprise, the actor must presuppose constantly operating causes. He would not interfere if he did not assume this would help bring about the desired result; and he would not prepare for and adjust to anything unless he thought the events on whose basis he began his preparations were indeed the constantly operating causal forces that would produce the result in question, and the preparation taken would indeed lead to the goal desired. Of course, an actor could go wrong with respect to his particular assumptions of cause-and-effect relations and a desired result might not come about in spite of the interference, or an anticipated event for which preparations had been made might fail to occur. But no matter what happens in this respect, whether or not the results conform to the expectations, whether or not actions regarding some given result or event are upheld for the future, any action, changed or unchanged, presupposes that there are constantly operating causes even if no particular cause for a particular event can be pre-known to any actor at any time. In fact, disproving that any natural phenomenon is governed by time-invariantly operating causes would require one to show that given phenomenon cannot be anticipated or produced on the basis of antecedent variables. But clearly, trying to prove this would again necessarily presuppose that the occurrence or nonoccurrence of the phenomenon under scrutiny could be effected by taking appropriate action and that the phenomenon must thus assumedly be embedded in a network of constantly operating causes. Hence, one is forced to conclude that the validity of the constancy principle cannot be falsified by any action as any action would have to presuppose it.[19] (There is only one way in which it might be said that "experience" could "falsify" the constancy principle: if the physical world were indeed so chaotic that one could no longer act at all, then of course it would not make much sense to speak of a world with constantly operating causes. But then human beings, whose essential characteristic is to act intentionally, would also no longer be the ones who *experience* this inconstancy. As long as one survives as a human being--and this is what the argument in effect says--the constancy principle must be assumed to be valid a priori, as any action must presuppose it and no experience that anyone could actually *have* could possibly disprove this.)[20]

Implied in the category of causality is that of time. Whenever one produces or prepares for a certain result and thereby categorizes events as causes and effects, one also distinguishes between earlier and later events. And to be sure, this categorization is not simply derived from experience, i.e., the mere observance of things and events. The sequence of experiences as it appears in the temporal order of one's observations is quite a different thing from the real sequence of events in real time. As a matter of fact, one can observe things in an order that is exactly the opposite of the real temporal order in which they stand to each other. That one knows how to interpret observations in a way that might deviate from and correct on the temporal order in which they were made and can even locate events in objective time requires that the observer be an actor and know what it means to produce or prepare for some result.[21] Only because one is an actor, and experiences are those of an acting person, can events be interpreted as occurring earlier and later. And, one cannot know from experience that experiences must be interpreted with reference to actions, as the performance of any action already presupposes the possession of experiences interpreted this way. No person who did not know what it means to act could ever experience events placed in real time, and hence the meaning of time must be assumed to be known a priori to any actor because of the fact that he is an actor.

Furthermore, actions not only presuppose causality and an objective time order, they also require values. Values, too, are not known to us through experience; rather, the opposite is true. One only experiences things because they are things on which positive or negative value can be placed in the course of action. Only by an *actor*, that is to say, can things be experienced as value-laden and, even more generally, only because one is an actor does one have conscious experiences at all, as they inform about things which might be valuable for an acting person to know. More precisely: with every action an actor pursues a goal.[22] He wants to produce a definite result or be prepared for a result that he cannot prevent from happening. Whatever the goal of his action (which, of course, one could only know from experience), the fact that it is pursued by an actor reveals that he places value on it. As a matter of fact, it reveals that at the very start of his action he places a relatively higher value on it than on any other goal of action he could think of, otherwise he would have acted differently. Furthermore, since in order to achieve his most highly valued goal any actor must interfere at an earlier point in time or must watch out for an earlier event in order to start preparations for some later occurrence, every action must also employ means (at least those of the actor's own body and the time absorbed by the interference or the preparations) to produce the desired end. And as these means are assumed to be causally necessary for achieving the valued goal, otherwise the actor would not employ them, value must also be placed on them. Not only the goals, then, have value for an actor, but the means do, too--a value that is derived from that of the desired end, as one could not reach an end without employing some means. In addition, as actions can only be performed sequentially by an actor, every action involves making a choice. It involves taking up that course of action which at the moment of acting promises the most highly valued result to the actor and hence is given preference by him; at the same time it involves excluding other possible actions with expected results of a lesser value. As a consequence of having to choose whenever one acts--of not being able to realize all valued goals simultaneously--the performance of each and every action implies the incurrence of costs. The cost of an action is the price that must be paid for having to prefer one course of action over another, and it amounts to the value attached to the most highly valued goal that cannot be realized or whose realization must now be deferred, because the means necessary to produce it are bound up in the production of another, even more highly valued end. And while this implies that at its starting point every action must be considered to be worth more than its costs and able to secure a profit to the actor, i.e., a result whose value is ranked higher than the costs, every action is also threatened by the possibility of a loss. Such a loss would occur if in retrospect an actor found that--contrary to his own previous expectation--the result in fact had a lower value than that of the relinquished alternative. And just as every action necessarily aims at a profit, the possibility of a loss, too, is a necessary accompaniment to any action. For an actor can always go wrong regarding his causal-technological knowledge, and the results aimed for cannot be produced successfully or the events for which they were produced do not occur; or he can go wrong because every action takes time to complete and the value attached to different goals can change in the meantime, making things less valuable now that earlier appeared to be highly valuable.

All of these categories--values, ends, means, choice, preference, cost, profit and loss--are implied in the concept of action. None of them is derived from experience. Rather, that one is able to interpret experiences in the above categories requires that one already know what it means to act. No one who is not an actor could understand them as they are not "given," ready to be experienced, but experience is cast in these terms as it is constructed by an actor according to the rules necessary for acting. And to be sure, as actions are real things and one cannot *not* act--as even the attempt to do so would itself be an action aimed at a goal, requiring means, excluding other courses of action, incurring costs, subjecting the actor to the possibility of not achieving the desired goal and so suffering a loss--the knowledge of what it means to act must be considered knowledge about reality which is a priori. The very possession of it could not be undone or disproved, since this would already presuppose its very existence. As a matter of fact, a situation in which these categories of action would cease to have a real existence could not itself ever be observed, as making an observation is itself an action.[23]

Economic analysis, and the economic analysis of socialism in particular, has as its foundation this a priori knowledge of the meaning of action as well as its logical constituents. Essentially, economic analysis consists of: (1) an understanding of the categories of action and an understanding of the meaning of a *change* in values, costs, technological knowledge, etc.; (2) a description of a situation in which these categories assume concrete meaning, where definite people are identified as actors with definite objects specified as their means of action, with definite goals identified as values and definite things specified as costs; and (3) a deduction of the consequences that result from the performance of some specified action in this situation, or of the consequences that result for an actor if this situation is changed in a specified way. And this deduction must yield a priori-valid conclusions, provided there is no flaw in the very process of deduction and the situation and the change introduced into it being given, and a priori-valid conclusions about *reality* if the situation and situation-change, as described, can themselves be identified as real, because then their validity would ultimately go back to the indisputable validity of the categories of action.

It is along this methodological path that in the preceding discussion of socialism the conclusion was derived, for instance, that if the labor expended by an actor was not itself his goal of action, but rather only his means of reaching the goal of producing income and if this income then is reduced against his consent--by taxation--then for him the cost of expending labor has been increased, as the value of other, alternative goals that can be pursued by means of his body and time has gone up in relative terms, and hence a reduced incentive to work must result. Along this path, too, the conclusion--as an a priori conclusion--was reached that, for instance, if the actual users of means of production do not have the right to sell them to the highest bidder, then no one can establish the monetary costs involved in producing what is actually produced with them (the monetary value, that is, of the opportunities foregone by not using them differently), and no one can assure any longer that these means are indeed employed in the production of those goods considered to be the most highly valued ones by the actors at the beginning of their productive efforts. Hence a reduced output in terms of purchasing power must ensue.

After this rather lengthy digression into the field of epistemology, let us now return to the discussion of the socialism of social engineering. This digression was necessary in order to refute the claim of empiricism-positivism, which if true would have saved socialism, that nothing categorical can be said against any policy-scheme, as only experience can reveal the real consequences of certain policies. Against this I have pointed out that empiricism clearly seems to contradict intuition. According to intuition, logic is more fundamental than experience and it is also knowledge about real things. Furthermore, empiricism-positivism turns out to be self-contradictory, as it itself must presuppose the existence of a priori knowledge as real knowledge. There indeed exists a stock of positive a priori knowledge which must be presupposed of every experiencing and acting person, because he knows what it means to act, and which cannot possibly be refuted by experience, as the very attempt to do so would itself presuppose the validity of what had been disputed.

The discussion has led us to a conclusion which can be summed up as follows: "Experience does not beat logic, but rather the opposite is true." Logic improves upon and corrects experience and tells us what kind of experiences we can possibly have and which ones are instead due to a muddled mind, and so would be better labeled "dreams" or "fantasies" rather than as experiences regarding "reality." With this reassurance about the solidity of the foundations on which the economic case against socialism has been built, a straightforward criticism of the socialism of social engineering is now possible; a criticism which is again a logical one, drawing on a priori knowledge, and demonstrating that the goals pursued by the socialism of social engineering can never be reached by its proposed means, since this would stand in contradiction to such knowledge. The following critique can now be brief, as the ideology of social engineering, *apart* from its empiricist-positivist methodology which has been proven faulty, is really no different from the other versions of socialism. Hence, the analyses provided in the preceding chapters regarding Marxist, social-democratic and conservative socialism find application here, too.

This becomes clear once the property rules of the socialism of social engineering are stated. First, the user-owners of scarce resources can do whatever they want with them. But secondly, whenever the outcome of this process is not liked by the community of social engineers (people, that is, who are not the user-owners of the things in question and who do not have a contractually acquired title to them), it has the right to interfere with the practices of the actual user-owners and determine the uses of these means, thereby restricting their property rights. Further, the community of social engineers has the right to determine unilaterally what is or is not a preferred outcome, and can thus restrict the property rights of natural owners whenever, wherever, and to the extent that it thinks necessary in order to produce a preferred outcome.

Regarding these property rules, one realizes at once that although socialism of social engineering allows for a gradual implementation of its goals with only a moderate degree of intervention in the property rights of natural owners, since the degree to which their rights can be curtailed is to be determined by society (the social engineers), private ownership is in principle abolished and peoples' productive enterprises take place under the threat of an ever-increasing or even total expropriation of private owners. In these respects there is no difference whatsoever between social-democratic and conservative socialism and socialism's socially engineered version. The difference again is reduced to one of social psychology. While Marxist, redistributive, and conservative socialism all want to achieve a general goal determined in advance--a goal of égalité or of the preservation of a given order--the socialism of social engineering does not have any such design. Its idea is one of punctuated, unprincipled intervention; flexible, piece-meal engineering. The engineering socialist is thus seemingly much more open to criticism, changing responses, new ideas--and this attitude certainly appeals to a lot of people who would not willingly subscribe to any of the other forms of socialism. On the other hand, though, and this should be kept in mind as well, there is almost nothing, including even the most ridiculous thing, that some social engineers would not like to try out on their fellowmen, whom they regard as bundles of variables to be technically manipulated like pawns on a chessboard by setting the right stimuli.

In any case, since the socialism of social engineering does not differ in principle from any of the other versions of socialism, in that it implies a redistribution of property titles away from the users and contractors of scarce resources and onto nonusers and noncontractors, it, too, raises the cost of production and so leads to a reduction in the production of wealth; and this is necessarily so and no one need try it out first to reach this conclusion. This general conclusion is true regardless of the specific course social engineering might take. Let us say that the community of social engineers does not approve of some people having a low income and so decides to fix minimum wages above the current market level.[24] Logic tells one that this implies a restriction of the property rights of the employers as well as the employees who are no longer allowed to strike certain kinds of mutually beneficial bargains. The consequence is and must be unemployment. Instead of getting paid at a lower market wage, some people now will not get paid at all, as some employers cannot pay the additional costs or hire as many people as they would be willing to hire at lower costs. The employers will be hurt as they can only employ fewer people and the output of production hence will be lower, in relative terms; and the employees will be hurt, as instead of some income, albeit low, they now have no income. It cannot be stated a priori *who* of the employees and the employers will suffer most from this, except that it will be those of the former whose specific labor services have a relatively low value on the market, and those of the latter who specifically hire precisely this type of labor. However, knowing from experience, for instance, that low-skilled labor services are particularly frequent among the young, among blacks, among women, among older people who want to reenter the labor force after a longer period of household-work, etc., it can be predicted with certainty that these will be the groups hit the hardest by unemployment. And to be sure, the very fact that the problem which intervention was originally supposed to cure (the low income of some people) is now even worse than before could have been known a priori, independent of *any* experience! To think that, misled by faulty empiricist methodology, all this first has to be tried out as it otherwise could not have been known is not only scientific humbug; like all acting based on ill-conceived intellectual foundations, it is extremely costly as well.

To look at yet another example, the community of social engineers does not like the fact that rents for houses or apartments are as high as they are, and hence some people are not able to live as comfortably as they think they should. Accordingly, rent-control legislation is passed, establishing maximum rents for certain apartments.[25] This is the situation, for instance, in New York City, or on a much grander scale, in all of Italy. Again, without having to wait for the consequences to become *real* one knows what they will be. The construction of new apartments will decrease, as the returns from investment are now lower. And with respect to old apartments, immediate shortages will appear, as the demand for them, their prices being lower, will rise. Some older apartments might not even be rented out anymore, if the fixed rents are so low that the rent would not even cover the cost of the deterioration that occurs by just living in and using the apartment. Then there would be a tremendous shortage of housing next to thousands of empty apartments (and New York City and Italy provide us with perfect illustrations of this). And there would be no way out of this, as it still would not pay to construct new apartments. In addition, the increased shortages would result in very costly inflexibilities, as people who had happily gotten into one of the low-priced apartments would be increasingly unwilling to move out again, in spite of the fact that, for instance, the family size normally changes during the life cycle and so different needs as regards housing emerge, and in spite of the fact that different job opportunities might appear at different places. And so a huge waste of rental space occurs, because old people, for example, who occupy large apartments that were just the right size when the children were still living at home but are much too big now, still will not move into smaller apartments as there are none available; and young families who are in need of larger premises cannot find those either, precisely because such places will not be vacated. Waste also occurs because people do not move to the places where there is the greatest demand for their specific labor services, or they spend large amounts of time commuting to rather distant places, merely because they cannot find a place to live where there is work for them, or they can only find accommodations at a much higher price than their presently fixed low rent. Clearly, the problem that the social engineers wanted to solve by means of introducing rent control legislation is much worse than before and the general standard of living, in relative terms, has declined. Once again, all of this could have been known a priori. For the social engineer, however, misled by an empiricist-positivist methodology which tells him that there is no way of knowing results unless things are actually tried out, this experience will probably only set the stage for the next intervention. Perhaps the results were not exactly as expected because one had forgotten to control some other important variable, and one should now go ahead and find out. But as this chapter has demonstrated, there *is* a way of knowing in advance that neither the first nor any subsequent acts of intervention will ever reach their goal, as they all imply an interference with the rights of the natural owners of things by nonusers and noncontractors.[26]

In order to understand this, it is only necessary to return to sound economic reasoning; to realize the unique epistemological nature of economics as an aprioristic science of human action that rests on foundations whose very denial must presuppose their validity; and to recognize, in turn, that a science of action grounded in an empiricist-positivist methodology is as ill-founded as the statement that "one can have his cake and eat it, too."

7

THE ETHICAL JUSTIFICATION OF CAPITALISM and WHY SOCIALISM IS MORALLY INDEFENSIBLE

The last four chapters have provided systematic reasons and empirical evidence for the thesis that socialism as a social system that is not thoroughly based on the "natural theory of property" (the first-use-first-own rule) which characterizes capitalism must necessarily be, and in fact is, an inferior system with respect to the production of wealth and the average standard of living. This may satisfy the person who believes that economic wealth and living standards are the most important criteria in judging a society--and there can be no doubt that for many, one's standard of living *is* a matter of utmost importance--and because of this it is certainly necessary to keep all of the above economic reasoning in mind. Yet there are people who do not attach much importance to economic wealth and who rank other values even higher--happily, one might say, for socialism, because it can thus quietly forget its original claim of being able to bring more prosperity to mankind, and instead resort to the altogether different but even more inspiring claim that whereas socialism might not be the key to prosperity, it would mean justice, fairness, and morality (all terms used synonymously here). And it can argue that a trade-off between efficiency and justice, an exchange of "less wealth" for "more justice" is justified, since justice and fairness, are fundamentally more valuable than economic wealth.

This claim will be examined in some detail in this chapter. In so doing, two separate but related claims will be analyzed: (1) the claim made in particular by socialists of the Marxist and the social-democratic camp, and to a lesser degree also by the conservatives, that a *principled* case in favor of socialism can be made because of the moral value of its principles and, mutatis mutandis, that capitalism cannot be defended morally; and (2) the claim of empiricist socialism that normative statements ("should" or "ought" statements)--since they neither solely relate to facts, nor simply state a verbal definition, and thus are neither empirical nor analytical statements--are not really statements at all, at least not statements that one could call "cognitive" in the widest of all senses, but rather mere "verbal expressions" used to express or arouse feelings (such as "wow" or "grrrrr").[1]

The second, empiricist or, as its position applied to the field of morals is called, "emotivist" claim will be dealt with first, as in a way it is more far-reaching.[2] The emotivist position is derived by accepting the central empiricist-positivist claim that the dichotomous distinction between empirical and analytical statements is of an all-inclusive nature; that is, that any statement whatsoever must be empirical or analytical and never can be both. This position, it will be seen, turns out to be self-defeating on closer inspection, just as empiricism in general turned out to be self-defeating.[3] If emotivism is a valid position, then its basic proposition regarding normative statements must itself be analytical or empirical, or else it must be an expression of emotions. If it is taken to be analytical, then it is mere verbal quibble, saying nothing about anything real, but rather only defining one sound by another, and emotivism would thus be a void doctrine. If, instead, it is empirical, then the doctrine would not carry any weight, as its central proposition could well be wrong. In any case, right or wrong, it would only be a proposition stating a historical fact, i.e., how certain expressions have been used in the past, which in itself would not provide any reason whatsoever why this would have to be the case in the future, too, and hence why one should or rather should not look for normative statements that are more than expressions of emotions in that they are meant to be justifiable. And the emotivist doctrine would also lose all its weight if it adopted the third alternative and declared its central tenet itself a "wow" statement, too. For if this were the case, then it would not contain any reason why one should relate to and interpret certain statements in certain ways, and so if one's own instincts or feelings did not happen to coincide with somebody else's "wowing," there would be nothing that could stop one from following one's own feelings instead. Just as a normative statement would be no more than the barking of a dog, so the emotivist position then is no more than a barking comment on barking.

On the other hand, if the central statement of empiricism-emotivism, i.e., that normative statements have no cognitive meaning but are simply expressions of feelings, is itself regarded as a meaningful statement communicating that one should conceive of all statements that are not analytical or empirical as mere expressive symbols, then the emotivist position becomes outrightly contradictory. This position must then assume, at least implicitly, that certain insights, i.e., those relating to normative statements, cannot simply be understood and meaningful, but can also be given justification as statements with specific meanings. Hence, one must conclude that emotivism falters, because if it were true, then it could not even say and mean what it says--it simply would not exist as a position that could be discussed and evaluated with regard to its validity. But if it is a meaningful position which can be discussed, then this fact belies its very own basic premise. Moreover, the fact that it is indeed such a meaningful position, it should be noted, cannot even be disputed, as one cannot communicate and argue that one cannot communicate and argue. Rather, it must be presupposed of *any* intellectual position, that it is meaningful and can be argued with regard to its cognitive value, simply because it is presented in a language and communicated. To argue otherwise would already implicitly admit its validity. One is forced, then, to accept a rationalist approach towards ethics for the very same reason that one was forced to adopt a rationalist instead of an empiricist epistemology.[4] Yet with emotivism so rebuffed, I am still far away, or so it seems, from my set goal, which I share with the Marxist and conservative socialists, of demonstrating that a principled case in favor of or against socialism or capitalism can be made. What I have reached so far is the conclusion that the question of whether or not normative statements are cognitive ones is itself a cognitive problem. However, it still seems to be a far cry from there to the proof that actual norm proposals can indeed be shown to be either valid or invalid.

Fortunately, this impression is wrong and there is already much more won here than might be suspected. The above argument shows us that any truth claim--the claim connected with any proposition that it is true, objective, or valid (all terms used synonymously here)--is and must be raised and decided upon in the course of an argumentation. And since it cannot be disputed that this is so (one cannot communicate and argue that one cannot communicate and argue), and it must be assumed that everyone knows what it means to claim something to be true (one cannot deny this statement without claiming its negation to be true), this has been aptly called "the apriori of communication and argumentation."[5]

Now, arguing never just consists of free-floating propositions claiming to be true. Rather, argumentation is always an activity, too. But given that truth claims are raised and decided upon in argumentation and that argumentation, aside from whatever is said in its course, is a practical affair, it follows that intersubjectively meaningful norms must exist--precisely those which make some action an argumentation--which have special cognitive status in that they are the practical preconditions of objectivity and truth.

Hence, one reaches the conclusion that norms must indeed be assumed to be justifiable as valid. It is simply impossible to argue otherwise, because the ability to argue so would in fact presuppose the validity of those norms which underlie any argumentation whatsoever.[6] The answer, then, to the question of which ends can or cannot be justified is to be derived from the concept of argumentation. And with this, the peculiar role of reason in determining the contents of ethics is given a precise description, too. In contrast to the role of reason in establishing empirical laws of nature, reason can claim to yield results in determining moral laws which can be shown to be valid a priori. It only makes explicit what is already implied in the concept of argumentation itself; and in analyzing any actual norm proposal, its task is merely confined to analyzing whether or not it is logically consistent with the very ethics which the proponent must presuppose as valid insofar as he is able to make his proposal at all.[7]

But what is the ethics implied in argumentation whose validity cannot be disputed, as disputing it would implicitly have to presuppose it? Quite commonly it has been observed that argumentation implies that a proposition claims *universal* acceptability, or, should it be a norm proposal, that it is "universalizable." Applied to norm proposals, this is the idea, as formulated in the Golden Rule of ethics or in the Kantian Categorical Imperative, that only those norms can be justified that can be formulated as general principles which are valid for everyone without exception.[8] Indeed, as argumentation implies that everyone who can understand an argument must in principle be able to be convinced of it simply because of its argumentative force, the universalization principle of ethics can now be understood and explained as grounded in the wider "apriori of communication and argumentation." Yet the universalization principle only provides a purely formal criterion for morality. To be sure, checked against this criterion all proposals for valid norms which would specify different rules for different classes of people could be shown to have no legitimate claim of being universally acceptable as fair norms, unless the distinction between different classes of people were such that it implied no discrimination, but could instead be accepted as founded in the nature of things again by everyone. But while some norms might not pass the test of universalization, if enough attention were paid to their formulation, the most ridiculous norms, and what is of course even more relevant, even openly incompatible norms could easily and equally well pass it. For example, "everybody must get drunk on Sundays or be fined" or "anyone who drinks alcohol will be punished" are both rules that do not allow discrimination among groups of people and thus could both claim to satisfy the condition of universalization.

Clearly then, the universalization principle alone would not provide one with any positive set of norms that could be demonstrated to be justified. However, there are other positive norms implied in argumentation aside from the universalization principle. In order to recognize them, it is only necessary to call three interrelated facts to attention. First, that argumentation is not only a cognitive but also a practical affair. Second, that argumentation, as a form of action, implies the use of the scarce resource of one's body. And third, that argumentation is a conflict-free way of interacting. Not in the sense that there is always agreement on the things said, but in the sense that as long as argumentation is in progress it is always possible to agree at least on the fact that there is disagreement about the validity of what has been said. And this is to say nothing else than that a mutual recognition of each person's exclusive control over his own body must be presupposed as long as there is argumentation (note again, that it is impossible to deny this and claim this denial to be true without implicitly having to admit its truth).

Hence, one would have to conclude that the norm implied in argumentation is that everybody has the right of exclusive control over his own body as his instrument of action and cognition. Only if there is at least an implicit recognition of each individual's property right in his own body can argumentation take place.[9] Only as long as this right is recognized is it possible for someone to agree to what has been said in an argument and hence can what has been said be validated, or is it possible to say "no" and to agree only on the fact that there is disagreement. Indeed, anyone who would try to justify any norm would already have to presuppose the property right in his body as a valid norm, simply in order to say, "This is what I claim to be true and objective." Any person who would try to dispute the property right in his own body would become caught up in a contradiction, as arguing in this way and claiming his argument to be true, would already implicitly accept precisely this norm as being valid.

Thus it can be stated that whenever a person claims that some statement can be justified, he at least implicitly assumes the following norm to be justified: "Nobody has the right to uninvitedly aggress against the body of any other person and thus delimit or restrict anyone's control over his own body." This rule is implied in the concept of justification as argumentative justification. Justifying *means* justifying without having to rely on coercion. In fact, if one formulates the opposite of this rule, i.e., "everybody has the right to uninvitedly aggress against other people" (a rule, by the way, that would pass the formal test of the universalization principle!), then it is easy to see that this rule is not, and never could be, defended in argumentation. To do so would in fact have to presuppose the validity of precisely its opposite, i.e., the aforementioned principle of nonaggression.

With this justification of a property norm regarding a person's body it may seem that not much is won, as conflicts over bodies, for whose possible avoidance the nonaggression principle formulates a universally justifiable solution, make up only a small portion of all possible conflicts. However, this impression is not correct. To be sure, people do not live on air and love alone. They need a smaller or greater number of other things as well, simply to survive--and of course only he who survives can sustain an argumentation, let alone lead a comfortable life. With respect to all of these other things norms are needed, too, as it could come to conflicting evaluations regarding their use. But in fact, any other norm must be logically compatible with the nonaggression principle in order to be justified itself, and, mutatis mutandis, every norm that could be shown to be incompatible with this principle would have to be considered invalid. In addition, as the things with respect to which norms have to be formulated are scarce goods--just as a person's body is a scarce good--and as it is only necessary to formulate norms at all because goods are *scarce* and not because they are *particular kinds* of scarce goods, the specifications of the nonaggression principle, conceived of as a special property norm referring to a specific kind of good, must in fact already contain those of a *general* theory of property.

I will first state this general theory of property as a set of rules applicable to *all* goods with the purpose of helping one to avoid *all* possible conflicts by means of *uniform* principles, and will then demonstrate how this general theory is implied in the nonaggression principle. Since according to the nonaggression principle a person can do with his body whatever he wants as long as he does not thereby aggress against another person's body, that person could also make use of other scarce means, just as one makes use of one's own body, provided these other things have not already been appropriated by someone else but are still in a natural, unowned state. As soon as scarce resources are visibly appropriated--as soon as someone "mixes his labor," as John Locke phrased it,[10] with them and there are objective traces of this--then property, i.e., the right of exclusive control, can only be acquired by a contractual transfer of property titles from a previous to a later owner, and any attempt to unilaterally delimit this exclusive control of previous owners or any unsolicited transformation of the physical characteristics of the scarce means in question is, in strict analogy with aggressions against other people's bodies, an unjustifiable action.[11]

The compatibility of this principle with that of nonaggression can be demonstrated by means of an argumentum a contrario. First, it should be noted that if no one had the right to acquire and control anything except his own body (a rule that would pass the formal universalization test), then we would all cease to exist and the problem of the justification of normative statements (or, for that matter, any other problem that is of concern in this treatise) simply would not exist. The existence of this problem is only possible because we are alive, and our existence is due to the fact that we do not, indeed *cannot*, accept a norm outlawing property in other scarce goods next and in addition to that of one's physical body. Hence, the right to acquire such goods must be assumed to exist. Now, if this is so, and if one does not have the right to acquire such rights of exclusive control over unused, nature-given things through one's own work, i.e., by doing something with things with which no one else had ever done anything before, and if other people *had* the right to disregard one's ownership claim with respect to such things which they had not worked on or put to some particular use before, then this would only be possible if one could acquire property titles not through labor, i.e., by establishing some objective, intersubjectively controllable link between a particular person and a particular scarce resource, but simply by verbal declaration; by decree.[12] However, acquiring property titles through declaration is incompatible with the above justified nonaggression principle regarding bodies. For one thing, if one could indeed appropriate property by decree, then this would imply that it would also be possible for one to simply declare another person's body to be one's own. Yet this, clearly enough, would conflict with the ruling of the nonaggression principle which makes a sharp distinction between one's own body and the body of another person. And this distinction can only be made in such a clear-cut and unambiguous way because for bodies, as for anything else, the separation between "mine" and "yours" is not based on verbal declarations but on action. (Incidentally, a decision between rival declarative claims could not be made unless there were some *objective* criterion other than declaration.) The separation is based on the observation that some particular scarce resource had in fact--for everyone to see and verify, as objective indicators for this would exist--been made an expression or materialization of one's own will, or, as the case may be, of someone else's will. Moreover, and more importantly, to say that property is acquired not through action but through a declaration involves an open practical *contradiction*, because nobody could say and declare so unless in spite of what was actually said his right of exclusive control over his body as his own instrument of saying *anything* was *in fact* already presupposed.

It has now been demonstrated that the right of original appropriation through actions is compatible with and implied in the nonaggression principle as the logically necessary presupposition of argumentation. Indirectly, of course, it has also been demonstrated that any rule specifying different rights, such as a socialist property theory, cannot be justified. Before entering a more detailed analysis, though, of *why* any socialist ethic is indefensible--a discussion which should throw some additional light on the importance of some of the stipulations of the "natural," capitalist theory of property--a few remarks about what is or is not implied by classifying these latter norms as justified seem to be in order.

In making this assertion, one need not claim to have derived an "ought" from an "is." In fact, one can readily subscribe to the almost generally accepted view that the gulf between "ought" and "is" is logically unbridgeable.[13] Rather, classifying the rulings of the natural theory of property in this way is a purely cognitive matter. It no more follows from the classification of the principle underlying capitalism as "fair" or "just" that one ought to act according to it, than it follows from the concept of validity or truth that one should always strive for it. To say that this principle is just also does not preclude the possibility of people proposing or even enforcing rules that are incompatible with it. As a matter of fact, with respect to norms the situation is very similar to that in other disciplines of scientific inquiry. The fact, for instance, that certain empirical statements are justified or justifiable and others are not does not imply that everyone only defends objective, valid statements. Rather, people can be wrong, even intentionally. But the distinction between objective and subjective, between true and false, does not lose any of its significance because of this. Rather, people who are wrong would have to be classified as either uninformed or intentionally lying. The case is similar with respect to norms. Of course there are many people who do not propagate or enforce norms which can be classified as valid according to the meaning of justification which I have given above. But the distinction between justifiable and nonjustifiable norms does not dissolve because of this, just as that between objective and subjective statements does not crumble because of the existence of uninformed or lying people. Rather, and accordingly, those people who would propagate and enforce such different, invalid norms would again have to be classified as uninformed or dishonest, insofar as one had explained to them and indeed made it clear that their alternative norm proposals or enforcements could not and never would be justifiable in argumentation. And there would be even more justification for doing so in the moral case than in the empirical one, since the validity of the nonaggression principle and that of the principle of original appropriation through action as its logically necessary corollary must be considered to be even more basic than any kind of valid or true statements. For what is valid or true has to be defined as that upon which everyone acting according to this principle can possibly agree. As a matter of fact, as has just been shown, at least the implicit acceptance of these rules is the necessary prerequisite to being able to live and to argue at all.[14]

Why is it, then, precisely, that socialist property theories of any kind fail to be justifiable as valid? First, it should be noted that all of the actually *practiced* versions of socialism and most of its theoretically proposed models as well would not even pass the first formal universalization test, and would fail for this fact alone! These versions all contain norms within their framework of legal rules which have the form "some people do, and some people do not." However, such rules, which specify different rights or obligations for different classes of people, have no chance of being accepted as fair by every potential participant in an argumentation for simply formal reasons. Unless the distinction made between different classes of people happens to be such that it is acceptable to both sides as grounded in the nature of things, such rules would not be acceptable because they would imply that one group is awarded legal privileges at the expense of complementary discriminations against another group. Some people, either those who are allowed to do something or those who are not, therefore could not agree that these were fair rules.[15] Since most kinds of socialism, as practiced or preached, have to rely on the enforcement of rules such as "some people have the obligation to pay taxes, and others have the right to consume them" or "some people know what is good for you and are allowed to help you get these alleged blessings even if you do not want them, but you are not allowed to know what is good for them and help them accordingly" or "some people have the right to determine who has too much of something and who too little, and others have the obligation to comply" or even more plainly, "the computer industry must pay to subsidize the farmers," "the employed for the unemployed," "the ones without kids for those with kids," etc., or vice versa, they all can be discarded easily as serious contenders to the claim of being part of a valid theory of norms qua property norms, because they all indicate by their very formulation that they are not universalizable.

But what is wrong with the socialist property theories if this is taken care of and there is indeed a theory formulated that contains exclusively universalizable norms of the type "nobody is allowed to" or "everybody can"? Even then--and this, more ambitiously, is what has been demonstrated indirectly above and shall be argued directly--socialism could never hope to prove its validity, no longer because of formal reasons, but because of its material specifications. Indeed, while those forms of socialism that can easily be refuted regarding their claim to moral validity on simple formal grounds can at least be practiced, the application of those more sophisticated versions that would pass the universalization test prove, for material reasons, to be fatal: even if we tried, they simply could never be put into effect.

There are two related specifications in the norms of the natural theory of property with at least one of which a socialist property theory comes into conflict. The first such specification is that according to the capitalistic ethic, aggression is defined as an invasion of the *physical* integrity of another person's property.[16] Socialism, instead, would define aggression as an invasion of the *value* or *psychic integrity* of another person's property. Conservative socialism, it should be recalled, aimed at preserving a given distribution of wealth and values, and attempted to bring those forces which could change the status quo under control by means of price controls, regulations, and behavioral controls. Clearly, in order to do so, property rights to the value of things must be assumed to be justifiable, and an invasion of values, mutatis mutandis, must be classified as unjustifiable aggression. Yet not only conservatism uses this idea of property and aggression. Social-democratic socialism does, too. Property rights to values must be assumed to be legitimate when social-democratic socialism allows me, for instance, to demand compensation from people whose chances or opportunities negatively affect mine. And the same is true when compensation for committing psychological or "structural violence"--a particularly dear term in the leftist political science literature--is permitted.[17]

In order to be able to ask for such compensation, what was done--affecting my opportunities, my psychic integrity, my feeling of what is owed to me--would have to be classified as an aggressive act.

Why is this idea of protecting the value of property unjustifiable? First, while every person, at least in principle, can have full control over whether or not his actions cause the *physical* characteristics of something to change, and hence also can have full control over whether or not those actions are justifiable, control over whether or not one's actions affect the *value* of some-one else's property does not rest with the acting person, but rather with other people and their subjective evaluations. Thus no one could determine ex ante if his actions would be classified as justifiable or unjustifiable. One would first have to interrogate the whole population to make sure that one's planned actions would not change another person's evaluations regarding his own property. And even then nobody could act until universal *agree-ment* was reached on who is supposed to do what with what, and at which point in time. Clearly, for all the practical problems involved, one would be long dead and nobody would argue anything any longer long before this was ever accomplished.[18] But more decisively still, the socialist position regarding property and aggression could not even be effectively *argued,* because arguing in favor of any norm, socialist or not, implies that there is conflict over the use of some scarce resource, otherwise there would simp-ly be no need for discussion. However, in order to argue that there is a way out of such conflicts, it must be presupposed that actions must be allowed to be performed *prior* to any actual agreement or disagreement, because if they were not, one could not even argue so. Yet if one can do this--and socialism too must assume that one can, insofar as it exists as an argued intellectual position--then this is only possible because the existence of *ob-jective borders* of property i.e., borders which every person can recognize as such *on his own*, without having to agree first with anyone else with respect to one's system of values and evaluations. Socialism, too, then, in spite of what it *says*, must *in fact* presuppose the existence of objective property borders, rather than of borders determined by subjective evaluations, if only in order to have any surviving socialist who can make his moral proposals.

The socialist idea of protecting value instead of physical integrity also fails for a second, related reason. Evidently, the value of a person, for example, on the labor or marriage market, can be and indeed is affected by other people's physical integrity or degree of physical integrity. Thus, if one wanted property *values* to be protected, one would have to allow *physical* aggression against people. However, it is only because of the very fact that a person's borders--that is, the borders of a person's property in his body as his domain of exclusive control with which another person is not allowed to interfere unless he wishes to become an aggressor--are physical borders (intersubjectively ascertainable, and not just subjectively fancied borders) that everyone can agree on anything independently (and, of course, agreement means agreement of independent decision-making units!). Only because the protected borders of property are objective then, i.e., fixed and recognizable as fixed prior to any conventional agreement, can there at all be argumentation, and possibly agreement, between independent decision-making units. There simply could not be anyone arguing anything unless his existence as an independent physical unit was first recognized. No one could argue in favor of a property system defining borders of property in subjective, evaluative terms--as does socialism--because simply to be able to say so presupposes that, contrary to what the theory says, one must in fact be a physically independent unit saying it.

The situation is no less dire for socialism when one turns to the second essential specification of the rulings of the natural theory of property. The basic norms of capitalism were characterized not only by the fact that property and aggression were defined in physical terms; it was of no less importance that in addition property was defined as private, individualized property and that the meaning of original appropriation, which evidently implies making a distinction between prior and later, had been specified. It is with this additional specification as well that socialism comes into conflict. Instead of recognizing the vital importance of the prior-later distinction in deciding between conflicting property claims, socialism proposes norms which in effect state that priority is irrelevant in making such a decision and that late-comers have as much of a right to ownership as first-comers. Clearly, this idea is involved when social-democratic socialism, for instance, makes the natural owners of wealth and/or their heirs pay a tax so that the unfortunate latecomers might be able to participate in its consumption. And this idea is also involved, for instance, when the owner of a natural resource is forced to reduce (or increase) its present exploitation in the interest of posterity. Both times it only makes sense to do so when it is assumed that the person accumulating wealth first, or using the natural resource first, thereby commits an aggression against some late-comers. If they have done nothing wrong, then the late-comers could have no such claim against them.[19]

What is wrong with this idea of dropping the prior-later distinction as morally irrelevant? First, if the late-comers, i.e., those who did not in fact do something with some scarce goods, had indeed as much of a right to them as the first-comers, i.e., those who did do something with the scarce goods, then literally no one would be allowed to do anything with anything, as one would have to have all of the late-comers' consent prior to doing whatever one wanted to do. Indeed, as posterity would include one's children's children--people, that is, who come so late that one could never possibly ask them--advocating a legal system that does not make use of the prior-later distinction as part of its underlying property theory is simply absurd in that it implies advocating death but must presuppose life to advocate anything. Neither we, our forefathers, nor our progeny could, do, or will survive and say or argue anything if one were to follow this rule. In order for any person--past, present, or future--to argue anything it must be possible to survive now. Nobody can wait and suspend acting until everyone of an indeterminate class of late-comers happens to appear and agree to what one wants to do. Rather, insofar as a person finds himself alone, he must be able to act, to use, produce, consume goods straightaway, prior to any agreement with people who are simply not around yet (and perhaps never will be). And insofar as a person finds himself in the company of others and there is conflict over how to use a given scarce resource, he must be able to resolve the problem at a definite point in time with a definite number of people instead of having to wait unspecified periods of time for unspecified numbers of people. Simply in order to survive, then, which is a prerequisite to arguing in favor of or against anything, property rights cannot be conceived of as being timeless and nonspecific regarding the number of people concerned. Rather, they must necessarily be thought of as originating through acting at definite points in time for definite acting individuals.[20]

Furthermore, the idea of abandoning the prior-later distinction, which socialism finds so attractive, would again simply be incompatible with the nonaggression principle as the practical foundation of argumentation. To argue and possibly agree with someone (if only on the fact that there is disagreement) means to recognize each other's prior right of exclusive control over his own body. Otherwise, it would be impossible for anyone to first say anything at a definite point in time and for someone else to then be able to reply, or vice versa, as neither the first nor the second speaker would be independent physical decisionmaking units anymore, at any time. Eliminating the prior-later distinction then, as socialism attempts to do, is tantamount to eliminating the possibility of arguing and reaching agreement. However, as one cannot argue that there is no possibility for discussion without the prior control of every person over his own body being recognized and accepted as fair, a late-comer ethic that does not wish to make this difference could never be agreed upon by anyone. Simply *saying* that it could implies a contradiction, as one's being able to say so would presuppose one's existence as an independent decision-making unit at a definite point in time.

Hence, one is forced to conclude that the socialist ethic is a complete failure. In all of its practical versions, it is no better than a rule such as "I can hit you, but you cannot hit me," which even fails to pass the universalization test. And if it did adopt universalizable rules, which would basically amount to saying "everybody can hit everybody else," such rulings could not conceivably be said to be universally acceptable on account of their very material specification. Simply to say and argue so must presuppose a person's property right over his own body. Thus, only the first-come-first-own ethic of capitalism can be defended effectively as it is implied in argumentation. And no other ethic could be so justified, as justifying something in the course of argumentation implies presupposing the validity of precisely this ethic of the natural theory of property.

8

THE SOCIO-PSYCHOLOGICAL FOUNDATIONS OF SOCIALISM or THE THEORY OF THE STATE

In the preceding chapters it has been demonstrated that socialism as a social system implying a redistribution of property titles away from user-owners and contractors to nonuser-owners and noncontractors necessarily involves a reduction in the production of wealth, since the use and contracting of resources are costly activities whose performance is made even more costly as compared with alternatives available to actors. Secondly, such a system cannot be defended as a fair or just social order from a moral point of view because to argue so, in fact to argue at all, in favor or against *anything,* be it a moral, nonmoral, empirical, or logico-analytical position, necessarily presupposes the validity of the first-use-first-own rule of the natural theory of property and capitalism, as otherwise no one could survive and then say, or possibly agree on, anything as an independent physical unit.

If neither an economic nor a moral case for socialism can be made, then socialism is reduced to an affair of merely social-psychological significance. What, then, are the socio-psychological foundations on which socialism rests? Or, since socialism has been defined as an *institutionalized* policy of redistribution of property titles away from user-owners and contractors, how is an institution that implements a more or less total expropriation of natural owners possible?

If an institution exists that is allowed to appropriate property titles other than through original appropriation or contract, it must assumedly damage some people who consider themselves to be the natural owners of these things. By securing and possibly increasing its monetary and/or nonmonetary income it reduces that of other people--something categorically different from the situation that exists when there is a contractual relationship among people in which no one gains at the expense of anyone else but everyone profits, as otherwise there simply would not be any exchange. In this case one can expect resistance to the execution of such a policy. This inclination to resist can, of course, be more or less intensive, and it can change over time and become either more or less pronounced and pose a greater or smaller threat to the institution carrying out the policy of redistribution. But as long as it exists at all, the institution must reckon with it. In particular, it must reckon with it if one assumes that the people representing this institution are ordinary people who, like everyone else, have an interest not only in stabilizing their current income which they are able to secure for themselves in their roles as representatives of this institution but also in increasing this income as much as possible. How, and this is precisely the problem, can they stabilize and possibly increase their income from noncontractual exchanges, even though this necessarily creates victims--and, over time, increasing numbers of victims, or victims who are increasingly hurt?

The answer can be broken down into three parts which will be discussed in turn: (1) by aggressive violence; (2) by corrupting the public through letting them or rather parts of them share in the enjoyment of the receipts coercively extracted from natural owners of things; and (3) by corrupting the public through letting them or parts of them participate in the specific policy of expropriation to be enacted.

To assure its very existence, any institution that enforces a socialist theory of property must rely on the continual threat of violence. Any such institution threatens people who are unwilling to accept its noncontractual appropriations of their natural property with physical assault, imprisonment, enslavement, or even death, and it must carry out such threats if necessary, in order to stay "trust-worthy" as the kind of institution that it is. Since one is dealing with an institution--an organization, that is, which performs these actions on a regular basis--it is almost self-explanatory that it refuses to call its own practice of doing things "aggression," and instead adopts a different name for it, with neutral or possibly even positive connotations. In fact, its representatives might not even think that they themselves are aggressors when acting in the name of this organization. However, it is not names or terms that matter here or elsewhere, but what they really mean.[1] Regarding the content of its actions, violence is the cornerstone of socialism's existence as an institution. And to leave no room for misunderstanding here, the violence on which socialism rests is not the kind of violence that a natural owner of things would use or threaten to use against aggressive intruders of his property. It is not the defensive threat toward a prospective murderer of, let us say, subjecting him to capital punishment, should he in fact murder someone. Rather, it is aggressive violence directed at innocent victims. An institution carrying out socialism literally rests on the threat posed by a prospective murderer against innocent people (i.e., people who have not done any physical harm whatsoever to anyone) to kill them should they not comply with his demands, or even to kill them just for the "fun" of killing.

It is not at all difficult to recognize the truth of this. In order to do so, it is only necessary to assume a boycott of any exchange-relation with the representatives of socialism because such an exchange, for whatever reasons, no longer seems profitable. It should be clear that in a social system based on the natural theory of property--under capitalism--anyone would have the right to boycott at any time, as long as he was indeed the person who appropriated the things concerned by using them before anyone else did or by acquiring them contractually from a previous owner. However much a person or institution might be affected by such a boycott, it would have to tolerate it and suffer silently, or else try to persuade the boycotter to give up his position by making a more lucrative offer to him. But it is not so with an institution that puts socialist ideas regarding property into effect. Try, for instance, to stop paying taxes or to make your future payments of taxes dependent on certain changes or improvements in the services that the institution offers in return for the taxes--it would fine, assault, imprison you, or perhaps do even worse things to you. Or to use another example, try to ignore this institution's regulations or controls imposed on your property. Try, that is to say, to make the point that you did not consent to these limitations regarding the use of your property and that you would not invade the physical integrity of anyone else's property by ignoring such impositions, and hence, that you have the right to secede from its jurisdiction, to "cancel your membership" so to speak, and from then on deal with it on equal footing, from one privileged institution to another. Again, assumedly without having aggressed against anyone through your secession, this institution would come and invade you and your property, and it would not hesitate to end your independence. As a matter of fact, if it did not do so, it would stop being what it is. It would abdicate and become a regular private property owner or a contractual association of such owners. Only because it does not so abdicate is there socialism at all. Indeed, and this is why the title of this chapter suggested that the question regarding the socio-psychological foundations of socialism is identical to that of the foundations of a state, if there were no institution enforcing socialistic ideas of property, there would be no room for a state, as a state is nothing else than an institution built on taxation and unsolicited, noncontractual interference with the use that private people can make of their natural property. There can be no socialism without a state, and as long as there is a state there is socialism. The state, then, is the very institution that puts socialism into action; and as socialism rests on aggressive violence directed against innocent victims, aggressive violence is the nature of any state.[2]

But socialism, or the state as the incorporation of socialist ideas, does not rest exclusively on aggression. The representatives of the state do not engage solely in aggressive acts in order to stabilize their incomes, though without it there would not be any state! As long as the relationship between the state and private property owners is exclusively a parasitic one, and the activities of the representatives of the state consist entirely of unsolicited interferences with other people's property rights, designed to increase the income of the former at the expense of a corresponding reduction in income of the latter, and these agents of socialism then do nothing else with their income than consume it for their own private purposes, then the chances for the state's growth and the spread of socialism are at least very limited and narrow. Certainly, one man, or one group of men, possessed with sufficient aggressive energies can inspire enough fear in one and possibly even in a few others, or in another more numerous group of men who, for whatever reason, lack such characteristics, and can establish a stable relationship of exploitation. But it is impossible to explain the fact, characteristic of all states and each and every socialist social system, that the group of men representing the state can hold people ten, a hundred, or even a thousand times more numerous than they themselves in submission, and extract from them the incredibly large amounts of income that they in fact do, only by instilling fear in them.

It might be thought that an increase in the degree of exploitation could explain the size of income. But from the economic reasoning of previous chapters we know that a higher degree of exploitation of natural owners necessarily reduces their incentive to work and produce, and so there is a narrow limit to the degree to which one person (or group of persons) can lead a comfortable life on the income coercively extracted from another person (or a roughly equally sized group of persons) who would have to support this life style through his (their) work. Hence, in order for the agents of socialism to be able to lead a comfortable life and prosper as they do, it is essential that the number of exploited subjects be considerably larger and grow over-proportionally as compared with those of the representatives of the state itself. With this, however, we are back to the question of how the few can rule the many.

There would also be no convincing way around this explanatory task by arguing that the state could simply solve this problem by improving its weaponry; by threatening with atomic bombs instead of with guns and rifles, so to speak, thereby increasing the number of its subjects. Since realistically one must assume that the technological know-how of such improved weaponry can hardly be kept secret, especially if it is in fact applied, then with the state's improved instruments for instilling fear, mutatis mutandis the victims' ways and means of resisting improve as well, and hence, such advances can hardly be thought of as explaining what has to be explained.[3] One must conclude, then, that the problem of explaining how the few can rule the many is indeed real, and that socialism and the state as the incorporation of socialism must rest in addition to aggression on some sort of active support among the public.

David Hume is one of the classic expositors of this insight. In his essay on "The first principles of government" he argues:

> Nothing appears more surprising to those who consider human affairs with a philosophical eye, than the easiness with which the many are governed by the few, and the implicit submission, with which men resign their own sentiments and passions to those of their rulers. When we inquire by what means this wonder is effected we shall find, that as Force is always on the side of the governed, the governors have nothing to support them but opinion. It is, therefore, on opinion only that government is founded, and this maxim extends to the most despotic and most military

> governments, as well as to the most free and most popular. The soldan of Egypt, or the emperor of Rome, might drive his harmless subjects, like brute beasts, against their sentiments and inclination. But he must, at least, have led his mamalukes or praetorian bands, like men, by their opinion.[4]

How indeed is this support brought about? One important component in the process of generating it is ideology. The state spends much time and effort persuading the public that it is not *really* what it is and that the consequences of its actions are positive rather than negative. Such ideologies, spread to stabilize a state's existence and increase its income, claim that socialism offers a superior economic system or a social order that is more just than capitalism, or claim that there is no such thing as justice at all prior to the state's stepping in and simply declaring certain norms to be just.[5] And such ideologies, too, less attractive now, but once extremely powerful, are those, for example, of the state being sanctified by religion, or of the rulers not being ordinary people but instead god-like superhumans, who must be obeyed because of their natural superiority. I have gone to great lengths in previous chapters to demonstrate that such ideas are false and unjustified, and I will return to the task of analyzing and unmasking another fashionable ideology in the final chapter of this treatise. But regardless of the falsity of these ideologies, it must be recognized that they certainly do have some effect on people, and that they do contribute--some more so than others--to their submission to a policy of aggressive invasion of the property rights of natural owners.

Yet there is another more important component contributing to public support and this is not verbal propaganda, but rather actions with a clear-cut, tangible impact. Instead of being a mere parasitic consumer of goods that other people have produced, the state, in order to stabilize itself and increase its income as much as possible, adds some positive ingredients to its policy, designed to be of use to some people outside the circle of its own personnel. Either it is engaged as an agent of income transfer, i.e., as an organization that hands out monetary or nonmonetary income to B that it has previously taken away from A without A's consent--naturally after subtracting a handling charge for the never costless act of such a transfer--or it engages in the production of goods or services, using the means expropriated earlier from natural owners, and thus contributes something of value to the users/buyers/consumers of these goods. Either way, the state generates support for its role. The recipients of transferred incomes as well as the users/consumers of state-produced goods and services become dependent to varying degrees on the continuation of a given state policy for their current incomes, and their inclination to resist the socialism embodied in state rule is reduced accordingly.

But this is only half of the picture. The positive achievements of the state are not undertaken simply to do something nice for some people, as, for instance, when someone gives somebody else a present. Nor are they done simply to gain as high an income as possible from the exchange for the organization doing them, as when an ordinary, profit-oriented institution engages in trade. Rather, they are undertaken in order to secure the existence and contribute to the growth of an institution that is built on aggressive violence. As such, the positive contributions emanating from the state must serve a *strategic purpose*. They must be designed to break up resistance to or add support for the continued existence of an aggressor as an aggressor. Of course, the state can err in this task, as can any ordinary business, because its decisions about what measures best serves its strategic purposes have to be made *in anticipation* of certain expected results. And if it errs with respect to the responses following its policy decisions, instead of rising its income can fall, jeopardizing its very existence, just as a profit-oriented institution can make losses or even go bankrupt if the public is not willing to deliberately buy what it was expected to buy. But only if the peculiar strategic purpose of state transfers and state production as compared with private transfers or production is understood does it become possible to explain typical, recurring structural patterns of a state's actions, and to explain why states generally and uniformly prefer to go into certain lines of activities rather than others.

As regards the first problem: it does not make sense for a state to exploit every individual to the same extent, since this would bring everyone against it, strengthen the solidarity among the victims, and in any case, it would not be a policy that would find many new friends. It also does not make sense for a state to grant its favors equally and indiscriminately to everybody. For if it did, the victims would still be victims, although perhaps to a lesser degree. However, there would then be less income left to be distributed to people who would truly profiteer from state action, and whose increased support could help compensate for the lack of support from victimized persons. Rather, state policy must be and indeed is guided by the motto "divide et impera": treat people differently, play them against each other, exploit one possibly smaller group and favor another possibly larger group at the former's expense, and so counterbalance increased resentment or resistance of some by increased support of others. Politics, as politics of a state, is not "the art of doing the possible," as statesmen prefer to describe their business. It is the art, building on an equilibrium of terror, of helping to stabilize state income on as high a level as possible by means of popular discrimination and a popular, discriminatory scheme of distributional favors. To be sure, a profit-oriented institution can also engage in discriminatory business policies, but to do so and to follow a discriminatory employment policy or not to sell indiscriminately to anyone who is willing to pay the price set for a given service or product is costly, and so an economic incentive to avoid such action exists. For the state, on the other hand, there is every incentive in the world to engage in such discriminatory practices.[6]

Regarding the kinds of services preferably offered by the state: clearly, the state cannot produce everything, or at least not everything to the same extent, for if it tried to do so its income would actually fall--as the state can only appropriate what has in fact been produced earlier by natural owners, and the incentive to produce anything in the future would be almost completely gone in a system of all-around socialization. It is of utmost importance in trying to implement socialism, then, that a state engage in and concentrate on the production and provision of such goods and services (and, mutatis mutandis, drive private competitors out of competition in such lines of productive activities, thereby monopolizing their provision) which are strategically relevant for preventing or suppressing any actual revolt, rebellion, or revolution.[7]

Thus, all states--some more extensively than others, but every state to a considerable degree--have felt the need to take the system of education, for one thing, into their own hands. It either directly operates the educational institutions, or indirectly controls such institutions by making their private operation dependent on the granting of a state license, thus insuring that they operate within a predefined framework of guidelines provided by the state. Together with a steadily extended period of compulsory schooling, this gives the state a tremendous head start in the competition among different ideologies for the minds of the people. Ideological competition which might pose a serious threat to state rule can thereby be eliminated or its impact considerably reduced, especially if the state as the incorporation of socialism succeeds in monopolizing the job market for intellectuals by making a state license the prerequisite for any sort of systematic teaching activity.[8]

The direct or indirect control of traffic and communication is of similar strategic importance for a state. Indeed, all states have gone to great pains to control rivers, coasts and seaways, streets and railroads, and especially, mail, radio, television, and telecommunication systems. Every prospective dissident is decisively restrained in his means of moving around and coordinating the actions of individuals if these things are in the hand or under the supervision of the state. The fact, well known from military history, that traffic and communication systems are the very first command posts to be occupied by any state attacking another vividly underlines their central strategic significance in imposing state rule on a society.

A third central concern of strategic relevance for any state is the control and possible monopolization of money. If the state succeeds in this task and, as is the case now all over the world, supplants a system of free banking and metal-based currency--most commonly the gold standard--with a monetary system characterized by a state-operated central bank and paper-money backed by nothing but paper and ink, a great victory has indeed been reached. In its permanent struggle for higher income, the state is no longer dependent on the equally unpopular means of increased taxation or currency depreciation (coin-clipping), which at all times has been unmasked quickly as fraudulent. Rather, it can now increase its own revenue and decrease its own debt almost at will by printing more money, as long as the additional money is brought into circulation before the inflationary consequences of this practice have taken effect or have been anticipated by the market.[9]

Fourth and last, there is the area of the production of security, of police, defense, and judicial courts. Of all the state-provided or controlled goods or services this is certainly the area of foremost strategic importance. In fact, it is of such great significance for any state to gain control of these things, to outlaw competitors, and to monopolize these activities, that "state" and "producer of law and order" have frequently been considered synonyms. Wrongly so, of course, as the state must be correctly described as an institution of organized aggression attempting only to *appear* as an ordinary producer in order to continue aggressing against innocent natural owners. But the fact that this confusion exists and is widely shared can be explained with reference to the observation that all states must monopolize the production of security because of its central strategic importance, and hence, these two terms, different as they are with respect to their intentional meaning, indeed have the same extensional meaning.

It is not difficult to see why in order to stabilize its existence, a state cannot, under any circumstances, leave the production of security in the hands of a market of private property owners.[10] Since the state ultimately rests on coercion, it requires armed forces. Unfortunately (for any given state, that is), other armed states exist which implies that there is a check on a state's desire to expand its reign over other people and thereby increase its revenue appropriated through exploitation. It is unfortunate for a given state, too, that such a system of competing states also implies that each individual state is somewhat limited regarding the degree to which it can exploit its own subjects, as their support might dwindle if its own rule is perceived as more oppressive than that of competing states. For then the likelihood of a state's subjects collaborating with a competitor in its desire to "take over," or that of voting with their feet (leaving one's own country and going to a different one) might increase.[11] It is even more important, then, for each individual state to avoid any such unpleasant competition from other potentially dangerous armed organizations at least *within* the very territory it happens to control. The mere existence of a private protection agency, armed as it would have to be to do its job of protecting people from aggression and employing people trained in the use of such arms, would constitute a potential threat to a state's ongoing policy of invading private people's property rights. Hence, such organizations, which would surely spring up on the market as the desire to be protected against aggressors is a genuine one, are eagerly outlawed, and the state arrogates this job to itself and its monopolistic control. As a matter of fact, states everywhere are highly intent on outlawing or at least controlling even the mere possession of arms by private citizens--and most states have indeed succeeded in this task--as an armed man is clearly more of a threat to any aggressor than an unarmed man. It bears much less risk for the state to keep things peaceful while its own aggression continues, if rifles with which the taxman could be shot are out of the reach of everyone except the taxman himself!

With respect to the judicial system matters are quite similar. If the state did not monopolize the provision of judicial services, it would be unavoidable that, sooner or later (and most likely sooner), the state would come to be regarded as the unjust institution it in fact is. Yet no unjust organization has any interest in being recognized as such. For one thing, if the state did not see to it that only judges appointed and employed by the state itself administered the law, it is evident that public law (those norms regulating the relationship between the state and private individuals or associations of such individuals) would have no chance of being accepted by the public, but instead would be unveiled immediately as a system of legalized aggression, existing in violation of almost everyone's sense of justice. And secondly, if the state did not also monopolize the administration of private law (those norms regulating the relationships among private citizens) but left this task to competing courts and judges, dependent on the public's deliberate financial support, it is doubtful that norms implying an asymmetrical distribution of rights or obligations between different persons or classes of persons would have even the slightest chance of becoming generally accepted as valid laws. Courts and judges who laid down such rules would immediately go bankrupt due to a lack of continued financial assistance.[12] However, since the state is dependent on a policy of *divide et impera* to maintain its power, it must stop the emergence of a competitive system of private law courts at all costs.

Without a doubt, all of these state-provided services--education, traffic and communication, money and banking, and, most importantly, security and the administration of justice--are of vital importance to any society whatsoever. All of them would certainly have to be provided, and would, in fact, be produced by the market if the state did not take these things into its own hands. But this does not mean that the state is simply a substitute for the market. The state engages in these activities for an entirely different reason than any private business would--not simply because there is a demand for them, but rather because these areas of activities are of essential strategic importance in assuring the state's continued existence as a privileged institution built on aggressive violence. And this different strategic intent is responsible for a peculiar kind of product. Since the educators, employees of traffic and communication systems, those of central banks, the police and judges, are all paid by taxes, the kind of products or services provided by a state, though certainly of some positive value to some people, can never be of such quality that *everyone* would deliberately spend his own money on them. Rather, these services all share the characteristic that they contribute to letting the state increase its own coercively extracted income by means of benefiting some while harming others.[13]

But there is even more to the socio-psychological foundations of the state as an institution of continued aggression against natural owners than the popular redistribution of strategically important goods and services. Equally important for the state's stability and growth is the decision-making structure which it adopts for itself: its constitution. An ordinary profit-oriented business would try to adopt a decision-making structure best suited to its goal of maximizing income through the perception and implementation of entrepreneurial opportunities, i.e., differences in production costs and anticipated product demand. The state, in comparison, faces the entirely different task of adopting a decision-making structure which allows it to increase maximally its coercively appropriated income--given its power to threaten and bribe persons into supporting it by granting them special favors.

I submit that the best decision-making structure for doing so is a democratic constitution, i.e., the adoption of majority rule. In order to realize the validity of this thesis, only the following assumption need be made. Not only the persons actually representing the state have the desire (which *they*, incidentally, are always permitted to satisfy) to increase their income at the expense of a corresponding income reduction of natural owners, producers, and contractors; this lust for power and the desire to rule others also exists among the people governed. Not everyone has this desire to the same extent; indeed some people might never have it. But most people have it quite normally on recurring occasions. If this is so (and experience informs us that this *is* indeed the case), then the state must reckon with resistance from two analytically distinct sources. On the one hand there is resistance by the victims which any state policy creates. The state can try to break this up by making supportive friends; and indeed it will succeed in doing so to the extent that people can be corrupted through bribery. On the other hand, if lust for power exists among the victims and/or the persons favored by a given state policy, then there must also be resistance or at least discontent originating from the fact that any given policy of expropriation and discriminatory distribution automatically excludes any other such policy with its advocates in the state-ruled population, and hence must frustrate their particular plan of how power should be used. By definition, no change in the expropriation-redistribution policy of the state can eliminate this sort of discontent, as any change would necessarily exclude a different policy. Thus, if the state wants to do something to reduce the resistance (stemming from the frustration of one's lust for power) that any one particular policy implies, it can only do so by adopting a decision-making structure which minimizes the disappointment of potential power wielders: by opening up a popular scheme of participation in decision making, so that everyone lusting for his particular power policy can hope to have a shot at it in the future.

This, precisely, is the function of a democracy. Since it is based on a respect for the majority, it is by definition a popular constitution for decision making. And as it indeed opens up the chance for everyone to lobby for his own specific plan of wielding power at regular intervals, it maximally reduces current frustrated lust for power through the prospect of a better future. Contrary to popular myth, the adoption of a democratic constitution has nothing to do with freedom or justice.[14] Certainly, as the state restrains itself in its use of aggressive violence when engaging in the provision of some positively valued goods and services, so it accepts additional constraints when the incumbent rulers subject themselves to the control of the majority of those being ruled. Despite the fact, though, that this constraint fulfills the positive function of satisfying certain desires of certain people by reducing the intensity of the frustrated lust for power, it by no means implies the state's forsaking its privileged position as an institution of legalized aggression. Rather, democratizing the state is an organizational measure undertaken for the strategic purpose of rationalizing the execution of power, thereby increasing the amount of income to be aggressively appropriated from natural owners. The form of power is changed, but majority rule is aggression, too. In a system based on the natural theory of property--under capitalism--majority rule does not and cannot play any role (apart from the fact, of course, that if accepted, anyone could join an association adopting majority rule, such as a sports club or an association of animal lovers, whose jurisdiction is deliberately accepted by members as binding for the duration of one's membership). In such a system, only the rules of original appropriation of goods through use or contractual acquisition from previous owners are valid. Appropriation by decree or without a previous user-owner's consent regardless of whether it was carried out by an autocrat, a minority, against a majority, or by a majority against a minority is without exception an act of aggressive violence. What distinguishes a democracy from an autocracy, monarchy, or oligarchy is not that the former means freedom, whereas the others mean aggression. The difference between them lies solely in the techniques used to manage, transform, and channel popular resistance fed by the frustrated lust for power. The autocrat does not allow the population to influence policy in any regular, formalized way, even though he, too, must pay close attention to public opinion in order to stabilize his existence. Thus, an autocracy is characterized by the lack of an institutionalized outlet for potential power wielders. A democracy, on the other hand, has precisely such an institution. It allows majorities, formed according to certain formalized rules, to influence policy changes regularly. Accordingly, if disappointed lust for power becomes more tolerable when there is a regular outlet for it, then there must be less resistance to democratic rule than to autocratic power. This important socio-psychological difference between autocratic and democratic regimes has been described masterfully by B. de Jouvenel:

> From the twelfth to the eighteenth century governmental authority grew continuously. The process was understood by all who saw it happening; it stirred them to incessant protest and to violent reaction. -- In later times its growth has continued at an accelerated pace, and its extension has brought a corresponding extension of war. And now we no longer understand the process, we no longer protest, we no longer react. This quiescence of ours is a new thing, for which Power has to thank the smoke-screen in which it has wrapped itself. Formerly it could be seen, manifest in the person of the king, who did not disclaim being the master he was, and in whom human passions were discern-

> ible. Now, masked in anonymity, it claims to have no existence of its own, and to be but the impersonal and passionless instrument of the general will. -- But that is clearly a fiction. -- ... Today as always Power is in the hands of a group of men who control the power house.... All that has changed is that it has now been made easy for the ruled to change the personnel of the leading wielders of Power. Viewed from one angle, this weakens Power, because the wills which control a society's life can, at the society's pleasure, be replaced by other wills, in which it feels more confidence. -- But by opening the prospect of Power to all the ambitious talents, this arrangement makes the extension of Power much easier. Under the "ancien regime," society's moving spirits, who had, as they knew, no chance of a share in Power, were quick to denounce its smallest encroachment. Now, on the other hand, when everyone is potentially a minister, no one is concerned to cut down an office to which he aspires one day himself, or to put sand in a machine which he means to use himself when his turn comes. Hence, it is that there is in the political circles of a modern society a wide complicity in the extension of Power.[15]

Given an identical population and an identical state policy of the discriminatory provision of goods and services, a democratic state has more opportunities for increasing its own aggressively appropriated income. And mutatis mutandis, an autocracy must settle for a relative lower income. In terms of the classics of political thought, it must rule more wisely, i.e., rule less. Since it does not allow any will other than that of the autocrat, and perhaps his immediate advisors, to gain power or influence policy on a regular basis, its execution of power appears less tolerable to those ruled. Thus, its stability can only be secured if the overall degree of exploitation enacted by the state is relatively reduced.

The situation over the last two centuries vividly illustrates the validity of this thesis. During this time we have experienced an almost universal substitution of relatively democratic regimes for relatively autocratic-monarchical systems.[16] (Even Soviet Russia is notably more democratic than czarist Russia ever was.) Hand in hand with this change has gone a process never experienced before regarding its speed and extent: a permanent and seemingly uncontrollable growth of the state. In the competition of different states for exploitable populations, and in these states' attempts to come to grips with internal resistance, the democratic state has tended to win outright over the autocratic one as the superior power-variant. Ceteris paribus, it is the democratic state--and the democratic socialism incorporated in it--which commands the higher income and so proves to be superior in wars with other states. And ceteris paribus, it is this state, too, that succeeds better in the management of internal resistance: it is, and historically this has been shown repeatedly, easier to save the power of a state by democratizing it than by doing the opposite and autocratizing its decision-making structure.

Here, then, we have the socio-psychological foundations of the state as the very institution enacting socialism. Any state rests on the monopolization or the monopolistic control of strategically important goods and services which it discriminately provides to favored groups of people, thereby breaking down resistance to a policy of aggression against natural owners. Furthermore, it rests on a policy of reducing the frustrated lust for power by creating outlets for public participation in future changes in a policy of exploitation. Naturally, every historical description of a state and its specific socialist policy and policy changes will have to give a more detailed account of what made it possible for socialism to become established and to grow. But if any such description is supposedly complete and is not to fall prey to ideological deception, then all measures taken by the state must be described as embedded in this very institutional framework of violence, *divide et impera*, and democratization.

Whatever any given state does in terms of positively evaluated contributions to society, and however great or small the extent of such contributions might be; whether the state provides help for working mothers with dependent children or gives medical care, engages in road or airport construction; whether it grants favors to farmers or students, devotes itself to the production of educational services, society's infrastructure, money, steel or peace; or even if it does all of these things and more, it would be completely fallacious to enumerate all of this and leave it at that. What must be said in addition is that the state can do *nothing* without the previous noncontractual expropriation of natural owners. Its contributions to welfare are never an ordinary present, even if they are given away free of charge, because something is handed out that the state does not rightfully own in the first place. If it sells its services at cost, or even at a profit, the means of production employed in providing them still must have been appropriated by force. And if it sells them at a subsidized price, aggression must continue in order to uphold the current level of production.

The situation is similar with respect to a state's decision-making structure. Whether a state is organized autocratically or democratically, has a centralized or decentralized decision-making structure, a single or multistage representational structure; whether it is organized as a system of parties or as a corporate state, it would be delusory to describe it in these terms and leave it at that. In order to be exhaustive, what must be added is that first and foremost, the constitution of a state is an organizational device for promoting its existence as an institution of aggression. And insofar as its stability rests on constitutionally guaranteed rights to participate in the inauguration of policy changes, it must be stressed that the state rests on an institutionalized appeal to motivational energies that people in their private lives would regard as criminal and accordingly would do everything to suppress. An ordinary business enterprise has a decision-making structure that must adapt to the purpose of enabling it to secure as high a profit as possible from sales to deliberately supportive customers. A state's constitution has nothing in common with this, and only superficial sociological "studies in organization" would engage in investigations of structural similarities or differences between the two.[17]

Only if this is thoroughly understood can the nature of the state and socialism be fully grasped. And only then can there be a complete understanding of the other side of the same problem: what it takes to overcome socialism. The state cannot be fought by simply boycotting it, as a private business could, because an aggressor does not respect the negative judgment revealed by boycotts. But it also cannot simply be fought by countering its aggression with defensive violence, because the state's aggression is supported by public opinion.[18] Thus, everything depends on a change in public opinion. More specifically, everything depends on two assumptions and the change that can be achieved regarding their status as realistic or unrealistic. One such assumption was implied when it was argued above that the state can generate support for its role by providing certain goods and services to favored groups of people. There, evidently, the assumption involved was that people can be corrupted into supporting an aggressor if they receive a share, however small, of the benefits. And, since states exist everywhere, this assumption, happily for the state, must indeed be said to be realistic everywhere, today. But then, there is no such thing as a law of nature stating that this must be so forever. In order for the state to fail in reaching its objective, no more and no less than a change in general public opinion must take place: state-supportive action must come to be regarded and branded as immoral because it is support given to an organization of institutionalized crime. Socialism would be at its end if only people stopped letting themselves be corrupted by the state's bribes, but would, let us say, if offered, take their share of the wealth in order to reduce the state's bribing power, while continuing to regard and treat it as an aggressor to be resisted, ignored, and ridiculed, at any time and in any place.

The second assumption involved was that people indeed lust for power and hence can be corrupted into state-supportive action if given a chance to satisfy this lust. Looking at the facts, there can hardly be any doubt that today this assumption, too, is realistic. But once again, it is not realistic because of natural laws, for at least in principle, it can deliberately be made unrealistic.[19] In order to bring about the end of statism and socialism, no more and no less must be accomplished than a change in public opinion which would lead people away from using the institutional outlets for policy participation for the satisfaction of power lust, but instead make them suppress any such desire and turn this very organizational weapon of the state against it and push uncompromisingly for an end to taxation and regulation of natural owners wherever and whenever there is a chance of influencing policy.[20]

9

CAPITALIST PRODUCTION AND THE PROBLEM OF MONOPOLY

The previous chapters have demonstrated that neither an economic nor a moral case for socialism can be made. Socialism is economically and morally inferior to capitalism. The last chapter examined why socialism is nonetheless a viable social system, and analyzed the socio-psychological characteristics of the state--the institution embodying socialism. Its existence, stability, and growth rest on aggression and on public support of this aggression which the state manages to effect. This it does, for one thing, through a policy of popular discrimination; a policy, that is, of bribing some people into tolerating and supporting the continual exploitation of others by granting them favors; and secondly, through a policy of popular participation in the making of policy, i.e., by corrupting the public and persuading it to play the game of aggression by giving prospective power wielders the consoling opportunity to enact their particular exploitative schemes at one of the subsequent policy changes.

We shall now return to economics, and analyze the workings of a capitalist system of production--a market economy--as the alternative to socialism, thereby constructively bringing my argument against socialism full circle. While the final chapter will be devoted to the question of how capitalism solves the problem of the production of so-called "public goods," this chapter will explain what might be termed the normal functioning of capitalist production and contrast it with the normal working of a system of state or social production. We will then turn to what is generally believed to be a special problem allegedly showing a peculiar economic deficiency in a pure capitalist production system: the so-called problem of monopolistic production.

Ignoring for the moment the special problems of monopolistic and public goods production, we will demonstrate why capitalism is economically superior as compared to its alternative for three structural reasons. First, only capitalism can rationally, i.e., in terms of consumer evaluations, allocate means of production; second, only capitalism can ensure that, with the quality of the people and the allocation of resources being given, the quality of the output produced reaches its optimal level as judged again in terms of consumer evaluations; and third, assuming a given allocation of production factors and quality of output, and judged again in terms of consumer evaluations, only a market system can guarantee that the value of production factors is efficiently conserved over time.[1]

As long as it produces for a market, i.e., for exchange with other people or businesses, and subject as it is to the rule of nonaggression against the property of natural owners, every ordinary business will use its resources for the production of such goods and such amounts of these goods which, in anticipation, promise a return from sales that surpasses as far as possible the costs which are involved in using these resources. If this were not so, a business would use its resources for the production of different amounts of such goods or of different goods altogether. And every such business has to decide repeatedly whether a given allocation or use of its means of production should be upheld and reproduced, or if, due to a change in demand or the anticipation of such a change, a reallocation to different uses is in order. The question of whether or not resources have been used in the most value-productive (the most profitable) way, or if a given reallocation was the most economic one, can, of course, only be decided in a more or less distant future under any conceivable economic or social system, because invariably time is needed to produce a product and bring it onto the market. However, and this is decisive, for every business there is an objective criterion for deciding the extent to which its previous allocational decisions were right or wrong. Bookkeeping informs us--and in principle anyone who wanted to do so could check and verify this information--whether or not and to what extent a given allocation of factors of production was economically rational, not only for the business in total but for each of its subunits, insofar as market prices exist for the production factors used in it. Since the profit-loss criterion is an ex post criterion, and must necessarily be so under any production system because of the time factor involved in production, it cannot be of any help when deciding on future ex ante allocations. Nevertheless, from the consumers' point of view it is possible to conceive of the process of resource allocation and reallocation as rational, because every allocational decision is constantly tested against the profit-loss criterion. Every business that fails to meet this criterion is in the short or long run doomed to shrink in size or be driven out of the market entirely, and only those enterprises that successfully manage to meet the profit-loss criterion can stay in operation or possibly grow and prosper. To be sure, then, the institutionalization of this criterion does not insure (and no other criterion ever could) that all individual business decisions will always turn out to be rational in terms of consumer evaluations. However, by eliminating bad forecasters and strengthening the position of consistently successful ones, it does insure that the structural changes of the whole production system which take place over time can be described as constant movements toward a more rational use of resources and as a never-ending process of directing and redirecting factors of production out of less value-productive lines of production into lines which are valued more highly by the consumer.[2]

The situation is entirely different and arbitrariness from the point of view of the consumer (for whom, it should be recalled, production is undertaken) replaces rationality as soon as the state enters the picture. Because it is different from ordinary businesses in that it is allowed to acquire income by noncontractual means, the state is not forced to avoid losses if it wants to stay in business as are all other producers. Rather, since it is allowed to impose taxes and/or regulations on people, the state is in a position to determine unilaterally whether or not, to what extent, and for what length of time to subsidize its own productive operations. It can also unilaterally choose which prospective competitor is allowed to compete with the state or possibly outcompete it. Essentially this means that the state becomes independent of cost-profit considerations. But if it is no longer forced to test continually any of its various uses of resources against this criterion, i.e., if it no longer need successfully adjust its resource allocations to the changes in demand of consumers in order to survive as a producer, then the sequence of allocational decisions as a whole must be regarded as an arbitrary, irrational process of decision making. A mechanism of selection forcing those allocational "mutations" which consistently ignore or exhibit a maladjustment to consumer demand out of operation simply no longer exists.[3] To say that the process of resource allocation becomes arbitrary in the absence of the effective functioning of the profit-loss criterion does not mean that the decisions which somehow have to be made are not subject to any kind of constraint and hence are pure whim. They are not, and any such decision faces certain constraints imposed on the decision maker. If, for instance, the allocation of production factors is decided democratically, then it evidently must appeal to the majority. But if a decision is constrained in this way or if it is made autocratically, respecting the state of public opinion as seen by the autocrat, then it is still arbitrary from the point of view of voluntarily buying or not-buying consumers.[4] Hence, the allocation of resources, whatever it is and however it changes over time, embodies a wasteful use of scarce means. Freed from the necessity of making profits in order to survive as a consumer-serving institution, the state necessarily substitutes allocational chaos for rationality. M. Rothbard nicely summarizes the problem as follows:

> How can it (i.e. the government, the state) know whether to build road A or road B, whether to invest in a road or in a school--in fact, how much to spend for all its activities? There is no rational way that it can allocate funds or even decide how much to have. When there is a shortage of teachers or schoolrooms or police or streets, the government and its supporters have only one answer: more money. Why is this answer never offered on the free market? The reason is that money must be *withdrawn* from some other uses in consumption or investment, ... and this withdrawal must be justified. This justification is provided by the test of profit and loss: the indication that the most urgent wants of the consumers are being satisfied. If an enterprise or product is earning high profits for its owners and these profits are expected to continue, more money will be forthcoming; if not, and losses are being incurred, money will flow out of the industry. The profit-and-loss-test serves as the critical guide for directing the flow of productive services. No such guide exists for the government, which has no rational way to decide how much money to spend, either in total, or in each specific line. The more money it spends, the more service it can supply--but where to stop?[5]

Besides the misallocation of factors of production that results from the decision to grant the state the special right to appropriate revenue in a non-contractual way, state production implies a reduction in the quality of the output of whatever it decides to produce. Again, an ordinary profit-oriented business can only maintain a given size or possibly grow if it can sell its products at a price and in such quantity that allow it to recover at least the costs involved in production and is hopefully higher. Since the demand for the goods or services produced depends either on their relative quality or on their price--this being one of many criteria of quality--as perceived by potential buyers, the producers must constantly be concerned about "perceived product quality" or "cheapness of product." A firm is dependent exclusively on voluntary consumer purchases for its continued existence, so there is no arbitrarily defined standard of quality for a capitalist enterprise (including so-called scientific or technological standards of quality) set by an alleged expert or committee of experts. For it there is only the quality as perceived and judged by the consumers. Once again, this criterion does not guarantee that there are no low-quality or overpriced products or services offered on the market because production takes time and the sales test comes only after the products have appeared on the market. And this would have to be so under any system of goods production. Nonetheless, the fact that every capitalist enterprise must undergo this sales test and pass it to avoid being eliminated from the market guarantees a sovereign position to the consumers and their evaluations. Only if product quality is constantly improved and adjusted to consumer tastes can a business stay in operation and prosper.

The story is quite different as soon as the production of goods is undertaken by the state. Once future revenue becomes independent of cost covering sales--as is typically the case when the state produces a good--there is no longer a reason for such a producer to be concerned about product quality in the same way that a sales-dependent institution would have to be. If the producer's future income can be secured, regardless of whether according to consumer evaluations the products or services produced are worth their money, why undertake special efforts to improve anything? More precisely, even if one assumes that the employees of the state as a productive enterprise with the right to impose taxes and to regulate unilaterally the competitiveness of its potential rivals are, on the average, just as much interested or uninterested in work as those working in a profit-dependent enterprise,[6] and if one further assumes that both groups of employees and workers are on the average equally interested or uninterested in an increase or decrease in their income, then the quality of products, measured in terms of consumer demand and revealed in actual purchases, must be lower in a state enterprise than in private business, because the income of the state employees would be far less dependent on product quality. Accordingly, they would tend to devote relatively less effort to producing quality products and more of their time and effort would go into doing what they, but not necessarily the consumer, happen to like.[7] Only if the people working for the state were superhumans or angels, while everyone else was simply an ordinary, inferior human being, could the result be any different. Yet the same result, i.e., the inferiority of product quality of any state-produced goods, would again ensue if the human race in the aggregate would somehow improve: if they were working in a state enterprise even angels would produce a lower quality output than their angel-colleagues in private business, if work implied even the slightest disutility for them.

Finally, in addition to the facts that only a market system can ensure a rational allocation of scarce resources, and that only capitalist enterprises can guarantee an output of products that can be said to be of optimal quality, there is a third structural reason for the economic superiority, indeed unsurpassability of a capitalist system of production. Only through the operation of market forces is it possible to utilize resources efficiently over time in any given allocation, i.e., to avoid overutilization as well as underutilization. This problem has already been addressed with reference to Russian style socialism in Chapter 3. What are the institutional constraints on an ordinary profit-oriented enterprise in its decisions about the degree of exploitation or conservation of its resources in the particular line of production in which they happen to be used? Evidently, the owner of such an enterprise would own the production factors or resources as well as the products produced with them. Thus, his income (used here in a wide sense of the term) consists of two parts: the income that is received from the sales of the products produced after various operating costs have been subtracted; and the value that is embodied in the factors of production which could be translated into current income should the owner decide to sell them. Institutionalizing a capitalist system--a social order based on private property--thus implies establishing an incentive structure under which people would try to maximize their income in both of these dimensions. What exactly does this mean?[8] Every act of production evidently affects both mentioned income dimensions. On one hand, production is undertaken to reach an income return from sales. On the other hand, as long as the factors of production are exhaustible, i.e., as long as they are scarce and not free goods, every production act implies a deterioration of the value of the production factors. Assuming that private ownership exists, this produces a situation in which every business constantly tries not to let the marginal costs of production (i.e., the drop in value of the resources that results from their usage) to become greater than the marginal revenue product, and where with the help of bookkeeping an instrument for checking the success or failure of these attempts exists. If a producer were not to succeed in this task and the drop in the value of capital were higher than the increase in the income returns from sales, the owner's total income (in the wider sense of the term) would be reduced. Thus, private ownership is an institutional device for safeguarding an existing stock of capital from being overexploited or if it is, for punishing an owner for letting this happen through losses in income. This helps make it possible for values produced to be higher than values destroyed during production. In particular, private ownership is an institution in which an incentive is established to efficiently adjust the degree of conserving or consuming a given stock of capital in a particular line of production to anticipated price changes. If, for instance, the future price of oil were expected to rise above its current level, then the value of the capital bound up in oil production would immediately rise as would the marginal cost involved in producing the marginal product. Hence, the enterprise would immediately be impelled to reduce production and increase conservation accordingly, because the marginal revenue product on the present market was still at the unchanged lower level. On the other hand, if in the future oil prices were expected to fall below their present level, this would result in an immediate drop in the respective capital values and in marginal costs, and hence the enterprise would immediately begin to utilize its capital stock more intensively since prices on the present market would still be relatively higher. And to be sure, both of these reactions are exactly what is desirable from the point of view of the consumers.

If the way in which a capitalist production system works is compared with the situation that becomes institutionalized whenever the state takes care of the means of production, striking differences emerge. This is true especially when the state is a modern parliamentary democracy. In this case, the managers of an enterprise may have the right to receive the returns from sales (after subtracting operation costs), but, and this is decisive, they do not have the right to appropriate privately the receipts from a possible sale of the production factors. Under this constellation, the incentive to use a given stock of capital economically over time is drastically reduced. Why? Because if one has the right to privately appropriate the income return from product sales but does not have the right to appropriate the gains or losses in capital value that result from a given degree of usage of this capital, then there is an incentive structure institutionalized not of maximizing total income--i.e., total social wealth in terms of consumer evaluations--but rather of maximizing income returns from sales at the expense of losses in capital value. Why, for instance, should a government official reduce the degree of exploitation of a given stock of capital and resort to a policy of conservation when prices for the goods produced are expected to rise in the future? Evidently, the advantage of such a conservationist policy (the higher capital value resulting from it) could not be reaped privately. On the other hand, by resorting to such a policy one's income returns from sales would be reduced, whereas they would not be reduced if one forgot about conserving. In short, to conserve would mean to have none of the advantages and all of the disadvantages. Hence, if the state managers are not super-humans but ordinary people concerned with their own advantages, one must conclude that it is an absolutely necessary consequence of any state production that a given stock of capital will be overutilized and the living standards of consumers impaired in comparison to the situation under capitalism.

Now it is fairly certain that someone will argue that while one would not doubt what has been stated so far, things would in fact be different and the deficiency of a pure market system would come to light as soon as one paid attention to the special case of monopolistic production. And by necessity, monopolistic production would have to arise under capitalism, at least in the long run. Not only Marxist critics but orthodox economic theorists as well make much of this alleged counter-argument.[9] In answer to this challenge four points will be made in turn. First, available historical evidence shows that contrary to these critics' thesis, there is no tendency toward increased monopoly under an unhampered market system. In addition, there are theoretical reasons that would lead one to doubt that such a tendency could ever prevail on a free market. Third, even if such a process of increasing monopolization should come to bear, for whatever reason, it would be harmless from the point of view of consumers provided that free entry into the market were indeed ensured. And fourth, the concept of monopoly prices as distinguished from and contrasted to competitive prices is illusory in a capitalist economy.

Regarding historical evidence, if the thesis of the critics of capitalism were true, then one would have to expect a more pronounced tendency toward monopolization under relatively freer, unhampered, unregulated laissez-faire capitalism than under a relatively more heavily regulated system of "welfare" or "social" capitalism. However, history provides evidence of precisely the opposite result. There is general agreement regarding the assessment of the historical period from 1867 to World War I as being a relatively more capitalist period in history of the United States, and of the subsequent period being one of comparatively more and increasing business regulations and welfare legislation. However, if one looks into the matter one finds that there was not only less development toward monopolization and concentration of business taking place in the first period than in the second but also that during the first period a constant trend towards more severe competition with continually falling prices for almost all goods could be observed.[10] And this tendency was only brought to a halt and reversed when in the course of time the market system became more and more obstructed and destroyed by state intervention. Increasing monopolization only set in when leading businessmen became more successful at persuading the government to interfere with this fierce system of competition and pass regulatory legislation, imposing a system of "orderly" competition to protect existing large firms from the so-called cutthroat competition continually springing up around them.[11] G. Kolko, a left-winger and thus certainly a trustworthy witness, at least for the critics from the left, sums up his research into this question as follows:

> There was during this [first] period a dominant trend toward growing competition. Competition was unacceptable to many key business and financial leaders, and the merger movement was to a large extent a reflection of voluntary, unsuccessful business effects to bring irresistible trends under control...As new competitors sprang up, and as economic power was diffused throughout an expanding nation, it became apparent to many important businessmen that only the national government could [control and stabilize] the economy...Ironically, contrary to the consensus of historians, it was not the existence of monopoly which caused the government to intervene in the economy, but the lack of it.[12]

In addition, these findings, which stand in clear contradiction to much of the common wisdom on the matter, are backed by theoretical considerations.[13] Monopolization means that some specific factor of production is withdrawn from the market sphere. There is no trading of the factor, but there is only the owner of this factor engaging in restraint of trade. Now if this is so, then no market price exists for this monopolized production factor. But if there is no market price for it, then the owner of the factor can also no longer assess the monetary costs involved in withholding it from the market and in using it as he happens to use it. In other words, he can no longer calculate his profits and make sure, even if only ex post facto, that he is indeed earning the highest possible profits from his investments. Thus, provided that the entrepreneur is really interested in making the highest possible profit (something, to be sure, which is always assumed by his critics), he would have to offer the monopolized production factors on the market continually to be sure that he was indeed using them in the most profitable way and that there was no other more lucrative way to use them, so as to make it more profitable for him to sell the factor than keep it. Hence, it seems, one would reach the paradoxical result that in order to maximize his profits, the monopolist must have a permanent interest in discontinuing his position as the owner of a production factor withheld from the market and, instead, desire its inclusion in the market sphere.

Furthermore, with every additional act of monopolization the problem for the owner of monopolized production factors--i.e., that because of the impossibility of economic calculation, he can no longer make sure that those factors are indeed used in the most profitable way--becomes ever more acute. This is so, in particular, because realistically one must assume that the monopolist is not only not omniscient but that his knowledge regarding future competing goods and services by the consumers in future markets becomes more and more limited as the process of monopolization advances. As production factors are withdrawn from the market, and as the circle of consumers served by the goods produced with these factors widens, it will be less likely that the monopolist, unable to make use of economic calculation, can remain in command of all the relevant information needed to detect the most profitable uses for his production factors. Instead, it becomes more likely in the course of such a process of monopolization, that other people or groups of people, given their desire to make profits by engaging in production, will perceive more lucrative ways of employing the monopolized factors.[14] Not necessarily because they are better entrepreneurs, but simply because they occupy different positions in space and time and thus become increasingly aware of entrepreneurial opportunities which become more and more difficult and costly for the monopolist to detect with every new step toward monopolization. Hence, the likelihood that the monopolist will be persuaded to sell his monopolized factors to other producers--*nota bene*: for the purpose of thereby increasing his profits--increases with every additional step toward monopolization.[15]

Now, let us assume that what historical evidence as well as theory proves to be unlikely happens anyway, for whatever reason. And let us assume straightaway the most extreme case conceivable: there is only one single business, one super-monopolist so to speak, that provides all the goods and services available on the market, and that is the sole employer of everyone. What does this state of affairs imply regarding consumer satisfaction, provided, of course, as assumed, that the super-monopolist has acquired his position and upholds it without the use of aggression? For one thing, it evidently means that no one has any valid claims against the owner of this firm; his enterprise is indeed fully and legitimately his own. And for another thing it means that there is no infringement on anyone's right to boycott any possible exchange. No one is forced to work for the monopolist or buy anything from him, and everyone can do with his earnings from labor services whatever he wants. He can consume or save them, use them for productive or nonproductive purposes, or associate with others and combine their funds for any sort of joint venture. But if this were so, then the existence of a monopoly would only allow one to say this: the monopolist clearly could not see any chance of improving his income by selling all or part of his means of production, otherwise he would do so. And no one else could see any chance of improving his income by bidding away factors from the monopolist or by becoming a capitalist producer himself through original saving, through transforming existing nonproductively used private wealth into productive capital, or through combining funds with others, otherwise it would be done. But then, if no one saw any chance of improving his income without resorting to aggression, it would evidently be absurd to see anything wrong with such a super-monopoly. Should it indeed ever come into existence within the framework of a market economy, it would only prove that this self-same super-monopolist was indeed providing consumers with the most urgently wanted goods and services in the most efficient way.

Yet the question of monopoly prices remains.[16] Doesn't a monopoly price imply a suboptimal supply of goods to consumers, and isn't there then an important exception from the generally superior economic working of capitalism to be found here? In a way this question has already been answered by the above explanation that even a super-monopolist establishing itself in the market cannot be considered harmful for consumers. But in any case, the theory that monopoly prices are (allegedly) categorically different from competitive prices has been presented in different, technical language and hence deserves special treatment. The result of this analysis, which is hardly surprising now, only reinforces what has already been discovered: monopoly does not constitute a special problem forcing anyone to make qualifying amendments to the general rule of a market economy being necessarily more efficient than any socialist or statist system. What is the definition of "monopoly price" and, in contrast to it, of "competitive price" according to economic orthodoxy (which in the matter under investigation includes the so-called Austrian school of economics as represented by L. v. Mises)? The following definition is typical:

> Monopoly is a prerequisite for the emergence of monopoly prices, but it is not the only prerequisite. There is a further condition required, namely a certain shape of the demand curve. The mere existence of monopoly does not mean anything in this regard. The publisher of a copyrighted book is a monopolist. But he may not be able to sell a single copy, no matter how low the price he asks. Not every price at which a monopolist sells a monopolized commodity is a monopoly price. Monopoly prices are only prices at which it is more advantageous for the monopolist to restrict the total amount to be sold than to expand its sales to the limit which a competitive market would allow.[17]

However plausible this distinction might seem, it will be argued that neither the producer himself nor any neutral outside observer could ever decide if the prices actually obtained on the market were monopoly or competitive prices, based on the criterion "restricted versus unrestricted supply" as offered in the above definition. In order to understand this, suppose a monopolist producer in the sense of "a sole producer of a given good" exists. The question of whether or not a given good is different from or homogeneous to other goods produced by other firms is not one that can be decided based on a comparative analysis of such goods in physical or chemical terms ex ante, but will always have to be decided ex post facto, on future markets, by the different or equal treatment and evaluations that these goods receive from the buying public. Thus every producer, no matter what his product is, can be considered a potential monopolist in this sense of the term, at the point of decision making. What, then, is the decision with which he and every producer is faced? He must decide how much of the good in question to produce in order to maximize his monetary income (with other, nonmonetary income considerations assumed to be given). To be able to do this he must decide how the demand curve for the product concerned will be shaped when the products reach the market, and he must take into consideration the various production costs of producing various amounts of the good to be produced. This done, he will establish the amount to be produced at that point where returns from sales, i.e., the amount of goods sold times price, minus production costs involved in producing that amount, will reach a maximum. Let us assume this happens and the monopolist also happens to be correct in his evaluation of the future demand curve in that the price he seeks for his products indeed clears the market. Now the question is, is this market price a monopoly or a competitive price? As M. Rothbard realized in his path-breaking but much neglected analysis of the monopoly problem, there is no way of knowing. Was the amount of the good produced "restricted" in order to take advantage of inelastic demand and was a monopoly price thus reaped, or was the price reached a competitive one established in order to sell an amount of goods that was expanded "to the limit that a competitive market would allow"? There is no way to decide the matter.[18] Clearly, every producer will always try to set the quantity produced at a level above which demand would become elastic and would hence yield lower total returns to him because of reduced prices paid. He thus engages in restrictive practices. At the same time, based on his estimate of the shape of future demand curves, every producer will always try to expand his production of any good up to the point at which the marginal cost of production (that is, the opportunity cost of not producing a unit of an alternative good with the help of scarce production factors now bound up in the process of producing another unit of x) equals the price per unit of x that one expects to be able to charge at the respective level of supply. Both restriction and expansion are part of profit-maximizing and market-price formation, and neither of these two aspects can be separated from the other to make a valid distinction between monopolistic and competitive action.

Now, suppose that at the next point of decision making the monopolist decides to reduce the output of the good produced from a previously higher to a new lower level, and assume that he indeed succeeds in securing higher total returns now than at the earlier point in time. Wouldn't this be a clear instance of a monopoly price? Again, the answer must be no. And this time the reason would be the indistinguishability of this reallocational "restriction" from a "normal" reallocation that takes account of changes in demand. Every event that can be interpreted in one way can also be interpreted in the other, and no means for deciding the matter exist, for once again both are essentially two aspects of one and the same thing: of action, of choosing. The same result, i.e., a restriction in supply coupled not only with higher prices but with prices high enough to increase total revenue from sales, would be brought about if the monopolist who, for example, produces a unique kind of apples faces an increase in the demand for his apples (an upward shift in the demand curve) and simultaneously an even higher increase in demand (an even more drastic upward shift of the demand curve) for oranges. In this situation he would reap greater returns from a reduced output of apples, too, because the previous market price for his apples would have become a subcompetitive price in the meantime. And if he indeed wanted to maximize his profits, instead of simply expanding apple production according to the increased demand, he now would have to use some of the factors previously used for the production of apples for the production of oranges, because in the meantime changes in the system of relative prices would have occurred. However, what if the monopolist who restricts apple production does not engage in producing oranges with the now available factors, but instead does nothing with them? Again, all that this would indicate is that besides the increase in demand for apples, in the meantime an even greater increase in the demand for yet another good--leisure (more precisely, the demand for leisure by the monopolist who is also a consumer)--had taken place. The explanation for the restricted apple supply is thus found in the relative price changes of leisure (instead of oranges) as compared with other goods.

Neither from the perspective of the monopolist himself nor from that of any outside observer could restrictive action then be distinguished conceptually from normal reallocations which simply follow anticipated changes in demand. Whenever the monopolist engages in restrictive activities which are followed by higher prices, by definition he must use the released factors for another more highly valued purpose, thereby indicating that he adjusts to changes in relative demand. As M. Rothbard sums up,

> We cannot use "restriction of production" as the test of monopoly vs. competitive price. A movement from a subcompetitive to a competitive price also involves a restriction of production of this good, coupled, of course, with an expansion of production in other lines by the released factors. There is no way whatever to distinguish such a restriction and corollary expansion from the alleged "monopoly price" situation. If the restriction is accompanied by increased leisure for the owner of the labor factor rather than increased production of some other good on the market, it is still the expansion of the yield of a consumer good--leisure. There is still no way of determining whether the "restriction" resulted in a "monopoly" or a "competitive" price or to what extent the motive of increased leisure was involved. To define a monopoly price as a price attained by selling a smaller quantity of a product at a higher price is therefore meaningless, since the same definition applies to the "competitive" price as compared with a subcompetitive price.[19]

The analysis of the monopoly question, then, provides no reason whatsoever to modify the description given above of the way a pure market economy normally works and its superiority over any sort of socialist or statist system of production. Not only is a process of monopolization highly unlikely to occur, empirically as well as theoretically, but even if it did, from the point of view of the consumers it would be harmless. Within the framework of a market system a restrictive monopolistic price could not be distinguished from a normal price hike stemming from higher demand and changes in relative prices. And as every restrictive action is simultaneously expansionary, to say that the curtailment of production in one production line coupled with an increase in total revenue implies a misallocation of production factors and an exploitation of consumers is simply nonsense. The misunderstanding involved in such reasoning has been accurately revealed in the following passage from one of L. v. Mises' later works in which he implicitly refutes his own above-cited orthodox position regarding the monopoly-price problem. He states:

> An entrepreneur at whose disposal are 100 units of capital employs, for instance, 50 units for the production of p and 50 units for the production of q. If both lines are profitable, it is odd to blame him for not having employed more, e.g., 75 units, for the production of p. He could increase the production of p only by curtailing correspondingly the production of q. But with regard to q the same fault could be found with the grumblers. If one blames the entrepreneur for not having produced more p, one must blame him also for not having produced more q. This means: one blames the entrepreneur for the fact that there is scarcity of factors of production and that the earth is not a land of Cockaigne.[20]

The monopoly problem as a special problem of markets requiring state action to be resolved does not exist.[21] In fact, only when the state enters the scene does a real, nonillusory problem of monopoly and monopoly prices emerge. The state is the only enterprise whose prices and business practices can be conceptually distinguished from all other prices and practices, and whose prices and practices can be called "too high" or "exploitative" in a completely objective, nonarbitrary way. These are prices and practices which consumers are not voluntarily willing to pay and accept, but which instead are forced upon them through threats of violence. And only for so privileged an institution as the state is it also normal to expect and to find a permanent process of increasing monopolization and concentration. As compared to all other enterprises, which are subject to the control of voluntarily buying or not-buying consumers, the enterprise "state" is an organization that can tax people and need not wait until they accept the tax, and can impose regulations on the use people make of their property without gaining their consent for doing so. This evidently gives the state, as compared to all other institutions, a tremendous advantage in the competition for scarce resources. If one only assumes that the representatives of the state are as equally driven by the profit motive as anyone else, it follows from this privileged position that the organization "state" must have a relatively more pronounced tendency toward growth than any other organization. And indeed, while there was not evidence for the thesis that a market system would bring about a tendency toward monopolistic growth, the thesis that a statist system would do so is amply supported by historical experience.

10

CAPITALIST PRODUCTION AND THE PROBLEM OF PUBLIC GOODS

We have tried to demolish socialism on the economic as well as moral fronts. Having reduced it to a phenomenon of exclusively socio-psychological significance, i.e., a phenomenon for whose existence neither good economic nor good moral reasons can be found, its roots were explained in terms of aggression and the corruptive influence that a policy of *divide et impera* exercises on public opinion. The last chapter returned to economics in order to give the final blows to socialism by engaging in the constructive task of explaining the workings of a capitalist social order as socialism's economically superior rival, ready for adoption at any time. In terms of consumer evaluations, capitalism was indicated as being superior with respect to the allocation of production factors, the quality of the output of goods produced, and the preservation of values embodied in capital over time. The so-called monopoly problem allegedly associated with a pure market system was in fact demonstrated not to constitute any special problem at all. Rather, everything said about the normally more efficient functioning of capitalism is true also with respect to monopolistic producers, as long as they are indeed subject to the control of voluntary purchases or voluntary abstentions from purchases by consumers.

This final chapter will analyze an even more frequently cited special case which allegedly requires one to make qualifying amendments regarding the thesis of the economic superiority of capitalism: the case of the production of so-called public goods. Considered in particular will be the production of security.

If what has been stated in the foregoing chapter regarding the working of a market economy is true, and if monopolies are completely harmless to consumers as long as the consumers have the right to boycott them and freely enter the market of competing producers themselves, then one must draw the conclusion that for economic as well as moral reasons, the production of all goods and services should be left in private hands. And in particular it follows that even the production of law and order, justice and peace--those things that one has come to think of as being the most likely candidates for state-provided goods for reasons explained in Chapter 8--should be provided privately, by a competitive market. This indeed is the conclusion that G. de Molinari, a renowned Belgian economist, formulated as early as 1849--at a time when classical liberalism was still the dominant ideological force, and "economist" and "socialist" were generally (and rightly so) considered to be antonyms:

> If there is one well established truth in political economy, it is this: That in all cases, for all commodities that serve to provide for the tangible or intangible need of the consumer, it is in the consumer's best interest that labor and trade remain free, because the freedom of labor and trade have as their necessary and permanent result the maximum reduction of price. And this: That the interests of the consumer of any commodity whatsoever should always prevail over the interests of the producer. Now, in pursuing these principles, one arrives at this rigorous conclusion: That the production of security should, in the interest of consumers of this intangible commodity, remain subject to the law of free competition. Whence it follows: That no government should have the right to prevent another government from going into competition with it, or require consumers of security to come exclusively to it for this commodity.[1]

And he comments on this argument by saying: "Either this is logical and true, or else the principles on which economic science is based are invalid."[2]

There is apparently only one way out of this unpleasant (for all socialists, that is) conclusion: to argue that there are particular goods to which for some special reasons the above economic reasoning does not apply. It is this that the so-called public goods theorists are determined to prove.[3] However, we will demonstrate that in fact no such special goods or special reasons exist, and that the production of security in particular does not pose any problem different from that of the production of any other good or service, be it houses, cheese, or insurance. In spite of its many followers, the whole public goods theory is faulty, flashy reasoning, ridden with internal inconsistencies, nonsequiturs, appealing to and playing on popular prejudices and assumed beliefs, but with no scientific merit whatsoever.[4]

What, then, does the "escape route" that socialist economists have found in order to avoid drawing Molinari's conclusion look like? Since Molinari's time it has become increasingly common to answer the question of whether there are goods to which different sorts of economic analyses apply in the affirmative. As a matter of fact, nowadays it is almost impossible to find a single economic textbook that does not make and stress the vital importance of the distinction between private goods, for which the truth of the economic superiority of a capitalist order of production is generally admitted, and public goods, for which it is generally denied.[5] Certain goods or services, and among them, security, are said to have the special characteristic that their enjoyment cannot be restricted to those persons who have actually financed their production. Rather, people who have not participated in their financing can draw benefits from them, too. Such goods are called public goods or services (as opposed to private goods or services, which exclusively benefit those people who actually paid for them). And it is due to this special feature of public goods, it is argued, that markets cannot produce them, or at least not in sufficient quantity or quality, and hence compensatory state action is required.[6] The examples given by different authors for alleged public goods vary widely. Authors often classify the same good or services differently, leaving almost no classification of a particular good undisputed.[7] This clearly foreshadows the illusory character of the whole distinction. Nonetheless, some examples that enjoy particularly popular status as public goods are the fire brigade that stops a neighbor's house from catching fire, thereby letting him profit from my fire brigade, even though he did not contribute anything to financing it; or the police that by walking around my property scare away potential burglars from my neighbor's property as well, even if he did not help finance the patrols; or the lighthouse, a particularly dear example to economists,[8] that helps ships find their way, even though they did not contribute a penny to its construction or upkeep.

Before continuing with the presentation and critical examination of the theory of public goods let us investigate how useful the distinction between private and public goods is in helping decide what should be produced privately and what by the state or with state help. Even the most superficial analysis could not fail to point out that using this alleged criterion, rather than presenting a sensible solution, would get one into deep trouble. While at least at first glance it seems that some of the state-provided goods and services might indeed qualify as public goods, it certainly is not obvious how many of the goods and services that are actually produced by states could come under the heading of public goods. Railroads, postal services, telephone, streets, and the like seem to be goods whose usage can be restricted to the persons who actually finance them, and hence appear to be private goods. And the same seems to be the case regarding many aspects of the multidimensional good "security": everything for which insurance could be taken out would have to qualify as a private good. Yet this does not suffice. Just as a lot of state-provided goods appear to be private goods, so many privately produced goods seem to fit in the category of a public good. Clearly my neighbors would profit from my well-kept rose garden--they could enjoy the sight of it without ever helping me garden. The same is true of all kinds of improvements that I could make on my property that would enhance the value of neighboring property as well. Even those people who do not throw money in his hat could profit from a street musician's performance. Those fellow travellers on the bus who did not help me buy it profit from my deodorant. And everyone who ever comes into contact with me would profit from my efforts, undertaken without their financial support, to turn myself into a most lovable person. Now, do all these goods--rose gardens, property improvements, street music, deodorants, personality improvements--since they clearly seem to possess the characteristics of public goods, then have to be provided by the state or with state assistance?

As these latter examples of privately produced public goods indicate, there is something seriously wrong with the thesis of public goods theorists that these goods cannot be produced privately but instead require state intervention. Clearly they *can* be provided by markets. Furthermore, historical evidence shows us that all of the alleged public goods which states now provide had at some time in the past actually been provided by private entrepreneurs or even today are so provided in one country or another. For example, the postal service was once private almost everywhere; streets were privately financed and still are sometimes; even the beloved lighthouses were originally the result of private enterprise;[9] private police forces, detectives, and arbitrators exist; and help for the sick, the poor, the elderly, orphans, and widows has been a traditional field for private charity organizations. To say, then, that such things cannot be produced by a pure market system is falsified by experience one hundredfold.

Apart from this, other difficulties arise when the public-private goods distinction is used to decide what to leave to the market and what not. What, for instance, if the production of so-called public goods did not have positive but negative consequences for other people, or if the consequences were positive for some and negative for others? What if the neighbor whose house was saved from burning by my fire brigade had wished (perhaps because he was overinsured) that it had burned down, or my neighbors hate roses, or my fellow travellers find the scent of my deodorant disgusting? In addition, changes in the technology can change the character of a given good. For example, with the development of cable TV, a good that was formerly (seemingly) public has become private. And changes in the laws of property--of the appropriation of property--can have the very same effect of changing the public-private character of a good. The lighthouse, for instance, is a public good only insofar as the sea is publicly (not privately) owned. But if it were permitted to acquire pieces of the ocean as private property, as it would be in a purely capitalist social order, then as the lighthouse only shines over a limited territory, it would clearly become possible to exclude nonpayers from the enjoyment of its services.

Leaving this somewhat sketchy level of discussion and looking into the distinction between private and public goods more thoroughly, it turns out to be a completely illusory distinction. A clear-cut dichotomy between private and public goods does not exist, and this is essentially why there can be so many disagreements on how to classify given goods. All goods are more or less private or public and can--and constantly do--change with respect to their degree of privateness/publicness with people's changing values and evaluations, and with changes in the composition of the population. They never fall, once and for all, into either one or the other category. In order to recognize this, one must only recall what makes something a good. For something to be a good it must be realized and treated as scarce by someone. Something is not a good-as-such, that is to say, but goods are goods only in the eyes of the beholder. Nothing is a good without at least one person subjectively evaluating it as such. But then, since goods are never goods-as-such--since no physico-chemical analysis can identify something as an economic good--there is clearly no fixed, objective criterion for classifying goods as either private or public. They can never be private or public goods as such. Their private or public character depends on how few or how many people consider them to be goods, with the degree to which they are private or public changing as these evaluations change, and ranging from one to infinity. Even seemingly completely private things like the interior of my apartment or the color of my underwear thus can become public goods as soon as somebody else starts caring about them.[10] And seemingly public goods, like the exterior of my house or the color of my overalls, can become extremely private goods as soon as other people stop caring about them. Moreover, every good can change its characteristics again and again; it can even turn from a public or private good to a public or private bad and vice versa, depending solely on the changes in this caring or uncaring. However, if this is so, no decision whatsoever can be based on the classification of goods as private or public.[11] In fact, to do so it would not only become necessary to ask virtually every individual person with respect to every single good whether or not he happened to care about it, positively or negatively and perhaps to what extent, in order to determine who might profit from what and should hence participate in its financing. (And how could one know if they were telling the truth?!) It would also become necessary to monitor all changes in such evaluations continually, with the result that no definite decision could ever be made regarding the production of anything, and as a consequence of a nonsensical theory all of us would be long dead.[12]

But even if one were to ignore all these difficulties, and were willing to admit for the sake of argument that the private-public good distinction did hold water, even then the argument would not prove what it is supposed to. It neither provides conclusive reasons why public goods--assuming that they exist as a separate category of goods--should be produced at all, nor why the state rather than private enterprises should produce them. This is what the theory of public goods essentially says, having introduced the above-mentioned conceptual distinction: The positive effects of public goods for people who do not contribute anything to their production or financing proves that these goods are desirable. But evidently, they would not be produced, or at least not in sufficient quantity and quality, in a free, competitive market, since not all of those who would profit from their production would also contribute financially to make the production possible. So in order to produce these goods (which are evidently desirable, but would not be produced otherwise), the state must jump in and assist in their production. This sort of reasoning, which can be found in almost every textbook on economics (Nobel laureates not excluded[13]) is completely fallacious, and fallacious on two counts.

For one thing, to come to the conclusion that the state has to provide public goods that otherwise would not be produced, one must smuggle a norm into one's chain of reasoning. Otherwise, from the statement that because of some special characteristics of theirs certain goods would not be produced, one could never reach the conclusion that these goods *should* be produced. But with a norm required to justify their conclusion, the public goods theorists clearly have left the bounds of economics as a positive, *wertfrei* science. Instead they have transgressed into the field of morals or ethics, and hence one would expect to be offered a theory of ethics as a cognitive discipline in order for them to legitimately do what they are doing and to justifiably derive the conclusion that they actually derive. But it can hardly be stressed enough that nowhere in the public goods theory literature can there be found anything that even faintly resembles such a cognitive theory of ethics.[14] Thus it must be stated at the outset, that the public goods theorists are misusing whatever prestige they might have as positive economists for pronouncements on matters on which, as their own writings indicate, they have no authority whatsoever. Perhaps, though, they have stumbled on something correct by accident, without supporting it with an elaborate moral theory? It becomes apparent that nothing could be further from the truth as soon as one explicitly formulates the norm that would be needed to arrive at the above-mentioned conclusion about the state's having to assist in the provision of public goods. The norm required to reach the above conclusion is this: whenever it can somehow be proven that the production of a particular good or service has a positive effect on someone but would not be produced at all, or would not be produced in a definite quantity or quality unless others participated in its financing, then the use of aggressive violence against these persons is allowed, either directly or indirectly with the help of the state, and these persons may be forced to share in the necessary financial burden. It does not need much comment to show that chaos would result from implementing this rule, as it amounts to saying that everyone can aggress against everyone else whenever he feels like it. Moreover, it should be sufficiently clear from the discussion of the problem of the justification of normative statements (Chapter 7) that this norm could never be justified as a fair norm. For to argue in that way and to seek agreement for this argument must presuppose, contrary to what the norm says, that everyone's integrity as a physically independent decision-making unit is assured.

But the public goods theory breaks down not just because of the faulty moral reasoning implied in it. Even the utilitarian, economic reasoning contained in the above argument is blatantly wrong. As the public goods theory states, it might well be that it would be better to have the public goods than not to have them, though it should not be forgotten that no a priori reason exists that this must be so of necessity (which would then end the public goods theorists' reasoning right here). For it is clearly possible, and indeed known to be a fact, that anarchists exist who so greatly abhor state action that they would prefer not having the so-called public goods at all to having them provided by the state![15] In any case, even if the argument is conceded so far, to leap from the statement that the public goods are desirable to the statement that they should therefore be provided by the state is anything but conclusive, as this is by no means the choice with which one is confronted. Since money or other resources must be withdrawn from possible alternative uses to finance the supposedly desirable public goods, the only relevant and appropriate question is whether or not these alternative uses to which the money could be put (that is, the private goods which could have been acquired but now cannot be bought because the money is being spent on public goods instead) are more valuable--more urgent--than the public goods. And the answer to this question is perfectly clear. In terms of consumer evaluations, however high its absolute level might be, the value of the public goods is relatively lower than that of the competing private goods, because if one had left the choice to the consumers (and had not forced one alternative upon them), they evidently would have preferred spending their money differently (otherwise no force would have been necessary). This proves beyond any doubt that the resources used for the provision of public goods are wasted, as they provide consumers with goods or services which at best are only of secondary importance. In short, even if one assumed that public goods which can be distinguished clearly from private goods existed, and even if it were granted that a given public good might be useful, public goods would still compete with private goods. And there is only one method for finding out whether or not they are more urgently desired and to what extent, or, mutatis mutandis, if, and to what extent, their production would take place at the expense of the nonproduction or reduced production of more urgently needed private goods: by having *everything* provided by freely competing private enterprises. Hence, contrary to the conclusion arrived at by the public goods theorists, logic forces one to accept the result that only a pure market system can safeguard the rationality, from the point of view of the consumers, of a decision to produce a public good. And only under a pure capitalist order could it be ensured that the decision about how much of a public good to produce (provided it should be produced at all) is rational as well.[16] No less than a semantic revolution of truly Orwellian dimensions would be required to come up with a different result. Only if one were willing to interpret someone's "no" as really meaning "yes," the "nonbuying of something" as meaning that it is really "preferred over that which the nonbuying person does instead of nonbuying," of "force" really meaning "freedom," of "non-contracting" really meaning "making a contract" and so on, could the public goods theorists' point be "proven."[17] But then, how could we be sure that they really mean what they seem to mean when they say what they say, and do not rather mean the exact opposite, or don't mean anything with a definite content at all, but are simply babbling? We could not! M. Rothbard is thus completely right when he comments on the endeavors of the public goods ideologues to prove the existence of so-called market failures due to the nonproduction or a quantitatively or qualitatively "deficient" production of public goods. He writes, "...such a view completely misconceives the way in which economic science asserts that free-market action is *ever* optimal. It is optimal, not from the standpoint of the personal ethical views of an economist, but from the standpoint of free, voluntary actions of all participants and in satisfying the freely expressed needs of the consumers. Government interference, therefore, will necessarily and always move away from such an optimum."[18]

Indeed, the arguments supposedly proving market failures are nothing short of being patently absurd. Stripped of their disguise of technical jargon all they prove is this: a market is not perfect, as it is characterized by the nonaggression principle imposed on conditions marked by scarcity, and so certain goods or services which could only be produced and provided if aggression were allowed will not be produced. True enough. But no market theorist would ever dare deny this. Yet, and this is decisive, this "imperfection" of the market can be defended, morally as well as economically, whereas the supposed "perfections" of markets propagated by the public goods theorists cannot.[19] It is true enough, too, that a termination of the state's current practice of providing public goods would imply some change in the existing social structure and the distribution of wealth. And such a reshuffling would certainly imply hardship for some people. As a matter of fact, this is precisely why there is widespread public resistance to a policy of privatizing state functions, even though in the long run overall social wealth would be enhanced by this very policy. Surely, however, this fact cannot be accepted as a valid argument demonstrating the failure of markets. If a man had been allowed to hit other people on the head and is now not permitted to continue with this practice, he is certainly hurt. But one would hardly accept *that* as a valid excuse for upholding the old (hitting) rules. He is harmed, but harming him means substituting a social order in which every consumer has an equal right to determine what and how much of anything is produced, for a system in which some consumers have the right to determine in what respect other consumers are not allowed to buy voluntarily what they want with the means justly acquired by them and at their disposal. And certainly, such a substitution would be preferable from the point of view of all consumers as voluntary consumers.

By force of logical reasoning, then, one must accept Molinari's above-cited conclusion that for the sake of consumers, all goods and services be provided by markets.[20] It is not only false that clearly distinguishable categories of goods exist, which would render special amendments to the general thesis of capitalism's economic superiority necessary; even if they did exist, no special reason could be found why these supposedly special public goods should not also be produced by private enterprises since they invariably stand in competition with private goods. In fact, in spite of all the propaganda from the side of the public goods theorists, the greater efficiency of markets as compared with the state has been realized with respect to more and more of the alleged public goods. Confronted daily with experience, hardly anyone seriously studying these matters could deny that nowadays markets could produce postal services, railroads, electricity, telephone, education, money, roads and so on more effectively, i.e., more to the liking of the consumers, than the state. Yet people generally shy away from accepting in one particular sector what logic forces upon them: in the field of the production of security. Hence, the rest of this chapter will explain the superior functioning of a capitalist economy in this particular area--a superiority whose logical case has already been made, but which shall be rendered more persuasive once some empirical material is added to the analysis and it is studied as a problem in its own right.[21]

How would a system of nonmonopolistic, competing producers of security work? It should be clear from the outset that in answering this question one is leaving the realm of purely logical analysis and hence the answers must necessarily lack the certainty, the apodictic character of pronouncements on the validity of the public goods theory. The problem faced is precisely analogous to that of asking how a market would solve the problem of hamburger production, especially if up to this point hamburgers had been produced exclusively by the state, and hence no one could draw on past experience. Only tentative answers could be formulated. No one could possibly know the exact structure of the hamburger industry--how many competing companies would come into existence, what importance this industry might have compared to others, what the hamburgers would look like, how many different sorts of hamburgers would appear on the market and perhaps disappear again because of a lack of demand, and so on. No one could know all of the circumstances and the changes which would influence the very structure of the hamburger industry that would take place over time--changes in demand of various consumer groups, changes in technology, changes in the prices of various goods that affect the industry directly or indirectly, and so on. It must be stressed that all this is no different when it comes to the question of the private production of security. But this by no means implies that nothing definitive can be said on the matter. Assuming certain general conditions of demand for security services which are known to be more or less realistic by looking at the world as it presently is, what can and will be said is how different social orders of security production, characterized by different structural constraints under which they have to operate, will respond differently.[22] Let us first analyze the specifics of monopolistic, state-run security production, as at least in this case one can draw on ample evidence regarding the validity of the conclusions reached, and then turn to comparing this with what could be expected if such a system were replaced by a nonmonopolistic one.

Even if security is considered to be a public good, in the allocation of scarce resources it must compete with other goods. What is spent on security can no longer be spent on other goods that also might increase consumer satisfaction. Moreover, security is not a single, homogeneous good, but rather consists of numerous components and aspects. There is not only prevention, detection, and enforcement but there is also security from robbers, rapists, polluters, natural disasters, and so on. Moreover, security is not produced in a "lump," but can be supplied in marginal units. In addition, different people attach different importance to security as a whole and also to different aspects of the whole thing, depending on their personal characteristics, their past experiences with various factors of insecurity, and the time and place in which they happen to live.[23] Now, and here we return to the fundamental economic problem of allocating scarce resources to competing uses, how can the state--an organization which is not financed exclusively by voluntary contributions and the sales of its products, but rather partially or even wholly by taxes--decide how much security to produce, how much of each of its countless aspects, to whom and where to provide how much of what? The answer is that it has no rational way to decide this question. From the point of view of the consumers its response to their security demands must thus be considered arbitrary. Do we need one policeman and one judge, or 100,000 of each? Should they be paid $100 a month, or $10,000? Should the policemen, however many we might have, spend more time patrolling the streets, chasing robbers, recovering stolen loot, or spying on participants in victimless crimes such as prostitution, drug use, or smuggling? And should the judges spend more time and energy hearing divorce cases, traffic violations, cases of shoplifting, murder, or antitrust cases? Clearly, all of these questions must be answered somehow because as long as there is scarcity and we do not live in the Garden of Eden, the time and money spent on one thing cannot be spent on another. The state must answer these questions, too, but whatever it does, it does it *without* being subject to the profit-and-loss criterion. Hence, its action is arbitrary and thus necessarily involves countless wasteful misallocations from the consumer's viewpoint.[24] Independent to a large degree of consumer wants, the state-employed security producers instead do, as everyone knows, what *they* like. They hang around instead of doing anything, and if they do work they prefer doing what is easiest or work where they can wield power rather than serve consumers. Police officers drive around a lot in cars, hassle petty traffic violators, and spend huge amounts of money investigating victimless crimes which a lot of people (i.e., nonparticipants) do not like, but which few would be willing to spend their money on to fight, as they are not immediately affected by it. Yet with respect to the one thing that consumers want most urgently--the prevention of hard-core crime (i.e., crimes *with* victims), the detection and effective punishment of hard-core criminals, the recovery of loot, and the securement of compensation to victims of crimes from the aggressors--they are notoriously inefficient, in spite of ever higher budget allocations.

Further, and here I return to the problem of a lowered quality of output (with given allocations), whatever state-employed police or judges happen to do (arbitrary as it must be), since their income is more or less independent of the consumers' evaluations of their respective services, they will tend to do poorly. Thus one observes police arbitrariness and brutality and the slowness in the judicial process. Moreover, it is remarkable that neither the police nor the judicial system offers consumers anything even faintly resembling a service contract in which it is laid down in unambiguous terms what procedure the consumer can expect to be set in motion in a specific situation. Rather, both operate in a contractual void which over time allows them to change their rules of procedure arbitrarily, and which explains the truly ridiculous fact that the settlement of disputes between police and judges on the one hand and private citizens on the other is not assigned to an independent third party, but to another police or judge who shares employers with one party--the government--in the dispute.

Third, anyone who has seen state-run police stations and courts, not to mention prisons, knows how true it is that the factors of production used to provide us with such security are overused, badly maintained, and filthy. There is no reason for them to satisfy the consumers who provide their income. And if, in an exceptional case, this happens not to be so, then it has only been possible at costs that are comparatively much higher than those of any similar private business.[25]

Without a doubt, all of these problems inherent in a system of monopolistic security production would be solved relatively quickly once a given demand for security services was met by a competitive market with its entirely different incentive structure for producers. This is not to say that a "perfect" solution to the problem of security would be found. There would still be robberies and murders; and not all loot would be recovered nor all murderers caught. But in terms of consumer evaluations the situation would improve to the extent that the nature of man would allow this. First, as long as there is a competitive system, i.e., as long as the producers of security services depend on voluntary purchases, most of which probably take the form of service and insurance contracts agreed to in advance of any actual "occurrence" of insecurity or aggression, no producer could increase its income without improving services or quality of product as perceived by the consumers. Furthermore, all security producers taken together could not bolster the importance of their particular industry unless, for whatever reason, consumers indeed started evaluating security more highly than other goods, thus ensuring that the production of security would never and nowhere take place at the expense of the non- or reduced production of, let us say, cheese, as a competing private good. In addition, the producers of security services would have to diversify their offerings to a considerable degree because a highly diversified demand for security products among millions and millions of consumers exists. Directly dependent on voluntary consumer support, they would immediately be hurt financially if they did not appropriately respond to the consumers' various wants or changes in wants. Thus, every consumer would have a direct influence, albeit small, on the output of goods appearing on or disappearing from the security market. Instead of offering a uniform "security packet" to everyone, as is characteristic of state production policy, a multitude of service packages would appear on the market. They would be tailored to the different security needs of different people, taking account of different occupations, different risk-taking behavior, different things to be protected and insured, and different geographical locations and time constraints.

But that is far from all. Besides diversification, the content and quality of the products would improve, too. Not only would the treatment of consumers by the employees of security enterprises improve immediately, the "I could care less" attitude, the arbitrariness and even brutality, the negligence and tardiness of the present police and judicial systems would ultimately disappear. Since they then would be dependent on voluntary consumer support, any maltreatment, impoliteness, or ineptitude could cost them their jobs. Further, the above-mentioned peculiarity--that the settlement of disputes between a client and his service provider is invariably entrusted to the latter's judgment--would almost certainly disappear from the books, and conflict arbitration by independent parties would become the standard deal offered by producers of security. Most importantly though, in order to attract and retain customers the producers of such services would have to offer *contracts* which would allow the consumer to know what he was buying and enable him to raise a valid, intersubjectively ascertainable complaint if the actual performance of the security producer did not live up to its obligations. And more specifically, insofar as they are not individualized service contracts where payment is made by the customers for covering their own risks exclusively, but rather insurance contracts proper which involve pooling one's own risks with those of other people, contrary to the present statist practice, these contracts most certainly would no longer contain any deliberately built-in redistributive scheme favoring one group of people at the expense of another. Otherwise, if anyone had the feeling that the contract offered to him involved his paying for other people's peculiar needs and risks--factors of possible insecurity, that is, that he did not perceive as applicable to his own case--he would simply reject signing it or discontinue his payments.

Yet when all this is said, the question will inevitably surface, "Wouldn't a competitive system of security production still necessarily result in permanent social conflict, in chaos and anarchy?" There are several points to be made regarding this alleged criticism. First, it should be noted that such an impression would by no means be in accordance with historical, empirical evidence. Systems of competing courts have existed at various places, such as in ancient Ireland or at the time of the Hanseatic league, before the arrival of the modern nation state, and as far as we know they worked well.[26] Judged by the then existent crime rate (crime per capita), the private police in the Wild West (which incidentally was not as wild as some movies insinuate) was relatively more successful than today's state-supported police.[27] And turning to contemporary experience and examples, millions and millions of international contacts exist even now--contacts of trade and travel--and it certainly seems to be an exaggeration to say, for instance, that there is more fraud, more crime, more breach of contract there than in domestic relations. And this is so, it should be noted, without there being one big monopolistic security producer and law-maker. Finally it is not to be forgotten that even now in a great number of countries there are various private security producers alongside to the state: private investigators, insurance detectives, and private arbitrators. Regarding their work, the impression seems to confirm the thesis that they are more, not less, successful in resolving social conflicts than their public counterparts.

However, this historical evidence is greatly subject to dispute, in particular regarding whether any general information can be derived from it. Yet there are systematic reasons, too, why the fear expressed in the above criticism is not well-founded. Paradoxical as it may seem at first, this is because establishing a competitive system of security producers implies erecting an institutionalized incentive structure to produce an order of law and law-enforcement that embodies the highest possible degree of consensus regarding the question of conflict resolution, and hence will tend to generate less rather than more social unrest and conflict than under monopolistic auspices![28] In order to understand this it is necessary to take a closer look at the only typical situation that concerns the skeptic and allows him to believe in the superior virtue of a monopolistically organized order of security production. This is the situation when a conflict arises between A and B, both are insured by different companies and the companies cannot come to an immediate agreement regarding the validity of the conflicting claims brought forward by their respective clients. (No problem would exist if such an agreement were reached, or if both clients were insured by one and the same company--at least the problem then would not be different in any way from that emerging under a statist monopoly!) Wouldn't such a situation always result in an armed confrontation? This is highly unlikely. First, any violent battle between companies would be costly and risky, in particular if these companies had reached a respectable size which would be important for them to have in order to appear as effective guarantors of security to their prospective clients in the first place. More importantly though, under a competitive system with each company dependent on the continuation of voluntary consumer payments, any battle would have to be deliberately supported by each and every client of both companies. If there were only one person who withdrew his payments because he was not convinced the battle was necessary in the particular conflict at hand, there would be immediate economic pressure on the company to look for a peaceful solution to the conflict.[29] Hence, any competitive producer of security would be extremely cautious about his dedication to engaging in violent measures in order to resolve conflicts. Instead, to the extent that it is peaceful conflict-resolution that consumers want, each and every security producer would go to great lengths to provide such measures to its clients and to establish in advance, for everyone to know, to what arbitration process it would be willing to submit itself and its clients in case of a disagreement over the evaluation of conflicting claims. And as such a scheme could only appear to the clients of different firms to be really working if there were agreement among them regarding such arbitrational measures, a system of law governing relations between companies which would be universally acceptable to the clients of all of the competing security producers would naturally evolve. Moreover, the economic pressure to generate rules representing consensus on how conflicts should be handled is even more far-reaching. Under a competitive system the independent arbitrators who would be entrusted with the task of finding peaceful solutions to conflicts would be dependent on the continued support of the two disagreeing companies insofar as they could and would select different judges if either one of them were sufficiently dissatisfied with the outcome of their arbitration work. Thus, these judges would be under pressure to find solutions to the problems handed over to them which, this time not with respect to the procedural aspects of law, but its content, would be acceptable to all of the clients of the firms involved in a given case as a fair and just solution.[30] Otherwise one or all of the companies might lose some of their customers, thus inducing those firms to turn to a different arbitrator the next time they were in need of one.[31]

But wouldn't it be possible under a competitive system for a security-producing firm to become an outlaw company--a firm, that is, which, supported by its own clients, started to aggress against others? There is certainly no way to deny that this might be possible, though again it must be emphasized that here one is in the realm of empirical social science and no one could know such a thing with certainty. And yet the tacit insinuation that the possibility of a security firm becoming an outlaw company would somehow indicate a severe deficiency in the philosophy and economics of a pure capitalist social order is fallacious.[32] First, it should be recalled that any social system, a statist-socialist order no less than a pure market economy, is dependent for its continued existence on public opinion, and that a given state of public opinion at all times delimits what can or cannot occur, or what is more or less likely to occur in a given society. The current state of public opinion in West Germany, for instance, makes it highly unlikely or even impossible that a statist-socialist system of the present-day Russian type could be imposed on the West German public. The lack of public support for such a system would doom it to failure and make it collapse. And it would be even more unlikely that any such attempt to impose a Russian-type order could ever hope to succeed among Americans, given American public opinion. Hence, in order to see the problem of outlaw companies correctly, the above question should be phrased as follows: How likely is it that any such event would occur in a given society with its specific state of public opinion? Formulated in this way, it is clear that the answer would have to be different for different societies. For some, characterized by socialist ideas deeply entrenched in the public, there would be a greater likelihood of the reemergence of aggressor companies, and for other societies there would be a much smaller chance of this happening. But then, would the prospect of a competitive system of security production in any given case be better or worse than that of the continuation of a statist system? Let us look, for instance, at the present-day United States. Assume that by a legislative act the state had abolished its right to provide security with tax funds, and a competitive system of security production were introduced. Given the state of public opinion, how likely would it then be that outlaw producers would spring up, and what if they did? Evidently, the answer would depend on the reactions of the public to this changed situation. Thus, the first reply to those challenging the idea of a private market for security would have to be: what about you? What would your reaction be? Does your fear of outlaw companies mean that you would then go out and engage in trade with a security producer that aggressed against other people and their property, and would you continue supporting it if it did? Certainly the critic would be much muted by this counterattack. But more important than this is the systematic challenge implied in this personal counterattack. Evidently, the described change in the situation would imply a change in the cost-benefit structure that everyone would face once he had to make his decisions. Before the introduction of a competitive system of security production it had been legal to participate in and support (state) aggression. Now such an activity would be an illegal activity. Hence, given one's conscience, which makes each of one's own decisions appear more or less costly, i.e., more or less in harmony with one's own principles of correct behavior, support for a firm engaging in the exploitation of people unwilling to deliberately support its actions would be more costly now than before. Given this fact, it must be assumed that the number of people--among them even those who otherwise would have readily lent their support to the state--who would now spend their money to support a firm committed to honest business would rise, and would rise everywhere this social experiment was tried. In contrast, the number of people still committed to a policy of exploitation, of gaining at the expense of others, would fall. How drastic this effect would be would, of course, depend on the state of public opinion. In the example at hand--the United States, where the natural theory of property is extremely widespread and accepted as a private ethic, the libertarian philosophy being essentially the ideology on which the country was founded and that let it develop to the height it reached[33]--the above-mentioned effect would naturally be particularly pronounced. Accordingly, security-producing firms committed to the philosophy of protecting and enforcing libertarian law would attract the greatest bulk of public support and financial assistance. And while it may be true that some people, and among them especially those who had profited from the old order, might continue their support of a policy of aggression, it is very unlikely that they would be sufficient in number and financial strength to succeed in doing so. Rather, the likely outcome would be that the honest companies would develop the strength needed--alone or in a combined effort and supported in this effort by their own voluntary customers--to check any such emergence of outlaw producers and destroy them wherever and whenever they came into existence.[34] And if against all odds the honest security producers should lose their fight to retain a free market in the production of security and an outlaw monopoly reemerged, one would simply have a state again.[35]

In any case, implementing a pure capitalist social system with private producers of security--a system permitting freedom of choice--would necessarily be better than what one has now. Even if such an order should then collapse because too many people were still committed to a policy of aggression against and exploitation of others, mankind would at least have experienced a glorious interlude. And should this order survive, which would seem to be the more likely outcome, it would be the beginning of a system of justice and unheard-of economic prosperity.

NOTES

CHAPTER 1

1. To avoid any misunderstanding from the outset: the thesis presented here is that any *given* society's overall wealth will be relatively increased, i.e., will grow more than it otherwise would, if the overall degree of socialism is decreased and vice versa. The United States, for instance, would improve their standards of living by adopting more capitalism (above the level that would be attained otherwise), and so would Germany, etc. It is a somewhat different task, though, to explain the relative position (as regards overall wealth) of *different* societies at any given time because then, of course, the "ceteris" are no longer necessarily "paribus," while, of course, other things, in addition to an *existing* degree of socialism, undoubtedly affect a society's overall wealth. A given society's *history*, for instance, has a tremendous effect on its present wealth. Every society is rich or poor not only because of present but also past conditions; because of capital having been accumulated or destroyed in the past by our fathers and forefathers. So it can easily happen that a society which is presently more capitalist can still be significantly poorer than a more socialist one. And the same, only seemingly paradoxical result can emerge because societies can (and do) differ with respect to other formerly or presently operating factors affecting the production of wealth. There can and do exist, for instance, differences in the work ethic and/or in prevalent world-views and habits among societies and these can and do account for divergencies (or similarities) in the production of wealth of societies alike or different with respect to their present degree of socialism. Thus, the most straightforward and best way to illustrate the validity of the thesis that the degree of socialism is inversely related to a society's wealth in any *comparative* social analysis, would be to compare societies which, except for differences in their degree of socialism, are paribus with respect to their history and the present socio-psychological characteristics of their people, or are at least very similar, like, for instance, West and East Germany: and here the predicted effect indeed shows in the most dramatic way, as will be dealt with in the following.

2. Incidentally, "socialism" in the United States is called "liberalism" and the socialist, or social democrat there, who calls himself "liberal" would generally detest being called "socialist."

3. Recall the repeated pronouncements in the early days of Soviet-Russian communism, up to the days of Khrushchev, that the capitalist world would soon be economically surpassed!

CHAPTER 2

1. Cf. D. Hume, *A Treatise of Human Nature* (ed. Selby- Bigge), Oxford, 1968, esp. 3, 2, p.484; and, "Enquiry Concerning the Principles of Morals," in: Hume, *Enquiries* (ed. Selby-Bigge), Oxford, 1970; cf. also: L. Robbins, *Political Economy: Past and Present*, London, 1977, esp. pp.29-33.

2. Incidentally, the *normative* character of the concept of property also makes the sufficient precondition for its emergence as a concept clear: Besides scarcity "rationality of agents" must exist, i.e., the agents must be capable of communicating, discussing, arguing, and in particular, *they must be able to engage in an argumentation of normative problems*. If there were no such capability of communication, normative concepts simply would not be of any use. We do not, for instance, try to avoid clashes over the use of a given scarce resource with, let us say, an elephant, by defining property rights, for we cannot argue with the elephant and hence arrive at an agreement on rights of ownership. The avoidance of future clashes in such a case is exclusively a *technical* (as opposed to a normative) problem.

3. It should be noted that a person cannot intentionally *not* act, as even the attempt not to act, i.e., one's decision *not* to do anything and instead remain in some previously occupied position or state would itself qualify as an action, thus rendering this statement aprioristically true, i.e., a statement that cannot be challenged by experience, as anyone who would try to disprove it thereby would have to choose and put his body willy-nilly to some specific use.

4. Cf. L. v. Mises, *Human Action*, Chicago, 1966, esp. part 1; M. N. Rothbard, *Man, Economy and State*, Los Angeles, 1970; also: L. Robbins, *Nature and Significance of Economic Science*, London, 1935.

5. On the concept of cost cf. in particular, M. Buchanan, *Cost and Choice*, Chicago, 1969; *L.S.E. Essays on Cost* (ed. Buchanan and Thirlby), Indianapolis, 1981.

6. It is worth mentioning here that the validity of all of what follows, of course, in no way depends on the correctness of the description of the natural position as "natural." Even if someone would only be willing to grant the so-called natural position the status of an arbitrary starting point, our

analysis assumes validity. Terms don't matter; what counts is what the natural position really is and implies as such. The following analyses are concerned exclusively with *this* problem.

7. Note again that the term "aggression" is used here without evaluative connotations. Only later in this treatise will I demonstrate that aggression as defined above is indeed morally indefensible. Names are empty; what alone is important is what it really *is* that is called aggression.

8. When I discuss the problem of moral justification in Chapter 7, I will return to the importance of the distinction just made of aggression as an invasion of the *physical* integrity of someone and, on the other hand, an invasion of the integrity of someone's value system, which is not classified as aggression. Here it suffices to notice that it is some sort of technical necessity for *any* theory of property (not just the natural position described here) that the delimitation of the property rights of one person against those of another be formulated in *physical, objective, intersubjectively ascertainable* terms. Otherwise it would be impossible for an actor to determine ex ante if any particular action of his were an aggression or not, and so the social function of property norms (*any* property norms), i.e., to make a conflict--free interaction possible, could not be fulfilled simply for technical reasons.

9. It is worth mentioning that the ownership right stemming from production finds its natural limitation only when, as in the case of children, the thing produced is itself another actor- producer. According to the natural theory of property, a child, once born, is just as much the owner of his own body as anyone else. Hence, not only can a child expect not to be physically aggressed against but as the owner of his body a child has the right, in particular, to abandon his parents once he is physically able to run away from them and say "no" to their possible attempts to recapture him. Parents only have special rights regarding their child--stemming from their unique status as the child's producers--insofar as they (and no one else) can rightfully claim to be the child's trustee as long as the child is physically unable to run away and say "no."

10. On the disutility of work and waiting cf. the theory of time-preference as espoused by L. v. Mises, *Human Action*, Chicago, 1966, chapters 5, 18, 21; the same, *Socialism*, Indianapolis, 1981, chapter 8; M. N. Rothbard, *Man, Economy and State*, Los Angeles, 1970, chapters 6, 9; also: E. v. Boehm-Bawerk, *Kapital und Kapitalzins. Positive Theory des Kapitals*, Meisenheim, 1967; F. Fetter, *Capital, Interest and Rent*, Kansas City, 1976.

On a critical assessment of the term "human capital," in particular of the absurd treatment that this concept has had at the hands of some Chicago-economists (notably G. Becker, *Human Capital*, New York, 1975), cf. A. Rubner, *The Three Sacred Cows of Economics*, New York, 1970.

11. On the theory of original appropriation cf. J. Locke, *Two Treatises of Government* (ed. Laslett), Cambridge, 1960, esp. 2, 5.

12. On the distinction, flowing naturally from the unique character of a person's body as contrasted with all other scarce goods, between "inalienable" and "alienable" property titles cf. W. Evers, "Toward a Reformation of a Law of Contracts," in: *Journal of Libertarian Studies*, 1977.

13. The superimposition of public on private law has tainted and compromised the latter to some extent everywhere. Nonetheless, it is not difficult to disentangle existing private law systems and find what is here called the natural position as constituting its central elements--a fact which once again underlines the "naturalness" of this property theory. Cf. also Chapter 8, n. 13.

CHAPTER 3

1. On Marxism and its development cf. L. Kolakowski, *Main Currents of Marxism*, 3 vols., Oxford, 1978; W. Leonhard, *Sovietideologie. Die politischen Lehren*, Frankfurt/M., 1963.

2. When one speaks of socialism Russian style it is evident that one abstracts from the multitude of concrete data which characterize any social system and with respect to which societies may differ. Russian style socialism is what has been termed by M. Weber an "ideal type." It "is arrived at through the one-sided intensification of one or several aspects and through integration into an immanently consistent conceptual representation of a multiplicity of scattered and discrete individual phenomena" (M. Weber, *Gesammelte Aufsaetze zur Wissenschaftslehre*, Tuebingen, 1922, p.191). But to stress the abstract character of the concept by no means implies any deficiency in it. On the contrary, it is the very purpose of constructing ideal types to bring out those features which the acting individuals themselves regard as constituting relevant resemblances or differences in meaning, and to disregard those which they themselves consider to be of little or no importance in understanding either one's own or another person's actions. More specifically, describing Russian style socialism on the level of abstraction chosen here and developing a typology of various forms of socialism later on should be understood as the attempt to reconstruct those conceptual distinctions which people use to attach themselves ideologically to various political parties or social movements, hence enabling an understanding of the ideological forces that in fact shape present-day societies. On ideal types as prerequisites for historico-sociological research cf. L. v. Mises, *Epistemological Problems of Economics*, New York, 1981, esp. pp.75ff; the same, *Human Action*, Chicago, 1966, esp. pp.59ff. On the methodology of "meaning reconstruction" of empirical social research cf. H. H. Hoppe, *Kritik der kausalwissenschaftlichen Sozialforschung*, Opladen, 1983, chapter 3, esp. pp.33ff.

3. For the following cf. in particular L. v. Mises, *Socialism*, Indianapolis, 1981.

4. Of course, this complete outlawing of private investment, as stated under (2) only applies strictly to a *fully* socialized economy. If next to a socialized part of the economy a private part also exists, then private investment would only become curtailed and hampered to the degree to which the economy

is socialized.

5. The related, crucial difference between capitalism and socialism is that under the former, the voluntary actions of consumers ultimately determine the structure and process of production, whereas it is the producer-caretakers who do so under socialism. Cf. in particular Chapter 9 below.

6. Writes Mises, "The essential mark of socialism is that *one will* alone acts. It is immaterial whose will it is. The director may be anointed king or a dictator, ruling by virtue of his *charisma*, he may be a Fuehrer or a board of Fuehrers appointed by the vote of the people. The main thing is that the employment of all factors of production is directed by one agency only" (L. v. Mises, *Human Action*, Chicago, 1966, p.695).

7. Cf. L. v. Mises, *Socialism*, Indianapolis, 1981, esp. part 2; also *Human Action*, Chicago, 1966, esp. Chapters 25, 26.

8. On the following cf. also F. A. Hayek (ed.), *Collectivist Economic Planning*, London, 1935; *Journal of Libertarian Studies* 5, 1, 1981 (An Economic Critique of Socialism).

9. On the free market as the necessary prerequisite for economic calculation and rational resource allocation cf. also Chapters 9, 10 below.

10. Incidentally, this proves that a socialized economy will be even less productive than a slave economy. In a slave economy, which of course also suffers from a relatively lower incentive to work on the part of the slaves, the slaveholder, who can sell the slave and capture his market value privately, would not have a comparable interest in extracting from his slave an amount of work which reduces the slave's value below the value of his marginal product. For a caretaker of labor no such disincentive exists. Cf. also G. Reisman, *Government Against the Economy*, New York, 1979.

11. Cf. H. H. Hoppe, *Eigentum, Anarchie und Staat*, Opladen, 1987, esp. Chapter 5, 3.2.

12. To be sure, Russia was a poor country to begin with, with little accumulated capital to be drawn on and consumed in an "emergency." On the socio-economic history of Soviet Russia cf. B. Brutzkus, *Economic Planning*

in Soviet Russia, London, 1935; also, e.g., A. Nove, *Economic History of the USSR*, Harmondsworth, 1969; also S. Wellisz, *The Economies of the Soviet Bloc*, New York, 1964.

13. On the economic system of the Soviet-dominated East bloc cf. T. Rakowska-Harmstone (ed)., *Communism in Eastern Europe*, Bloomington, 1984; H. H. Hohmann, M. Kaser, and K. Thalheim (eds.), *The New Economic Systems of Eastern Europe*, London, 1975; C.M. Cipolla (ed.), *Economic History of Europe. Contemporary Economies, vol. 2*, Glasgow, 1976.

14. On everyday life in Russia cf., e.g., H. Smith, *The Russians*, New York, 1983; D.K. Willis, *Klass. How Russians Really Live*, New York, 1985; S. Pejovich, *Life in the Soviet Union*, Dallas, 1979; M. Miller, *Rise of the Russian Consumer*, London, 1965.

15. Cf. L. Erhard, the initiator and major political exponent of post-war economic policy, *Prosperity through Competition*, New York, 1958; and *The Economics of Success*, London, 1968. For theoreticians of the German "soziale Marktwirtschaft" cf. W. Eucken, *Grundsaetze der Wirtschaftspolitik*, Hamburg, 1967; W. Roepke, *A Humane Economy*, Chicago, 1960; the same, *Economics of a Free Society*, Chicago, 1963. For a critique of the West German economic policy as insufficiently capitalist and ridden with inconsistencies which would lead to increasingly socialist interventions in the course of time cf. the prophetic observations by L. v. Mises, *Human Action*, Chicago, 1966, p.723.

16. For comparative studies on the two Germanys cf. E. Jesse (ed.), *BRD und DDR*, Berlin, 1982; H. v. Hamel (ed.), *BRD-DDR. Die Wirtschaftssysteme*, Muenchen, 1983; also K. Thalheim, *Die wirtschaftliche Entwicklung der beiden Staaten in Deutschland*, Opladen, 1978.

An honest but naive empirically minded comparative study which illustrates that at best, economic statistics has very little to do with reality as perceived by acting persons is P. R. Gregory and R.C. Stuart, *Comparative Economic Systems*, Boston, 1985, Chapter 13 (East and West Germany). For a valuable critique of economic statistics cf. O. Morgenstern, *National Income Statistics: A Critique of Macroeconomic Aggregation*, San Francisco, 1979. For an even more fundamental criticism cf. L. v. Mises, *Theory of Money and Credit*, Irvington, 1971, part II, Chapter 5.

17. On life in East Germany cf. E. Windmoeller and T. Hoepker, *Leben in der DDR*, Hamburg, 1976.

CHAPTER 4

1. Cf. L. Kolakowski, *Main Currents of Marxism*, 3 vols., Oxford, 1978; also W. Leonhard, *Sovietideologie heute. Die politischen Lehren*, Frankfurt/M., 1963.

2. Cf. note 16 below on the assessment of the somewhat different practice.

3. Cf. E. Bernstein, *Die Voraussetzungen des Sozialismus und die Aufgaben der Sozialdemokratie*, Bonn, 1975, as a major expositor of the reformist-revisionist course; K. Kautsky, *Bernstein und das sozialdemokratische Programm*, Bonn, 1976, as exponent of the Marxist orthodoxy.

4. On the idea of a "market-socialism" cf. one of its leading representatives, O. Lange, "On the Economic Theory of Socialism," in M. I. Goldman (ed.), *Comparative Economic Systems*, New York, 1971.

5. On the ideology of the German Social Democrats cf. T. Meyer (ed.), *Demokratischer Sozialismus*, Muenchen, 1980; G. Schwan (ed.), *Demokratischer Sozialismus fuer Industriegesellschaften*, Frankfurt/M., 1979.

6. Indicators for the social-democratization of the socialist movement are the rise of the socialist party and the corresponding decline of the orthodox communist party in France; the emergence of a social-democratic party as a rival to the more orthodox labour party in Great Britain; the moderation of the communists in Italy as the only remaining powerful communist party in Western Europe toward an increasingly social-democratic policy; and the growth of the socialist-social-democratic parties in Spain and Portugal under Gonzales and Soares, both with close ties to the German SPD. Furthermore, the socialist parties of Scandinavia, which traditionally had closely followed the German path and which later provided safe haven to a number of prominent socialists during the Nazi persecution (most notably W. Brandt and B. Kreisky), have long given credence to the revisionist beliefs.

7. On the social-democratic position regarding the North-South conflict cf. *North-South: A Programme for Survival*, Independent Commission on International Development Issues (Chair: W. Brandt), 1980.

8. Note again that this characterization of social-democratic socialism has the status of an "ideal type" (cf. Chapter 3, n. 2). It is not to be taken as a description of the policy or ideology of any actual party. Rather, it should be understood as the attempt to reconstruct what has become the essence of modern social-democratic style socialism, underlying a much more diverse reality of programs and policies of various parties or movements of different names as the ideologically unifying core.

9. On the following cf. L. v. Mises, *Socialism*, Indianapolis, 1981, esp. part V; *Human Action*, Chicago, 1966, esp. part 6.

10. Cf. M. N. Rothbard, *Power and Market*, Kansas City, 1977.

11. In addition, it should not be overlooked that even if it led to increased work by those taxed, a higher degree of taxation would in any case reduce the amount of leisure available to them and thereby reduce their standard of living. Cf. M.N. Rothbard, *Power and Market,* Kansas City, 1977, pp.95f.

12. A fictional account of the implementation of such a policy, supervised by "the unceasing vigilance of agents of the United States Handicapper General" has been given by K. Vonnegut in "Harrison Bergeron," in: K. Vonnegut, *Welcome to the Monkey House*, New York, 1970.

13. On the phenomenon of politicalization cf. also K. S. Templeton (ed.), *The Politicalization of Society*, Indianapolis, 1977.

14. On the concern of orthodox and social-democratic socialism for equality cf. S. Lukes, "Socialism and Equality," in: L. Kolakowski and S. Hampshire (eds.), *The Socialist Idea*, New York, 1974; also B. Williams, "The Idea of Equality," in P. Laslett and W. G. Runciman (eds.), *Philosophy, Politics, and Society*, 2nd series, Oxford, 1962.

For a critique of the socialist concept of equality cf. M. N. Rothbard, "Freedom, Inequality, Primitivism and the Division of Labor," in K. S. Templeton (ed.), *The Politicalization of Society*, Indianapolis, 1977; and *Egalitarianism as a Revolt Against Nature*, (title essay), Washington, 1974; H. Schoeck, *Envy*, New York, 1966; and *Ist Leistung unanstaendig*?, Osnabrueck, 1971; A. Flew, *The Politics of Procrustes*, London, 1980; and *Sociology, Equality and Education*, New York, 1976.

15. Traditionally, this approach has been favored, at least in theory, by orthodox Marxist socialism--in line with Marx' famous dictum in his "Critique of the Gotha Programme," (K. Marx, *Selected Works*, vol. 2, London, 1942, p.566), "from each according to his ability, to each according to his needs." Economic reality, however, has forced the Russian-style countries to make considerable concessions in practice. Generally speaking, an effort has indeed been made to equalize the (assumedly highly visible) monetary income for various occupations, but in order to keep the economy going, considerable difference in (assumedly less visible) nonmonetary rewards (such as special privileges regarding travel, education, housing, shopping, etc.) have had to be introduced.

Surveying the literature, P. Gregory and R. Stuart (*Comparative Economic Systems*, Boston, 1985), state: "... earnings are more equally distributed in Eastern Europe, Yugoslavia and the Soviet Union than in the United States. For the USSR, this appears to be a relatively new phenomenon, for as late as 1957, Soviet earnings were more unequal than the United States." However, in Soviet-style countries "a relatively larger volume of resources ... is provided on an extra market bases ..." (p.502). In conclusion: "Income is distributed more unequally in the capitalist countries in which the state plays a relatively minor redistributive role ... (United States, Italy, Canada). Yet even where the state plays a major redistributive role (United Kingdom, Sweden), the distribution of incomes appears to be slightly more unequal than in the planned socialist countries (Hungary, Czechoslovakia, Bulgaria). The Soviet Union in 1966 appears to have a less egalitarian distribution of income than its East European counterparts" (p.504). Cf. also, F. Parkin, *Class Inequality and Political Order*, New York, 1971, esp. Chapter 6.

16. This approach is traditionally most typical for social-democratic socialism. In recent years it has been given much publicized support--from the side of the economics profession--by M. Friedman with his proposal for a "negative income tax" (Friedman, *Capitalism and Freedom*, Chicago, 1962, Chapter 12); and by J. Rawls--from the philosophical side--with his "difference principle" (Rawls, *A Theory of Justice*, Cambridge, 1971, pp.60, 75ff, 83). Accordingly, both authors have received much attention from social-democratic party intellectuals. Generally, Friedman was only found "guilty" of not wanting to set the minimum income high enough--but then, he had no principled criterion for setting it at any specific point anyway. Rawls, who wants to coerce the "most advantaged person" into letting the "least advantaged one" share in his fortune whenever he happens to improve his own position, was at times even found to have gone too far with his egalitarianism. Cf. G. Schwan, *Sozialismus in der Demokratie. Theorie eine*

konsequent sozialdemokratischen Politik, Stuttgart, 1982, Chapter 3. D.

17. A representative example of social-democratically inclined research on equality of opportunity, in particular regarding education, is C. Jencks, and others, *Inequality*, London, 1973; the increasing prominence of the idea of equalizing opportunity also explains the flood of sociological studies on "quality of life" and "social indicators" that has appeared since the late 1960s. Cf., for instance, A. Szalai and F. Andrews (eds.), *The Quality of Life*, London, 1980.

18. On the following cf. also R. Merklein, *Griff in die eigene Tasche*, Hamburg, 1980; and *Die Deutschen werden aermer*, Hamburg, 1982.

19. Cf. as a representative example, W. Zapf (ed.), *Lebensbedingungen in der Bundesrepublik*, Frankfurt/M., 1978.

20. Cf. on this A. Alchian, "The Economic and Social Impact of Free Tuition" in: A. Alchian, *Economic Forces at Work*, Indianapolis, 1977.

CHAPTER 5

1. On the following cf. in particular M. N. Rothbard's brilliant essay "Left and Right: The Prospects for Liberty" in the same, *Egalitarianism as a Revolt Against Nature*, Washington, 1974.

2. On the social structure of feudalism cf. M. Bloch, *Feudal Society*, Chicago, 1961; P. Anderson, *Passages from Antiquity to Feudalism*, London, 1974; R. Hilton (ed.), *The Transition from Feudalism to Capitalism*, London, 1978.

3. Cf. H. Pirenne, *Medieval Cities. Their Origins and the Revival of Trade*, Princeton, 1974, Chapter 5, esp. pp.126ff; also cf. M. Tigar and M. Levy, *Law and the Rise of Capitalism*, New York, 1977.

4. It is worth stressing that contrary to what various nationalist historians have taught, the revival of trade and industry was caused by the *weakness* of central states, by the essentially *anarchistic character* of the feudal system. This insight has been emphasized by J. Baechler in *The Origins of Capitalism*, New York, 1976, esp. Chapter 7. He writes: "The constant expansion of the market, both in extensiveness and in intensity, was the result of an absence of a political order extending over the whole of Western Europe." (p.73) "The expansion of capitalism owes its origin and raison d'eetre to political anarchy.... Collectivism and State management have only succeeded in school text-books (look, for example, at the constantly favourable judgement they give to Colbertism)." (p.77) "All power tends toward the absolute. If it is not absolute, this is because some kind of limitations have come into play ... those in positions of power at the centre ceaselessly tried to erode these limitations. They never succeeded, and for a reason that also seems to me to be tied to the international system: a limitation of power to act externally and the constant threat of foreign assault (the two characteristics of a multi-polar system) imply that power is also limited internally and must rely on autonomous centres of decisionmaking and so may use them only sparingly." (p.78)

On the role of ecological and reproductive pressures for the emergence of capitalism cf. M. Harris, *Cannibals and Kings*, New York, 1978, Chapter 14.

5. Cf. on this the rather enthusiastic account given by H. Pirenne, *Medieval Cities*, Princeton, 1974, pp.208ff.

6. On this coalition cf. H. Pirenne, *Medieval Cities*, Princeton, 1974. "The clear interest of the monarchy was to support the adversaries of high feudalism. Naturally, help was given whenever it was possible to do so without becoming obligated to these middle classes who in arising against their lords fought, to all intents and purposes, in the interests of royal prerogatives. To accept the king as arbitrator of their quarrel was, for the parties in conflict, to recognize his sovereignty ... It was impossible that royalty should not take count of this and seize every chance to show its goodwill to the communes which, without intending to do so, labored so usefully in its behalf" (p.179-80; cf. also pp.227f).

7. Cf. P. Anderson, *Lineages of Absolutism*, London, 1974.

8. Cf. L. Tigar and M. Levy, *Law and the Rise of Capitalism*, New York, 1977.

9. Cf. L. v. Mises, *Liberalismus*, Jena, 1929; also E. K. Bramsted and K. J. Melhuish (eds.), *Western Liberalism*, London, 1978.

10. Cf. F. A. Hayek (ed.), *Capitalism and the Historians*, Chicago, 1963.

11. On the social dynamics of capitalism as well as the resentment caused by it cf. D. Mc. C. Wright, *Democracy and Progress*, New York, 1948; and *Capitalism*, New York, 1951.

12. In spite of their generally progressive attitude, the socialist left is not entirely free of such conservative glorifications of the feudal past, either. In their contempt for the "alienation" of the producer from his product, which of course is the normal consequence of any market system based on division of labor, they have frequently presented the economically self-sufficient feudal manor as a cozy, wholesome social model. Cf., for instance, K. Polanyi, *The Great Transformation*, New York, 1944.

13. Cf. R. Nisbet, "Conservatism," in: R. Nisbet and T. Bottomore, *History of Sociological Analysis*, New York, 1978; also G. K. Kaltenbrunner (ed.), *Rekonstruktion des Konservatismus*, Bern, 1978; on the relationship be-

tween liberalism and conservatism cf. F. A. Hayek, *The Constitution of Liberty*, Chicago, 1960 (Postscript).

14. On the inconsistencies of liberalism cf. Chapter 10, n. 21.

15. Normally, peoples' attitudes toward change are ambivalent: on the one hand, in their role as consumers people see change as a positive phenomenon since it brings about a greater variety of choice. On the other hand, in their role as producers people tend to embrace the ideal of stability, as this would save them from the need to continually adapt their productive efforts to changed circumstances. It is, then, largely in their capacity as producers that people lend support to the various socialist stabilization schemes and promises, only to thereby harm themselves as consumers. Writes D. Mc. C. Wright in *Democracy and Progress*, New York, 1948, p.81: "From freedom and science came rapid growth and change. From rapid growth and change came insecurity. From insecurity came demands which ended growth and change. Ending growth and change ended science and freedom."

16. On liberalism, its decline, and the rise of socialism cf. A. V. Dicey, *Lectures on the Relation Between Law and Public Opinion in England during the Nineteenth Century*, London, 1914; W. H. Greenleaf, *The British Political Tradition*, 2 vols., London, 1983.

17. I might again mention that the characterization of conservatism, too, has the status of an ideal-type (cf. Chapter 3, n. 2; Chapter 4, n. 8). It is the attempt to reconstruct those ideas which people either consciously or unconsciously accept or reject in attaching or detaching themselves to or from certain social policies or movements.

The idea of a conservative policy as described here and in the following can also be said to be a fair reconstruction of the underlying, unifying ideological force of what is indeed labeled "conservative" in Europe. However, the term "conservative" is used differently in the United States. Here, quite frequently, everyone who is not a left-liberal-(social)-democrat is labeled a conservative. As compared with this terminology, our usage of the term conservative is much narrower, but also much more in line with ideological reality. Labeling everything that is not "liberal" (in the American sense) "conservative" glosses over the fundamental ideological differences that--despite some partial agreement regarding their opposition to "liberalism"--exist in the United States between libertarians, as advocates of a pure capitalist order based on the natural theory of property, and conservatives proper, who, from W. Buckley to I. Kristol, nominally hail the institution of private property, only to disregard private owners' rights whenever it is deemed necessary in order to protect established economic and political powers from eroding in the process of peaceful competition. And in the field of foreign affairs they exhibit the same disrespect for private property rights through their advocacy of a policy of aggressive interventionism. On the polar difference between libertarianism and conservatism cf. G. W. Carey (ed.), *Freedom and Virtue. The Conservative/Libertarian Debate,* Lanham, 1984.

18. D. Mc. C. Wright (*Capitalism*, New York, 1951, p.198) correctly describes that both--left-liberalism, or rather social democracy, and conservatism--imply a partial expropriation of producers/contractors. He then misinterprets the difference, though, when he sees it as a disagreement over the question of how *far* this expropriation should go. In fact, there is disagreement about this among social-democrats *and* conservatives. Both groups have their "radicals" and "moderates." What makes them social-democrats or conservatives is a different idea about which groups are to be favored at the expense of others.

19. Note the interesting relationship between our sociological typology of socialist policies and the logical typology of market interventions as developed by M. N. Rothbard. Rothbard (*Power and Market*, Kansas City, 1977, pp.10ff) distinguishes between "autistic intervention" where "the intervener may command an individual subject to do or not to do certain things when these actions directly involve the individual's person or property *alone* ... (i.e.) when exchange is not involved"; "binary intervention" where "the intervener may enforce a coerced *exchange* between the individual subject and himself"; and "triangular intervention" where "the intervener may either compel or prohibit an exchange between a *pair* of subjects" (p.10). In terms of this distinction, the characteristic mark of conservatism then is its preference for "triangular intervention"--and as will be seen later in this Chapter, "autistic intervention" insofar as autistic actions also have natural repercussions on the pattern of inter-individual exchanges--for such interventions are uniquely suited, in accordance with the social psychology of conservatism, to helping "freeze" a given pattern of social exchanges. As compared with this, egalitarian socialism, in line with its described "progressive" psychology, exhibits a preference for "binary interventions" (taxation). Note, however, that the actual policies of socialist and social-democratic parties do not always coincide precisely with our ideal-typical description of socialism social-democratic style. While they generally do, the socialist par-

ties--most notably under the influence of labor unions--have also adopted typically conservative policies to a certain extent and are by no means totally opposed to any form of triangular intervention.

20. Cf. on the following M. N. Rothbard, *Power and Market*, Kansas City, 1977, pp.24ff.

21. While in order to stabilize social positions, price-freezing is needed and price-freezing can result in maximum or minimum prices, conservatives distinctly favor minimum price controls to the extent that it is commonly considered even more urgent that one's absolute--rather than one's relative--wealth position be prevented from eroding.

22. To be sure, conservatives are by no means always actually willing to go quite as far. But they recurringly do so--the last time in the United States being during the Nixon presidency. Moreover, conservatives have always exhibited a more or less open admiration for the great unifying social spirit brought about by a war-economy which is typically characterized precisely by full-scale price controls.

23. Cf. G. Reisman, *Government Against the Economy*, New York, 1979. For an apologetic treatment of price-controls cf. J. K. Galbraith, *A Theory of Price Control*, Cambridge, 1952.

24. G. Reisman, *Government Against the Economy*, New York, 1979, p.141.

25. On the politics and economics of regulation cf. G. Stigler, *The Citizen and the State. Essays on Regulation*, Chicago, 1975; M. N. Rothbard, *Power and Market*, Kansas City, 1977, Chapter 3.3; on licenses cf. also M. Friedman, *Capitalism and Freedom*, Chicago, 1962, Chapter 9.

26. Cf. also B. Badie and P. Birnbaum, *The Sociology of the State*, Chicago, 1983, esp. pp.107f.

27. Cf. on this R. Radosh and M. N. Rothbard (eds.), *A New History of Leviathan*, New York, 1972.

28. Cf. Badie and Birnbaum, *The Sociology of the State*, Chicago, 1983.

29. Cf. L. v. Mises, *Omnipotent Government*, New Haven, 1944; F. A. Hayek, *The Road to Serfdom*, Chicago, 1956; W. Hock, *Deutscher Antikapitalismus*, Frankfurt/M., 1960.

30. Cf. one of the foremost representatives of the German "Historical School," the "Kathedersozialist" and naziapologist: W. Sombart, *Deutscher Sozialimus*, Berlin, 1934.

31. Cf. W. Fischer, *Die Wirtschaftspolitik Deutschlands 1918-45*, Hannover, 1961; W. Treue, *Wirtschaftsgeschichte der Neuzeit, vol. 2,* Stuttgart, 1973; R. A. Brady, "Modernized Cameralism in the Third Reich: The Case of the National Industry Group," in: M. I. Goldman (ed.), *Comparative Economic Systems*, New York, 1971.

32. The average gross income of employed persons in Germany in 1938 (last figure available) was (in absolute terms, i.e., not taking inflation into account!) still lower than that of 1927. Hitler then started the war and resources were increasingly shifted from civilian to non-civilian uses, so that it can safely be assumed that the standard of living decreased even further and more drastically from 1939 on. Cf. *Statistisches Jahrbuch fuer die BRD,* 1960, p.542; cf. also V. Trivanovitch, *Economic Development of Germany Under National Socialism*, New York, 1937, p.44.

CHAPTER 6

1. Cf. on the classical positivist position A.J. Ayer, *Language, Truth and Logic*, New York, 1950; on critical rationalism K. R. Popper, *Logic of Scientific Discovery*, London, 1959; *Conjectures and Refutations*, London, 1969; and *Objective Knowledge*, Oxford, 1973; on representative statements of empiricism-positivism as the appropriate methodology of economics cf. e.g. M. Blaug, *The Methodology of Economics*, Cambridge, 1980; T. W. Hutchinson, *The Significance and Basic Postulates of Economic Theory*, London, 1938; and *Positive Economics and Policy Objectives*, London, 1964; and *Politics and Philosophy of Economics,* New York, 1981; also M. Friedman, "The Methodology of Positive Economics," in: M. Friedman, *Essays in Positive Economics*, Chicago, 1953; H. Albert, *Marktsoziologie und Entscheidungslogik*, Neuwied, 1967.

2. On piecemeal social engineering cf. K. R. Popper, The *Poverty of Historicism*, London, 1957.

3. Cf. G. Luehrs (ed.), *Kritischer Rationalismus und Sozialdemokratie*, 2 vols., Bonn, 1975-76.

4. On the following cf. M. Hollis and E. Nell, *Rational Economic Man,* Cambridge, 1975, pp.3ff.

5. Cf. D. Hume, *A Treatise of Human Nature* and *Enquiry Concerning Human Understanding*, in: Selby-Bigge (ed.), *Hume's Enquiries*, Oxford, 1970; also H. H. Hoppe, *Handeln und Erkennen*, Bern, 1976.

6. Cf. I. Lakatos, "Falsification and the Methodology of Scientific Research Programmes," in: Lakatos and Musgrave (eds.), *Criticism and the Growth of Knowledge*, Cambridge, 1970.

7. All of this has been brought home to Popperianism, mainly by T. S. Kuhn, *The Structure of Scientific Revolutions*, Chicago, 1964; and it was then P. Feyerabend who drew the most radical conclusion: to throw out science's claim to rationality altogether, and to embrace nihilism under the banner "everything goes" (P. Feyerabend, *Against Method*, London, 1978; and *Science in a Free Society*, London, 1978). For a critique of this unfounded

conclusion cf. note 20 below.

8. Cf. on this and the following A. Pap, *Semantics and Necessary Truth*, New Haven, 1958; M. Hollis and E. Nell, *Rational Economic Man*, Cambridge, 1975; B. Blanshard, *Reason and Analysis*, La Salle, 1964.

9. Cf. on this W. Kamlah and P. Lorenzen, *Logische Propaedeutik*, Mannheim, 1967.

10. Cf. L. v. Mises, *The Ultimate Foundation of Economic Science*, Kansas City, 1978, p.5: "The essence of logical positivism is to deny the cognitive value of a priori knowledge by pointing out that all a priori propositions are merely analytic. They do not provide new information, but are merely verbal or tautological ... Only experience can lead to synthetic propositions. There is an obvious objection against this doctrine, viz., that this proposition is in itself a--as the present writer thinks, false--synthetic a priori proposition, for it can manifestly not be established by experience."

11. M. Hollis and E. Nell remark: "Since every significant statement is, for a positivist, analytic or synthetic and none is both, we can ask for a classification .... We know of no positivist who has tried to produce empirical evidence for statements of (the sort in question). Nor can we see how to do so, unless by arguing that this is a matter of fact how people use terms ... which would prompt us to ask simply 'So what'?" (M. Hollis and E. Nell, *Rational Economic Man*, Cambridge, 1975, p.110).

12. Cf. on this H. H. Hoppe, *Kritik der kausalwissenschaftlichen Sozialforschung*, Opladen, 1983; and "Is Research Based on Causal Scientific Principles Possible in the Social Sciences," in *Ratio*, XXV, 1, 1983.

13. Cf. I. Kant, *Kritik der reinen Vernunft*, in Kant, *Werke* (ed. Weischedel), Wiesbaden, 1956, vol. II, p.45.

14. This, of course, is a Kantian idea, expressed in Kant's dictum that "reason can only understand what it has itself produced according to its own design" (*Kritik der reinen Vernunft*, in: Kant, *Werke* (ed. Weischedel), Wiesbaden, 1956, vol. II, p.23).

15. Cf. on this P. Lorenzen, "Wie ist Objektivitaet in der Physik moeglich";

"Das Begruendungsproblem der Geometrie als Wissenschaft der raeumlichen Ordnung," in: *Methodisches Denken*, Frankfurt/M., 1968; and *Normative Logic and Ethics*, Mannheim, 1969; F. Kambartel, *Erfahrung und Struktur*, Frankfurt/M., 1968, Kap. 3; also H. Dingler, *Die Ergreifung des Wirklichen*, Muenchen, 1955; P. Janich, *Protophysik der Zeit,* Mannheim, 1969.

16. On the problem of real vs. conventional or stipulated definitions cf. M. Hollis and E. Nell, *Rational Economic Man*, Cambridge, 1975, pp.177ff. "Honest definitions are, from an empiricist point of view, of two sorts, lexical and stipulative." (p.177) But "when it comes to justifying (this) view, we are presumably being offered a definition of 'definition'. Whichever category of definition the definition ... falls in, we need not accept it as of any epistemological worth. Indeed, it would not be even a possible epistemological thesis, unless it were neither lexical nor stipulative. The view is both inconvenient and self-refuting. A contrary opinion with a long pedigree is that there are 'real' definitions, which capture the essence of the thing defined" (p.178); cf. also B. Blanshard, *Reason and Analysis*, La Salle, 1964, pp.268f.

17. Cf. A. v. Melsen, *Philosophy of Nature*, Pittsburgh, 1953, esp. Chapters 1, 4.

18. Cf. also H. H. Hoppe. *Kritik der kausalwissenschaftlichen Sozialforschung*, Opladen, 1983; and "Is Research Based on Causal Scientific Principles Possible in the Social Sciences" in *Ratio* XXV, 1, 1983. Here the argument is summed up thus (p.37): "(1) I and--as possible opponents in an argument--other people are able to learn. (This statement cannot be challenged without implicitly admitting that it is correct. Above all, it must be assumed by anyone undertaking research into causes. To this extent, proposition (1) is valid *a priori.*) (2) If it is possible to learn, one cannot know at any given time what one will know at any later time and how one will act on the basis of this knowledge. (If one did know at any given time what one will come to know at some later time, it would be impossible ever to learn anything--but see proposition (1) on this point.) (3) The assertion that it is possible to predict the future state of one's own and/or another's knowledge and the corresponding actions manifesting that knowledge (i.e. find the variables which can be interpreted as the causes) involves a contradiction. If the subject of a given state of knowledge or of an intentional act can learn, then there are no causes for this; however, if there are causes, then the subject cannot learn--but see again proposition (1)."

19. M. Singer, *Generalization in Ethics*, London, 1863; P. Lorenzen, *Normative Logic and Ethics*, Mannheim, 1969; S. Toulmin, *The Place of Reason in Ethics*, Cambridge, 1970; F. Kambartel (ed.), *Praktische Philosophie und konstruktive Wissenschaftstheorie*, Frankfurt/M., 1974; A. Gewirth, *Reason and Morality*, Chicago, 1978.

20. Causality, then, is not a contingent feature of physical reality, but rather a category of action, and as such, a logically necessary trait of the physical world. This fact explains why in spite of the possibility explained above of immunizing any hypothesis against possible refutations by postulating ever new uncontrolled variables, no nihilistic consequences regarding the undertaking of causal scientific research follow (cf. note 7 above). For if it is understood that natural science is not a contemplative enterprise but ultimately an instrument of action (cf. on this also J. Habermas, *Knowledge and Human Interests*, Boston, 1971, esp. Chapter 6), then neither the fact that hypotheses can be immunized nor that a selection between rival theories may not always seem possible (because theories are, admittedly, underdetermined by data) ever affects the permanent existence of the rationality criterion of "instrumental success." Neither immunizing hypotheses nor referring to paradigmatic differences makes anyone less subject to this criterion in whose light every theory ultimately proves commensurable. It is the inexorability of the rationality criterion of instrumental success which explains why--not withstanding Kuhn, Feyerabend et al.--the development of the natural sciences could bring about an ultimately undeniable, constant technological progress.

On the other hand, in the field of human action, where, as has been demonstrated above, no causal scientific research is possible, where predictive knowledge can never attain the status of empirically testable scientific hypotheses but rather only that of informed, not-systematically teachable foresight, and where in principle the criterion of instrumental success is thus inapplicable, the spectre of nihilism would seem indeed to be real, if one were to take the empiricist methodological prescriptions seriously. However, not only are these prescriptions inapplicable to the social sciences as *empirical* sciences (cf. on this H. H. Hoppe, *Kritik der kausalwissenschaftlichen Sozialforschung*, Opladen, 1983, esp. Chapter 2); as I show here, contrary to the empiricist doctrine according to which everything must be tried out before its outcome can be known, a priori knowledge regarding action exists, and apodictically true predictions regarding the social world can be made based on this a priori knowledge. It is this, then, that proves all nihilistic temptations unfounded.

21. Cf. also, H. H. Hoppe, *Handeln und Erkennen*, Bern, 1976, pp.62f.

22. Cf. also L. v. Mises, *Human Action*, Chicago, 1966; *Epistemological Problems of Economics*, New York, 1981; and *The Ultimate Foundation of Economic Science*, Kansas City, 1978.

23. The aprioristic character of the concept of action--i.e., the impossibility of disproving the proposition that man acts and acting involves the categories explained above, because even the attempt to disprove it would itself be an action--has its complement in the field of epistemology, in the law of contradiction and the unthinkability of its denial. Regarding this law B. Blanshard writes: "To deny the law means to say that it is false *rather than* true, that its being false excludes its being true. But this is the very thing that is supposedly denied. One cannot deny the law of contradiction without presupposing its validity in the act of denying it" (B. Blanshard, *Reason and Analysis*, La Salle, 1964, p.276).

In fact, as L. v. Mises indicates, the law of contradiction is implied in the epistemologically more fundamental "axioms of action." (L. v. Mises, *The Ultimate Foundation of Economic Science*, Kansas City, 1978, p.35). On the relation between praxeology and epistemology cf. also Chapter 7, n. 5.

24. On the effects of minimum wages cf. also Y. Brozen and M. Friedman, *The Minimum Wage: Who Pays?*, Washington, 1966.

25. On the effects of rent control cf. also C. Baird, *Rent Control: The Perennial Folly*, San Francisco, 1980; F. A. Hayek et al., *Rent Control: A Popular Paradox*, Vancouver, 1975.

26. Cf. also L. v. Mises, *A Critique of Interventionism*, New Rochelle, 1977.

CHAPTER 7

1. For such a position cf. A. J. Ayer, *Language, Truth and Logic*, New York, 1950.

On the emotivist position cf. C. L. Stevenson, *Facts and Values*, New Haven, 1963; and *Ethics and Language*, London, 1945; cf. also the instructive discussion by G. Harman, *The Nature of Morality*, New York, 1977; the classical exposition of the idea that "reason is and can be no more than the slave of the passions" is to be found in D. Hume, *Treatise on Human Nature*, (ed. Selby-Bigge), Oxford, 1970.

3. Cf. also Chapter 6 above.

4. For various "cognitivist" approaches toward ethics cf. K. Baier, *The Moral Point of View*, Ithaca, 1958; M. Singer, *Generalization in Ethics*, London, 1863; P. Lorenzen, *Normative Logic and Ethics*, Mannheim, 1969; S. Toulmin, *The Place of Reason in Ethics*, Cambridge, 1970; F. Kambartel (ed.), *Praktische Philosophie und konstruktive Wissenschaftstheorie*, Frankfurt/M., 1974; A. Gewirth, *Reason and Morality*, Chicago, 1978.
Another cognitivist tradition is represented by various "natural rights" theorists. Cf. J. Wild, *Plato's Modern Enemies and the Theory of Natural Law*, Chicago, 1953; H. Veatch, *Rational Man. A Modern Interpretation of Aristotelian Ethics*, Bloomington, 1962; and *For An Ontology of Morals. A Critique of Contemporary Ethical Theory*, Evanston, 1968; and *Human Rights. Fact or Fancy?*, Baton Rouge, 1985; L. Strauss, *Natural Right and History*, Chicago, 1970.

5. Cf. K. O. Apel, *Transformation der Philosophie*, Vol. 2, Frankfurt/M., 1973, in particular the essay "Das Apriori der Kommunikationsgemeinschaft und die Grundlagen der Ethik"; also J. Habermas, "Wahrheitstheorien," in: H. Fahrenbach (ed.), *Wirklichkeit und Reflexion*, Pfullingen, 1974; *Theorie des kommunikativen Handelns, Vol. 1*, Frankfurt/M., 1981, pp.44ff; and *Moralbewusstsein und kommunikatives Handeln*, Frankfurt/M., 1983.
Note the structural resemblance of the "a priori of argumentation" to the "a priori of action," i.e., the fact, as explained in Chapter 6 above, that there is no way of disproving the statement that everyone knows what it means to act, since the attempt to disprove this statement would presuppose one's knowledge of how to perform certain activities. Indeed, the indisputability of the knowledge of the meaning of validity claims and action are intimately related. On the one hand, actions are more fundamental than argumen-

tation with whose existence the idea of validity emerges, as argumentation is clearly only a subclass of action. On the other hand, to say what has just been said about action and argumentation and their relation to each other already requires argumentation and so in this sense--epistemologically, that is--argumentation must be considered to be more fundamental than nonargumentative action. But then, as it is epistemology, too, which reveals the insight that although it might not be *known* to be so prior to any argumentation, *in fact* the development of argumentation *presupposes* action in that validity claims can only be explicitly discussed in an argument if the persons doing so already know what it means to have knowledge implied in actions; both, the meaning of action in general and argumentation in particular, must be thought of as logically necessary interwoven strands of a priori knowledge.

6. Methodologically, our approach exhibits a close resemblance to what A. Gewirth has described as the "dialectically necessary method" (*Reason and Morality*, Chicago, 1978, p.42-47)--a method of a priori reasoning modeled after the Kantian idea of transcendental deductions. Unfortunately, though, in his important study Gewirth chooses the wrong starting point for his analyses. He attempts to derive an ethical system not from the concept of argumentation, but from that of action. However, this surely cannot work, because from the correctly stated fact that in action an agent must, by necessity, presuppose the existence of certain values or goods, it does not follow that such goods then are universalizable and should thus be respected by others as the agent's goods by right. (On the requirement of normative statements to be universalizable cf. the following discussion in the text.) Rather, the idea of truth, or regarding morals, of universalizable rights or goods only emerges with argumentation as a special subclass of actions but not with action as such, as is clearly revealed by the fact that Gewirth, too, is not engaged simply in action, but more specifically in argumentation when he tries to convince us of the necessary truth of his ethical system. However, with argumentation recognized as the one and only appropriate starting point for the dialectically necessary method, a capitalist (i.e., non-Gewirthian) ethic follows, as will be seen. On the faultiness of Gewirth's attempt to derive universalizable rights from the notion of action cf. also the perceptive remarks by M. MacIntyre, *After Virtue*, Notre Dame, 1981, pp.64-65; J. Habermas, *Moralbewusstsein und kommunikatives Handeln*, Frankfurt/M., 1983, pp.110-111; and H. Veatch, *Human Rights*, Baton Rouge, 1985, pp.159-160.

7. The relationship between our approach and a "natural rights" approach can now be described in some detail, too. The natural law or natural rights

tradition of philosophic thought holds that universally valid norms can be discerned by means of reason as grounded in the very nature of man. It has been a common quarrel with this position, even on the part of sympathetic readers, that the concept of human nature is far "too diffuse and varied to provide a determinate set of contents of natural law" (A. Gewirth, "Law, Action, and Morality" in: *Georgetown Symposium on Ethics. Essays in Honor of H. Veatch* (ed. R. Porreco), New York, 1984, p.73). Furthermore, its description of rationality is equally ambiguous in that it does not seem to distinguish between the role of reason in establishing empirical laws of nature on the one hand, and normative laws of human conduct on the other. (Cf., for instance, the discussion in H. Veatch, *Human Rights*, Baton Rouge, 1985, p.62-67.)

In recognizing the narrower concept of argumentation (instead of the wider one of human nature) as the necessary starting point in deriving an ethic, and in assigning to moral reasoning the status of a priori reasoning, clearly to be distinguished from the role of reason performed in empirical research, our approach not only claims to avoid these difficulties from the outset, but claims thereby to be at once more straightforward and rigorous. Still, to thus dissociate myself from the natural rights tradition is not to say that I could not agree with its critical assessment of most of contemporary ethical theory; indeed I do agree with H. Veatch's complementary refutation of all desire (teleological, utilitarian) ethics as well as all duty (deontological) ethics (see *Human Rights*, Baton Rouge, 1985, Chapter 1). Nor do I claim that it is impossible to interpret my approach as falling in a "rightly conceived" natural rights tradition after all. What I claim, though, is that the following approach is clearly out of line with what the natural rights approach has actually come to be, and that it owes nothing to this tradition as it stands.

8. The universalization principle figures prominently indeed among all cognitivist approaches to morals. For the classical exposition cf. I. Kant, "Grundlegung zur Metaphysik der Sitten" and "Kritik der praktischen Vernunft" in: Kant, *Werke* (ed. Weischedel), vol. IV, Wiesbaden, 1956.

9. It might be noted here that only because scarcity exists is there even a problem of formulating moral laws; insofar as goods are superabundant ("free" goods) no conflict over the use of goods is possible and no action-coordination is needed. Hence, it follows that *any* ethic, correctly conceived, must be formulated as a theory of property, i.e., a theory of the assignment of rights of exclusive control over scarce means. Because only then does it become possible to avoid otherwise inescapable and unresolvable conflict. Unfortunately, moral philosophers, in their widespread ignorance of economics, have hardly ever seen this clearly enough. Rather,

like H. Veatch (*Human Rights*, Baton Rouge, 1985, p.170), for instance, they seem to think that they can do without a precise definition of property and property rights only to then necessarily wind up in a sea of vagueness and ad-hoceries. On human rights as property rights cf. also M. N. Rothbard, *The Ethics of Liberty*, Atlantic Highlands, 1982, Chapter 15.

10. Cf. J. Locke, *Two Treatises on Government* (ed. P. Laslett), Cambridge, 1970, esp. 2, 5.

11. On the nonaggression principle and the principle of original appropriation cf. also M. N. Rothbard, *For A New Liberty*, New York, 1978, Chapter 2; and *The Ethics of Liberty*, Atlantic Highlands, 1982, Chapters 6-8.

12. This, for instance, is the position taken by J. J. Rousseau, when he asks us to resist attempts to privately appropriate nature given resources by, for example, fencing them in. In his famous dictum, he says, "Beware of listening to this impostor; you are undone if you once forget that the fruits of the earth belong to us all, and the earth itself to nobody" ("Discourse upon the Origin and Foundation of Inequality among Mankind" in: J. J. Rousseau, *The Social Contract and Discourses* (ed. G. Cole), New York, 1950, p.235). However, it is only possible to argue so if it is assumed that property claims can be justified by decree. Because how else could "all" (i.e., even those who never did anything with the resources in question) or "nobody" (i.e., not even those who actually made use of it) own something--unless property claims were founded by mere decree?!

13. On the problem of the deriveability of "ought" from "is" statements cf. W. D. Hudson (ed.), *The Is-Ought Question*, London, 1969; for the view that the fact-value dichotomy is an ill-conceived idea cf. the natural rights literature cited in note 4 above.

14. Writes M. N. Rothbard in *The Ethics of Liberty*, Atlantic Highlands, 1982, p.32: "Now, *any* person participating in any sort of discussion, including one on values, is, by virtue of so participating, alive and affirming life. For if he were *really* opposed to life he would have no business in such a discussion, indeed he would have no business continuing to be alive. Hence, the *supposed* opponent of life is really affirming it in the very process of discussion, and hence the preservation and furtherance of one's life takes on the stature of an incontestable axiom." Cf. also D. Osterfeld, "The Natural Rights Debate" in: *Journal of Libertarian Studies*, VII, I, 1983, pp.106f.

15. Cf. also M. N. Rothbard, *The Ethics of Liberty*, Atlantic Highlands, 1982, p.45.

16. On the importance of the definition of aggression as physical aggression cf. also M. N. Rothbard, *The Ethics of Liberty*, Atlantic Highlands, 1982, Chapters 8-9; the same, "Law, Property Rights and Pollution," in: *Cato Journal*, Spring 1982, esp. pp.60-63.

17. On the idea of structural violence as distinct from physical violence cf. D. Senghaas (ed.), *Imperialismus und strukturelle Gewalt*, Frankfurt/M., 1972.
The idea of defining aggression as an invasion of property *values* also underlies the theories of justice of both J. Rawls and R. Nozick, however different these two authors may have appeared to be to many commentators. For how could he think of his so-called difference-principle--"Social and economic inequalities are to be arranged so that they are ... reasonably expected to be to everyone's--including the least advantaged one's--advantage or benefit" (J. Rawls, *A Theory of Justice*, Cambridge, 1971, pp.60-83; see also pp.75ff)--as justified unless Rawls believes that simply by increasing his relative wealth a more fortunate person commits an aggression, and a less fortunate one then has a valid claim against the more fortunate person only because the former's relative position in terms of value has deteriorated?! And how could Nozick claim it to be justifiable for a "dominant protection agency" to outlaw competitors, regardless of what their actions would have been like (R. Nozick, *Anarchy, State and Utopia*, New York, 1974, pp.55f)? Or how could he believe it to be morally correct to outlaw so-called nonproductive exchanges, i.e., exchanges where one party would be better off if the other one did not exist at all, or at least had nothing to do with it (as, for instance, in the case of a blackmailee and a blackmailer), regardless of whether or not such an exchange involved physical invasion of any kind (*ibid.*, pp.83- 86), unless he thought that the right existed to have the integrity of one's property *values* (rather than its physical integrity) preserved?! For a devastating critique of Nozick's theory in particular cf. M. N. Rothbard, *The Ethics of Liberty*, Atlantic Highlands, 1982, Chapter 29; on the fallacious use of the indifference curve analysis, employed both by Rawls and Nozick, cf. the same, "Toward a Reconstruction of Utility and Welfare Economics," *Center for Libertarian Studies, Occasional Paper No. 3*, New York, 1977.

18. Cf. also M. N. Rothbard, *The Ethics of Liberty*, Atlantic Highlands, 1982,

p.46.

19. For an awkward philosophical attempt to justify a late-comer ethic cf. J. Rawls, *A Theory of Justice*, Cambridge, 1971, pp.284ff; J. Sterba, *The Demands of Justice*, Notre Dame, 1980, esp. pp.58ff, pp.137ff; On the absurdity of such an ethic cf. M. N. Rothbard, *Man, Economy and State*, Los Angeles, 1972, p.427.

20. It should be noted here, too, that only if property rights are conceptualized as private property rights originating in time, does it then become possible to make contracts. Clearly enough, contracts are agreements between enumerable physically independent units which are based on the mutual recognition of each contractor's private ownership claims to things acquired prior to the agreement, and which then concern the transfer of property titles to definite things from a specific prior to a specific later owner. No such thing as contracts could conceivably exist in the framework of a late-comer ethic!

CHAPTER 8

1. On the difference between institutional aggression committed by the state as the very incorporation of socialism and common, criminal action cf. L. Spooner, *No Treason*, Colorado Springs, 1973, pp.19-20.: ."..the government, like a highwayman, says to a man: "Your money, or your life." And many, if not most, taxes are paid under the compulsion of that threat. The government does not, indeed, waylay a man in a lonely place, spring upon him from the roadside, and, holding a pistol to his head, proceed to rifle his pockets. But the robbery is none the less a robbery on that account; and it is far more dastardly and shameful. The highwayman takes solely upon himself the responsibility, danger, and crime of his own act. He does not pretend that he has any rightful claim to your money, or that he intends to use it for your own benefit. He does not pretend to be anything but a robber. He has not acquired impudence enough to profess to be merely a "protector," and that he takes men's money against their will, merely to enable him to "protect" those infatuated travellers, who feel perfectly able to protect themselves, or do not appreciate his peculiar system of protection. He is too sensible a man to make such professions as these. Furthermore, having taken your money, he leaves you, as you wish him to do. He does not persist in following you on the road, against your will; assuming to be your rightful "sovereign," on account of the "protection" he affords you. He does not keep "protecting" you, by commanding you to bow down and serve him; by requiring you to do this, and forbidding you to do that; by robbing you of more money as often as he finds it for his interest or pleasure to do so; and by brandishing you as a rebel, a traitor, and an enemy to your country, and shooting you down without mercy, if you dispute his authority or resist his demands. He is too much of a gentleman to be guilty of such impostures and insults and villainies as these. In short, he does not, in addition to robbing you, attempt to make you either his dupe or his slave. The proceedings of those robbers and murderers, who call themselves "the government," are directly the opposite of these of the "single highwayman."

2. On the theory of the state cf. M. N. Rothbard, "The Anatomy of the State," in: the same, *Egalitarianism As A Revolt Against Nature*, Washington, 1974; *For A New Liberty*, New York, 1978; and *The Ethics of Liberty,* Atlantic Highlands, 1982; H. H. Hoppe, *Eigentum, Anarchie und Staat*, Opladen, 1987; cf. also A. Herbert, *The Right and Wrong of Compulsion by the State* (ed. E. Mack), Indianapolis, 1978; H. Spencer, *Social Statics*, London, 1851; F. Oppenheimer, *The State*, New York, 1926; A. J. Nock, *Our Enemy, the State*,

Delevan, 1983; cf. also J. Schumpeter's remark directed against then as now prevalent views, notably among economists, that "the theory which construes taxes on the analogy of club dues or the purchase of a service of, say, a doctor only proves how far removed this part of the social sciences is from scientific habits of minds" (J. Schumpeter, *Capitalism, Socialism and Democracy*, New York, 1942, p.198).

3. In addition, the use of at least some weaponry, such as atomic bombs, against one's subjects would be prohibitive, since the rulers could hardly prevent that they themselves would be hurt or killed by it, too.

4. D. Hume, *Essays, Moral, Political and Literary*, Oxford, 1971, p.19; cf. also E. de La Boetie, *The Politics of Obedience: The Discourse of Voluntary Servitude*, New York, 1975.

5. The classical exposition of the idea that in the "state of nature" no distinction between "just" and "unjust" can be made and that only the state creates justice is to be found in T. Hobbes, *Leviathan*, Oxford, 1946. That this "positivistic" theory of law is untenable has been implicitly demonstrated in Chapter 7 above. In addition, it should be noted that such a theory does not even succeed in doing what it is supposed to do: in *justifying* the state. Because the transition from the state of nature to a statist system can of course only be called justified (as opposed to arbitrary) if natural (pre-statist) norms exist that are the justificatory basis for this very transition.

For modern positivists cf. G. Jellinek, *Allgemeine Staatslehre*, Bad Homburg, 1966; H. Kelsen, *Reine Rechtslehre*, Wien, 1976; for a critique of legal positivism cf. F. A. Hayek, *Law, Legislation and Liberty*, 3 vols., Chicago, 1973-79.

6. For the classical exposition of this view of politics cf. N. Machiavelli, *The Prince*, Harmondsworth, 1961; cf. also Q. Skinner, *The Foundations of Modern Political Thought*, Cambridge, 1978.

7. Cf. on this and the following, M. N. Rothbard, *Power and Market*, Kansas City, 1977, pp.182f.

8. On the role of the intellectuals and teachers as advocates of socialism and statism cf. B. de Jouvenel, "The Treatment of Capitalism by Continental Intellectuals," in: F. A. Hayek, *Capitalism and the Historians*, Chicago, 1954; L. v. Mises, *The Anti-Capitalist Mentality*, South Holland, 1972.

9. On a free market monetary system and the effects of government intervention on this system cf. R. Paul and L. Lehrman, *The Case For Gold*, San Francisco, 1983, Chapters 2, 3; M. N. Rothbard, *What Has Government Done to Our Money?*, Novato, 1973.

10. On the problem of a free market production of law and order cf. Chapter 10 below.

11. Cf. on this also Chapter 5, n. 4.

12. On this point cf. also Chapter 10 below.

13. F. Oppenheimer, *System der Soziologie, Vol. II, Der Staat*, Stuttgart, 1964. Oppenheimer sums up the peculiar, discriminatory character of state-provided goods, in particular of its production of law and order, in this way (pp.322-323): "the basic norm of the state is power. That is, seen from the side of its origin: violence transformed into might. Violence is one of the most powerful forces shaping society, but is not itself a form of *social* interaction. It must become law in the positive sense of this term, that is, sociologically speaking, it must permit the development of a system of 'subjective reciprocity': and this is only possible through a system of self-imposed restrictions on the use of violence and the assumption of certain obligations in exchange for its arrogated rights. In this way violence is turned into might, and a relationship of domination emerges which is accepted not only by the rulers, but under not too severely oppressive circumstances by their subjects as well, as expressing a 'just reciprocity.' Out of this basic norm secondary and tertiary norms now emerge as implied in it: norms of private law, of inheritance, criminal, obligational, and constitutional law, which all bear the mark of the basic norm of power and domination, and which are all designed to influence the structure of the state in such a way as to increase economic exploitation to the maximum level which is compatible with the continuation of legally regulated domination." The insight is fundamental that "law grows out of two essentially different roots (...): on the one hand, out of the law of the association of equals, which can be called a 'natural' right, even if it is no 'natural right,' and on the other hand, out of the law of violence transformed into regulated might, the law of unequals."

14. Only the fact that democracy has become a sacred cow in modern politics can explain why the extent to which the idea of majority rule is rid-

den with inner contradictions is almost generally overlooked: first, and this is already decisive, if one accepts democracy as justified, then one would also have to accept a democratic abolishment of democracy and a substitution of either an autocracy or a libertarian capitalism for democracy--and this would demonstrate that democracy as such cannot be regarded as a moral value. In the same way it would have to be accepted as justified if majorities decided to eliminate minorities until the point at which there were only two people, the last majority, left, for which majority rule could no longer be applied, for logico-arithmetic reasons. This would prove once again that democracy cannot in itself be regarded as justifiable. Or, if one did not want to accept these consequences and instead adopted the idea of a constitutionally limited, liberal democracy, one would at the same time have to admit that the principles from which these limitations are derived must then be logically more fundamental than the majority rule--and this again would point to the fact that there can be nothing of particular moral value in democracy. Second, by accepting majority rule it is not automatically clear what the population is to which it should be applied. (The majority of *which* population is to decide?) Here there are exactly three possibilities. Either one applies the democratic principle once again with regard to this question, and decides to opt for the idea that greater majorities should always prevail over smaller ones--but then, of course, there would be no way of saving the idea of national or regional democracy, as one would have to choose the total, global population as one's group of reference. Or, one decides that determining the population is an arbitrary matter--but in this case, one would have to accept the possibility of increasingly smaller minorities seceding from larger ones, with every individual being his own self-determining majority, as the logical end point of such a process of secession--and once again the unjustifiability of democracy as such would have been demonstrated. Third, one could adopt the idea that selecting the population to which the majority principle is applied is neither done democratically nor arbitrarily, but somehow differently--but then again, one would have to admit that whatever this different principle that would justify such a decision might be, it must be more fundamental than the majority rule itself, and majority rule in itself must be classified as completely arbitrary. Cf. on this M. N. Rothbard *Power and Market*, Kansas City, 1977, pp.189ff., H. H. Hoppe, *Eigentum, Anarchie und Staat*, Opladen, 1987, Chapter 5.

15. B. de Jouvenel, *On Power*, New York, 1949, pp.9-10; on the social psychology of democracy cf. also the same, *On Sovereignty*, Cambridge, 1957; G. Mosca, *The Ruling Class*, New York, 1939; H. A. Mencken, *Notes on Democracy*, New York, 1926; on the tendency of democratic rule to "degenerate" to oligarchic rule cf. R. Michels, *Zur Soziologie des Par-*

teiwesens in der modernen Demokratie, Stuttgart, 1957.

16. Cf. on this process, R. Bendix, *Kings or People*, Berkeley, 1978.

17. On the fundamental difference between private business organizations and the state cf. L. v. Mises, *Bureaucracy*, New Haven, 1944.

18. L. Spooner describes the supporters of the state as falling into two categories: "1. Knaves, a numerous and active class, who see in the government an instrument which they can use for their own aggrandizement or wealth. 2. Dupes--a large class, no doubt--each of whom, because he is allowed one voice out of millions in deciding what he may do with his own person and his own property, and because he is permitted to have the same voice in robbing, enslaving, and murdering others, that others have in robbing, enslaving and murdering himself, is stupid enough to imagine that he is a 'free man,' a 'sovereign,' that this is a 'free government,' 'the best government on earth,' and such like absurdities" (L. Spooner, *No Treason. The Constitution of No Authority*, Colorado Springs, 1973, p.18).

19. Writes E. de la Boetie (*The Politics of Obedience: The Discourse of Voluntary Servitude*, New York, 1975, pp.52-53): "He who domineers over you ... has indeed nothing more than the power that you confer upon him to destroy you .... Resolve to serve no more, and you are at once freed. I do not ask that you place hands upon the tyrant to topple him over, but simply that you support him no longer; then you will behold him, like a great Colossus whose pedestal has been pulled away, fall of his own weight and break into pieces."

20. On a strategy for liberty, and in particular on the importance of a libertarian movement for the achievement of these goals, cf. M. N. Rothbard, *For A New Liberty*, New York, 1978, Chapter 15; and *The Ethics of Liberty*, Atlantic Highlands, 1982, part 5.

CHAPTER 9

1. Cf. on this also Chapter 3 above and Chapter 10 below.

2. On the function of profit and loss cf. L. v. Mises, *Human Action*, Chicago, 1966, Chapter 15; and "Profit and Loss," in: the same, *Planning for Freedom*, South Holland, 1974; M. N. Rothbard, *Man, Economy and State*, Los Angeles, 1970, Chapter 8.

3. On the economics of government cf., esp. M. N. Rothbard, *Power and Market*, Kansas City, 1977, Chapter 5.

4. Regarding democratically controlled allocations, various deficiencies have become quite evident. For instance J. Buchanan and R. Wagner write (*The Consequences of Mr. Keynes*, London, 1978, p.19), "Market competition is continuous; at each purchase, a buyer is able to select among competing sellers. Political competition is intermittent; a decision is binding generally for a fixed number of years. Market competition allows several competitors to survive simultaneously,...Political competition leads to an all-or-nothing outcome....in market competition the buyer can be reasonably certain as to just what it is that he will receive from his purchase. In political competition, the buyer is in effect purchasing the services of an agent, whom he cannot bind....Moreover, because a politician needs to secure the cooperation of a majority of politicians, the meaning of a vote for a politician is less clear than that of a 'vote' for a private firm." (Cf. on this also J. Buchanan, "Individual Choice in Voting and the Market," in: the same, *Fiscal Theory and Political Economy*, Chapel Hill, 1962; for a more general treatment of the problem J. Buchanan and G. Tullock, *The Calculus of Consent*, Ann Arbor, 1962.)

What has commonly been overlooked, though--especially by those who try to make a virtue of the fact that a democracy gives equal voting power to everyone, whereas consumer sovereignty allows for unequal "votes"--is the most important deficiency of all: that under a system of consumer sovereignty people might cast unequal votes but, in any case, they exercise control exclusively over things which they acquired through original appropriation or contract and hence are forced to act morally. Under a democracy of production everyone is assumed to have something to say regarding things one did not so acquire, and hence one is permanently invited thereby not only to create legal instability with all its negative effects on the process of capital formation, but, moreover, to act immorally. Cf. on this also L. v. Mises, *Socialism*, Indianapolis, 1981, Chapter 31; also cf. Chapter 8 above.

5. M. N. Rothbard, *Power and Market*, Kansas City, 1977, p.176.

6. This is a very generous assumption, to be sure, as it is fairly certain that the so-called public sector of production attracts a different type of person from the very outset and boasts an unusually high number of inefficient, lazy, and incompetent people.

7. Cf. L. v. Mises, *Bureaucracy*, New Haven, 1944; Rothbard, *Power and Market*, Kansas City, 1977, pp.172ff; and *For A New Liberty New York, 1978, Chapter 10; also M. and R. Friedman, The Tyranny of the Status Quo*, New York, 1984, pp.35-51.

8. On the following cf. L. v. Mises, *Human Action*, Chicago, 1966, Chapter 23.6; M.N. Rothbard, *Man Economy and State*, Los Angeles, 1970, Chapter 7, esp. 7.4-6; "Conservation in the Free Market," in: *Egalitarianism As A Revolt Against Nature*, Washington, 1974; and *For A New Liberty*, New York, 1978, Chapter 13.

9. On this and the following cf. L. v. Mises, *Socialism*, Indianapolis, 1981, part 3.2.

10. Thus states J. W. McGuire, *Business and Society*, New York, 1963, pp.38-39: "From 1865 to 1897, declining prices year after year made it difficult for businessmen to plan for the future. In many areas new railroad links had resulted in a nationalization of the market east of the Mississippi, and even small concerns in small towns were forced to compete with other, often larger firms located at a distance. At the same time there were remarkable advances in technology and productivity. In short it was a wonderful era for the consumer and a frightful age for the producers especially as competition became more and more severe."

11. Cf. on this G. Kolko, *The Triumph of Conservatism*, Chicago, 1967; and *Railroads and Regulation*, Princeton, 1965; J. Weinstein, *The Corporate Ideal in the Liberal State*, Boston, 1968; M. N. Rothbard and R. Radosh (eds.), *A New History of Leviathan*, New York, 1972.

12. G. Kolko, *The Triumph of Conservatism*, Chicago, 1967, pp.4-5; cf. also the investigations of M. Olson, *The Logic of Collective Action*, Cambridge, 1965, to the effect that mass organizations (in particular labor unions), too, are not market phenomena but owe their existence to legislative action.

13. On the following cf. L. v. Mises, *Socialism*, Indianapolis, 1981, part 3.2; and IHuman Action, Chicago, 1966, Chapters 25-26; M. N. Rothbard, *Man, Economy and State*, Los Angeles, 1970, pp.544ff; pp.585ff; and "Ludwig von Mises and Economic Calculation under Socialism," in: L. Moss (ed.), *The Economics of Ludwig von Mises*, Kansas City, 1976, pp.75-76.

14. Cf. F. A. Hayek, *Individualism and Economic Order*, Chicago, 1948, esp. Chapter 9; I. Kirzner, *Competition and Entrepreneurship*, Chicago, 1973.

15. Regarding large-scale ownership, in particular of land, Mises observes that it is normally only brought about and upheld by nonmarket forces: by coercive violence and a state-enforced legal system outlawing or hampering the selling of land. "Nowhere and at no time has the large scale ownership of land come into being through the working of economic forces in the market. Founded by violence, it has been upheld by violence and that alone. As soon as the latifundia are drawn into the sphere of market transactions they begin to crumble, until at last they disappear completely....That in a market economy it is difficult even now to uphold the latifundia, is shown by the endeavors to create legislation institutions like the 'Fideikommiss' and related legal institutions such as the English 'entail'....Never was the ownership of the means of production more closely concentrated than at the time of Pliny, when half the province of Africa was owned by six people, or in the day of the Merovingian, when the church possessed the greater part of all French soil. And in no part of the world is there less large-scale land ownership than in capitalist North America," *Socialism*, Indianapolis, 1981, pp.325-326.

16. Cf. on the following in M. N. Rothbard, *Man, Economy and State*, Los Angeles, 1970, Chapter 10, esp. pp.586ff; also W. Block, "Austrian Monopoly Theory. A Critique," in: *Journal of Libertarian Studies*, 1977.

17. L. v. Mises, *Human Action*, Chicago, 1966, p.359; cf. also any current textbook, such as P. Samuelson, *Economics*, New York, 1976, p.500.

18. Cf. M. N. Rothbard, *Man, Economy and State*, Los Angeles, 1970, Chapter 10, esp. pp.604-614.

19. M. N. Rothbard, *Man, Economy and State*, Los Angeles, 1970, p.607.

20. L. v. Mises, "Profit and Loss," in: *Planning for Freedom*, South Holland, 1974, p.116.

21. In fact, historically, governmental anti-trust policy has almost exclusively been a practice of providing less successful competitors with the legal tools needed to hamper the operation of their more successful rivals. For an impressive assembly of case studies to this effect cf. D. Armentano, *Antitrust and Monopoly*, New York, 1982; also Y. Brozen, *Is Government the Source of Monopoly? And Other Essays*, San Francisco, 1980.

CHAPTER 10

1. G. de Molinari, "The Production of Security," Center for Libertarian Studies, Occasional Paper No. 2, New York, 1977, p.3.

2. *Ibid*., p.4.

3. For various approaches of public goods theorists cf. J. Buchanan and G. Tullock, *The Calculus of Consent*, Ann Arbor, 1962; J. Buchanan, *The Public Finances*, Homewood, 1970; and *The Limits of Liberty*, Chicago, 1975; G. Tullock, *Private Wants, Public Means*, New York, 1970; M. Olson, *The Logic of Collective Action*, New York, 1965; W. Baumol, *Welfare Economics and the Theory of the State*, Cambridge, 1952.

4. Cf. on the following M. N. Rothbard, *Man, Economy and State*, Los Angeles, 1970, pp.883ff; and "The Myth of Neutral Taxation," in: *Cato Journal*, 1981; W. Block, "Free Market Transportation: Denationalizing the Roads," in: *Journal of Libertarian Studies*, 1979; and "Public Goods and Externalities: The Case of Roads," in: *Journal of Libertarian Studies*, 1983.

5. Cf. for instance, W. Baumol and A. Blinder, *Economics, Principles and Policy*, New York, 1979, Chapter 31.

6. Another frequently used criterion for public goods is that of "non-rivalrous consumption." Generally, both criteria seem to coincide: when free riders cannot be excluded, nonrivalrous consumption is possible; and when they can be excluded, consumption becomes rivalrous, or so it seems. However, as public goods theorists argue, this coincidence is not perfect. It is, they say, conceivable that while the exclusion of free riders might be possible, their inclusion might not be connected with any additional cost (the marginal cost of admitting free riders is zero, that is), and that the consumption of the good in question by the additionally admitted free rider will not necessarily lead to a subtraction in the consumption of the good available to others. Such a good would be a public good, too. And since exclusion would be practiced on the free market and the good would not become available for nonrivalrous consumption to everyone it otherwise could--even though this would require no additional costs--this, according to statist- socialist logic, would prove a market failure, i.e., a suboptimal level

of consumption. Hence, the state would have to take over the provision of such goods. (A movie theater, for instance, might only be half-full, so it might be "costless" to admit additional viewers free of charge, and their watching the movie also might not affect the paying viewers; hence the movie would qualify as a public good. Since, however, the owner of the theater would be engaging in exclusion, instead of letting free riders enjoy a "costless" performance, movie theaters would be ripe for nationalization.) On the numerous fallacies involved in defining public goods in terms of nonrivalrous consumption cf. notes 12 and 16 below.

7. Cf. on this W. Block, "Public Goods and Externalities," in: *Journal of Libertarian Studies*, 1983.

8. Cf. for instance, J. Buchanan, *The Public Finances*, Homewood, 1970, p.23; P. Samuelson, *Economics*, New York, 1976, p.160.

9. Cf. R. Coase, "The Lighthouse in Economics," in: *Journal of Law and Economics*, 1974.

10. Cf. for instance, the ironic case that W. Block makes for socks being public goods in "Public Goods and Externalities," in: *Journal of Libertarian Studies*, 1983.

11. To avoid any misunderstanding here, every single producer and every association of producers making joint decisions can, at any time, decide whether or not to produce a good based on an evaluation of the privateness or publicness of the good. In fact, decisions on whether or not to produce public goods privately are constantly made within the framework of a market economy. What is impossible is to decide whether or not to ignore the outcome of the operation of a free market based on the assessment of the degree of privateness or publicness of a good.

12. In fact, then, the introduction of the distinction between private and public goods is a relapse into the presubjectivist era of economics. From the point of view of subjectivist economics no good exists that can be categorized objectively as private or public. This, essentially, is why the second proposed criterion for public goods, i.e., permitting nonrivalrous consumption (cf. note 6 above), breaks down, too. For how could any outside observer determine whether or not the admittance of an additional free rider at no charge would not indeed lead to a reduction in the enjoyment of

a good by others?! Clearly, there is no way that he could objectively do so. In fact, it might well be that one's enjoyment of a movie or driving on a road would be considerably reduced if more people were allowed in the theater or on the road. Again, to find out whether or not this is the case one would have to ask every individual--and not everyone might agree. (What then?) Furthermore, since even a good that allows nonrivalrous consumption is not a free good, as a consequence of admitting additional free riders "crowding" would *eventually* occur, and hence everyone would have to be asked about the appropriate "margin." In addition, my consumption may or may not be affected, depending on *who* it is that is admitted free of charge, so I would have to be asked about this, too. And finally, everyone might change his opinion on all of these questions over time. It is thus in the same way impossible to decide whether or not a good is a candidate for state (rather than private) production based on the criterion of nonrivalrous consumption as on that of nonexcludability. (Cf. also note 16 below).

13. Cf. P. Samuelson, "The Pure Theory of Public Expenditure," in: *Review of Economics and Statistics*, 1954; and *Economics*, New York, 1976, Chapter 8; M. Friedman, *Capitalism and Freedom*, Chicago, 1962, Chapter 2; F. A. Hayek, *Law, Legislation and Liberty*, vol. 3, Chicago, 1979, Chapter 14.

14. In recent years economists, in particular of the so-called Chicago-school, have been increasingly concerned with the analysis of property rights (cf. H. Demsetz, "The Exchange and Enforcement of Property Rights," in: *Journal of Law and Economics*, 1964; and "Toward a Theory of Property Rights," in: *American Economic Review*, 1967; R. Coase, "The Problem of Social Cost," in: *Journal of Law and Economics*, 1960; A. Alchian, *Economic Forces at Work*, Indianapolis, 1977, part 2; R. Posner, *Economic Analysis of Law*, Boston, 1977). Such analyses, however, have nothing to do with ethics. On the contrary, they represent attempts to substitute economic efficiency considerations for the establishment of justifiable ethical principles (on the critique of such endeavors cf. M. N. Rothbard, *The Ethics of Liberty*, Atlantic Highlands 1982, Chapter 26; W. Block, "Coase and Demsetz on Private Property Rights," in: *Journal of Libertarian Studies*, 1977; R. Dworkin, "Is Wealth a Value," in: *Journal of Legal Studies*, 1980; M. N. Rothbard, "The Myth of Efficiency," in: M. Rizzo (ed.), *Time, Uncertainty, and Disequilibrium*, Lexington, 1979). Ultimately, all efficiency arguments are irrelevant because there simply exists no nonarbitrary way of measuring, weighing, and aggregating individual utilities or disutilities that result from some given allocation of property rights. Hence, any attempt to recommend some particular system of assigning property rights in terms of its alleged maximization of "social welfare" is pseudo-scientific humbug (see

in particular, M. N. Rothbard, "Toward a Reconstruction of Utility and Welfare Economics," Center for Libertarian Studies, Occasional Paper No. 3, New York, 1977; also, L. Robbins, "Economics and Political Economy," in: *American Economic Review*, 1981).

The "Unanimity Principle" which J. Buchanan and G. Tullock, following K. Wicksell (*Finanztheoretische Untersuchungen*, Jena, 1896), have repeatedly proposed as a guide for economic policy is also not to be confused with an ethical principle proper. According to this principle only such policy changes should be enacted which can find unanimous consent--and that surely sounds attractive; but then, mutatis mutandis, it also determines that the status quo be preserved if there is less than unanimous agreement on any proposal of change--and that sounds far less attractive because it implies that any given, present state of affairs regarding the allocation of property rights must be legitimate either as a point of departure or as a to-be-continued state. However, the public choice theorists offer no justification in terms of a normative theory of property rights for this daring claim as would be required. Hence, the unanimity principle is ultimately without ethical foundation. In fact, because it would legitimize any conceivable status quo, the Buchananites most favored principle is no less than outrightly absurd as a moral criterion (cf. on this also M. N. Rothbard, *The Ethics of Liberty*, Atlantic Highlands, 1982, Chapter 26; and "The Myth of Neutral Taxation," in: *Cato Journal*, 1981, pp.549f).
Whatever might still be left for the unanimity principle, Buchanan and Tullock, following the lead of Wicksell again, then give away by reducing it in effect to one of "relative" or "quasi" unanimity.

15. Cf. on this argument M. N. Rothbard, "The Myth of Neutral Taxation," in: *Cato Journal*, 1981, p.533. Incidentally, the existence of one single anarchist also invalidates all references to Pareto-optimality as a criterion for economically legitimate state action.

16. Essentially the same reasoning that leads one to reject the socialist-statist theory built on the allegedly unique character of public goods as defined by the criterion of nonexcludability, also applies when instead, such goods are defined by means of the criterion of nonrivalrous consumption (cf. notes 6 and 12 above). For one thing, in order to derive the normative statement that they *should* be so offered from the statement of fact that goods which allow nonrivalrous consumption would *not* be offered on the free market to as many consumers as could be, this theory would face exactly the same problem of requiring a justifiable ethics. Moreover, the utilitarian reasoning is blatantly wrong, too. To reason, as the public goods theorists do, that the free-market practice of excluding free riders from the

enjoyment of goods which would permit nonrivalrous consumption at zero marginal costs would indicate a suboptimal level of social welfare and hence would require compensatory state action is faulty on two related counts. First, cost is a subjective category and can never be objectively measured by any outside observer. Hence, to say that additional free riders could be admitted at no cost is totally inadmissible. In fact, if the subjective costs of admitting more consumers at no charge were indeed zero, the private owner-producer of the good in question would do so. If he does not do so, this reveals that to the contrary, the costs for him are *not* zero. The reason for this may be his belief that to do so would reduce the satisfaction available to the other consumers and so would tend to depress the price for his product; or it may simply be his dislike for uninvited free riders as, for instance, when I object to the proposal that I turn over my less-than-capacity-filled living room to various self-inviting guests for nonrivalrous consumption. In any case, since for whatever reason the cost cannot be assumed to be zero, it is then fallacious to speak of a market failure when certain goods are not handed out free of charge. On the other hand, welfare losses would indeed become unavoidable if one accepted the public goods theorists' recommendation of letting goods that allegedly allow for nonrivalrous consumption to be provided free of charge by the state. Besides the insurmountable task of determining what fulfills this criterion, the state, independent of voluntary consumer purchases as it is, would first face the equally insoluble problem of rationally determining *how much* of the public good to provide. Clearly, since even public goods are not free goods but are subject to "crowding" at some level of use, there is no stopping point for the state, because at any level of supply there would still be users who would have to be excluded and who, with a larger supply, could enjoy a free ride. But even if this problem could be solved miraculously, in any case the (necessarily inflated) cost of production and operation of the public goods distributed free of charge for nonrivalrous consumption would have to be paid for by taxes. And this then, i.e., the fact that consumers would have been coerced into enjoying their free rides, again proves beyond any doubt that from the consumers' point of view these public goods, too, are inferior in value to the competing private goods that they now no longer can acquire.

17. The most prominent modern champions of Orwellian double talk are J. Buchanan and G. Tullock (cf. their works cited in note 3 above). They claim that government is founded by a "constitutional contract" in which everyone "conceptually agrees" to submit to the coercive powers of government with the understanding that everyone else is subject to it, too. Hence, government is only seemingly coercive but really voluntary. There are several evi-

dent objections to this curious argument. First, there is no empirical evidence whatsoever for the contention that any constitution has ever been voluntarily accepted by everyone concerned. Worse, the very idea of all people voluntarily coercing themselves is simply inconceivable, much in the same way that it is inconceivable to deny the law of contradiction. For if the voluntarily accepted coercion is voluntary, then it would have to be possible to revoke one's subjection to the constitution and the state would be no more than a voluntarily joined club. If, however, one does not have the "right to ignore the state"--and that one does not have this right is, of course, the characteristic mark of a state as compared to a club--then it would be logically inadmissible to claim that one's acceptance of state coercion is voluntary. Furthermore, even if all this were possible, the constitutional contract could still not claim to bind anyone except the original signers of the constitution.

How can Buchanan and Tullock come up with such absurd ideas? By a semantic trick. What was "inconceivable" and "no agreement" in pre-Orwellian talk is for them "conceptually possible" and a "conceptual agreement." For a most instructive short exercise in this sort of reasoning in leaps and bounds cf. J. Buchanan, "A Contractarian Perspective on Anarchy," in: *Freedom in Constitutional Contract*, College Station, 1977. Here we learn (p.17) that even the acceptance of the 55 m.p.h. speed limit is possibly voluntary (Buchanan is not quite sure), since it ultimately rests on all of us conceptually agreeing on the constitution, and that Buchanan is not really a statist, but in truth an anarchist (p.11).

18. M. N. Rothbard, *Man, Economy and State*, Los Angeles, 1970, p.887.

19. This, first of all, should be kept in mind whenever one has to assess the validity of statist-interventionist arguments such as the following, by J. M. Keynes ("The End of Laissez Faire," in: J. M. Keynes, *Collected Writings*, London 1972, vol. 9, p.291): "The most important Agenda of the state relate not to those activities which private individuals are already fulfilling but to those functions which fall outside the sphere of the individual, to those decisions which are made by *no one* if the state does not make them. The important thing for government is not to do things which individuals are doing already and to do them a little better or a little worse: but to do those things which are not done at all." This reasoning not only *appears* phony, it truly is.

20. Some libertarian minarchists object that the existence of a market presupposes the recognition and enforcement of a common body of law, and hence a government as a monopolistic judge and enforcement agen-

cy. (Cf., for instance, J. Hospers, *Libertarianism*, Los Angeles, 1971; T. Machan, *Human Rights and Human Liberties*, Chicago, 1975.) Now, it is certainly correct that a market presupposes the recognition and enforcement of those rules that underlie its operation. But from this it does not follow that this task must be entrusted to a monopolistic agency. In fact, a common language or sign-system is also presupposed by the market; but one would hardly think it convincing to conclude that hence the government must ensure the observance of the rules of language. Just as the system of language then, the rules of market behavior emerge spontaneously and can be enforced by the "invisible hand" of self-interest. Without the observance of common rules of speech people could not reap the advantages that communication offers, and without the observance of common rules of conduct, people could not enjoy the benefits of the higher productivity of an exchange economy based on the division of labor. In addition, as I have demonstrated in Chapter 7, independent of any government, the rules of the market can be defended a priori as just. Moreover, as I will argue in the conclusion of this Chapter, it is precisely a competitive system of law administration and law enforcement that generates the greatest possible pressure to elaborate and enact rules of conduct that incorporate the highest degree of *consensus* conceivable. And, of course, the very rules that do just this are those that a priori reasoning establishes as the logically necessary presupposition of argumentation and argumentative agreement.

21. Incidentally, the same logic that would force one to accept the idea of the production of security by private business as economically the best solution to the problem of consumer satisfaction also forces one, as far as moral-ideological positions are concerned, to abandon the political theory of classical liberalism and take the small but nevertheless decisive step (from there) to the theory of libertarianism, or private property anarchism. Classical liberalism, with L. v. Mises as its foremost representative in this century, advocates a social system based on the fundamental rules of the natural theory of property. And these are also the rules that libertarianism advocates. But classical liberalism then wants to have these laws enforced by a monopolistic agency (the government, the state)--an organization, that is, which is not exclusively dependent on voluntary, contractual support by the consumers of its respective services, but instead has the right to unilaterally determine its own income, i.e., the taxes to be imposed on consumers in order to do its job in the area of security production. Now, however plausible this might sound, it should be clear that it is inconsistent. Either the principles of the natural property theory are valid, in which case the state as a privileged monopolist is immoral, or business built on and

around aggression--the use of force and of noncontractual means of acquiring resources--is valid, in which case one must toss out the first theory. It is impossible to sustain both contentions and not be inconsistent unless, of course, one could provide a principle that is more fundamental than both the natural theory of property and the state's right to aggressive violence and from which both, with the respective limitations regarding the domains in which they are valid, can be logically derived. However, liberalism never provided any such principle, nor will it ever be able to do so, since, as I demonstrated in Chapter 7, to argue in favor of anything presupposes one's right to be free of aggression. Given the fact then that the principles of the natural theory of property cannot be argumentatively contested as morally valid principles without implicitly acknowledging their validity, by force of logic one is committed to abandoning liberalism and accepting instead its more radical child: libertarianism, the philosophy of pure capitalism, which demands that the production of security be undertaken by private business, too.

22. Cf. on the problem of competitive security production G. de Molinari, "The Production of Security" Center for Libertarian Studies, Occasional Paper No. 2, New York, 1977; M. N. Rothbard, *Power and Market*, Kansas City, 1977, Chapter 1; and *For A New Liberty*, New York, 1978, Chapter 12; also: W.C. Wooldridge, *Uncle Sam the Monopoly Man*, New Rochelle, 1970, Chapters 5-6; M. and L. Tannehill, *The Market for Liberty*, New York, 1984, part 2.

23. Cf. M. Murck, *Soziologie der oeffentlichen Sicherheit*, Frankfurt/M., 1980.

24. On the deficiencies of democratically controlled allocation decisions cf. above, Chapter 9, n. 4.

25. Sums up Molinari ("Production of Security," Center for Libertarian Studies, Occasional Paper No. 2, New York, 1977, pp.13-14): "If...the consumer is not free to buy security wherever he pleases, you forthwith see open up a large profession dedicated to arbitrariness and bad management. Justice becomes slow and costly, the police vexatious, individual liberty is no longer respected, the price of security is abusively inflated and inequitably apportioned, according to the power and influence of this or that class of consumers."

26. Cf. the literature cited in note 21 above; also: B. Leoni, *Freedom and the Law*, Princeton, 1961; J. Peden, "Property Rights in Celtic Irish Law," in: *Journal of Libertarian Studies*, 1977.

27. Cf. T. Anderson and P. J. Hill, "The American Experiment in Anarcho-Capitalism: The Not So Wild, Wild West," in: *Journal of Libertarian Studies*, 1980.

28. Cf. on the following H. H. Hoppe, *Eigentum, Anarchie und Staat*, Opladen, 1987, Chapter 5.

29. Contrast this with the state's policy of engaging in battles without having everyone's deliberate support because it has the right to tax people; and ask yourself if the risk of war would be lower or higher if one had the right to stop paying taxes as soon as one had the feeling that the state's handling of foreign affairs was not to one's liking!

30. And it may be noted here again that norms that incorporate the highest possible degree of consensus are, of course, those that are presupposed by argumentation and whose acceptance makes consensus on anything at all possible, as shown in Chapter 7.

31. Again, contrast this with state-employed judges who, because they are paid from taxes and so are relatively independent of consumer satisfaction, can pass judgments which are clearly not acceptable as fair by everyone; and ask yourself if the risk of not finding the truth in a given case would be lower or higher if one had the possibility of exerting economic pressure whenever one had the feeling that a judge who one day might have to adjudicate in one's own case had not been sufficiently careful in assembling and judging the facts of a case, or simply was an outright crook.

32. Cf. on the following in particular, M. N. Rothbard, *For A New Liberty*, New York, 1978, pp.233ff.

33. Cf. B. Bailyn, *The Ideological Origins of the American Revolution*, Cambridge, 1967; J. T. Main, *The Anti-Federalists: Critics of the Constitution*, Chapel Hill, 1961; M. N. Rothbard, *Conceived in Liberty*, 4 vols., New Rochelle, 1975-1979.

34. Naturally, insurance companies would assume a particularly important role in checking the emergence of outlaw companies. Note M. and L. Tannehill: "Insurance companies, a very important sector of any totally free economy, would have a special incentive to dissociate themselves from any aggressor and, in addition, to bring all their considerable business influence to bear against him. *Aggressive violence causes value loss*, and the insurance industry would suffer the major cost in most such value losses. An unrestrained aggressor is a walking liability, and no insurance company, however remotely removed from his original aggression, would wish to sustain the risk that he might aggress against one of its own clients next. Besides, aggressors and those who associate with them are more likely to be involved in situations of violence and are, thus, bad insurance risks. An insurance company would probably refuse coverage to such people out of a foresighted desire to minimize any future losses which their aggressions might cause. But even if the company were not motivated by such foresight, it would still be forced to raise their premiums up drastically or cancel their coverage altogether in order to avoid carrying the extra risk involved in their inclination to violence. In a competitive economy, no insurance company could afford to continue covering aggressors and those who had dealings with aggressors and simply pass the cost on to its honest customers; it would soon lose these customers to more reputable firms which could afford to charge less for their insurance coverage.

What would loss of insurance coverage mean in a free economy? Even if [the aggressor] could generate enough force to protect itself against any aggressive or retaliatory force brought against it by any factor or combination of factors, it would still have to go completely without several economic necessities. It could not purchase insurance protection against auto accidents, natural disasters, or contractual disputes. It would have no protection against damage suits resulting from accidents occurring on its property. It is very possible that [it] would even have to do without the services of a fire extinguishing company, since such companies are natural outgrowths of the fire insurance business.

In addition to the terrific penalties imposed by the business ostracism which would naturally follow its aggressive act [it] would have trouble with its employees....[For] if a defense service agent carried out an order which involved the intentional initiation of force, both the agent and the entrepreneur or manager who gave him the order, as well as any other employees knowledgeably involved, would be liable for any damages caused" (M. and L. Tannehill, *The Market for Liberty*, New York, 1984, pp.110-111).

35. The process of an outlaw company emerging as a state would be even

further complicated, since it would have to reacquire the "ideological legitimacy" that marks the existence of the presently existing states and which took them centuries of relentless propaganda to develop. Once this legitimacy is lost through the experience with a pure free market system, it is difficult to imagine how it could ever be easily regained.

REFERENCES

Albert, H. *Marktsoziologie und Entscheidungslogik*. Neuwied, 1967.

Alchian, A. *Economic Forces at Work*. Indianapolis, 1977.

Anderson, P. *Passages from Antiquity to Feudalism*. London, 1974.

____. *Lineages of Absolutism*. London, 1974.

Anderson, T. and Hill, P. J. "The American Experiment in Anarcho-Capitalism: The Not So Wild, Wild West." *Journal of Libertarian Studies*, 1980.

Apel, K. O. *Transformation der Philosophie* (2 vols.). Frankfurt/M., 1973.

Armentano, D. *Antitrust and Monopoly*. New York, 1982.

Ayer, A. J. *Language, Truth and Logic*. New York, 1950.

Badie, B. and Birnbaum, P. *The Sociology of the State*. Chicago, 1983.

Baechler, J. *The Origins of Capitalism*. New York, 1976.

Baier, K. *The Moral Point of View*. Ithaca, 1958.

Bailyn, B. *The Ideological Origins of the American Revolution*. Cambridge, 1967.

Baird, C. *Rent Control: The Perennial Folly*. San Francisco, 1980.

Baumol, W. *Welfare Economics and the Theory of the State*. Cambridge, 1952.

____. and Blinder, A. *Economics. Principles and Policy*. New York, 1979.

Becker, G. *Human Capital*. New York, 1975.

Bendix, R. *Kings or People*. Berkeley, 1978.

Bernstein, E. *Die Voraussetzungen des Sozialismus und die Aufgaben der Sozialdemokratie*. Bonn, 1975.

Blanshard, B. *Reason and Analysis*. La Salle, 1964.

Blaug, M. *The Methodology of Economics*. Cambridge, 1980.

Bloch, M. *Feudal Society*. Chicago, 1961.

Block, W. "Public Goods and Externalities: The Case of Roads." *Journal of Libertarian Studies*, 1983.

____. "Free Market Transportation: Denationalizing the Roads." *Journal of Libertarian Studies*, 1979.

____. "Austrian Monopoly Theory. A Critique." *Journal of Libertarian Studies*, 1977.

____. "Coase and Demsetz on Private Property Rights." *Journal of Libertarian Studies*, 1977.

Boehm-Bawerk, E. v. *Kapital und Kapitalzins. Positive Theorie des Kapitals*. Meisenheim, 1967.

Boetie, E. de La. *The Politics of Obedience: The Discourse of Voluntary Servitude* (ed. M. N. Rothbard). New York, 1975.

Brady, R. A. "Modernized Cameralism in the Third Reich: The Case of the National Industry Group." in: M. I. Goldman (ed.) *Comparative Economic Systems*. New York, 1971.

Bramsted, E. K. and Melhuish, K. J. (eds.). *Western Liberalism*. London, 1978.

Brandt, W. (ed.). *North-South: A Programme for Survival*. 1980.

Brozen, Y. *Is Government the Source of Monopoly? And Other Essays*. San Francisco, 1980.

____ and Friedman, M. *The Minimum Wage: Who Pays*? Washington, 1966.

Brutzkus, B. *Economic Planning in Soviet Russia*. London, 1935.

Buchanan, J. *Freedom in Constitutional Contract*. College Station, 1977.

____. *The Limits of Liberty*. Chicago, 1975.

____. *The Public Finances*. Homewood, 1970.

____. *Cost and Choice*. Chicago, 1969.

____. *Fiscal Theory and Political Economy*. Chapel Hill, 1962.

____/Thirlby (ed.). *L. S. E. Essays on Cost*. Indianapolis, 1981.

____ and Tullock, G. *The Calculus of Consent*. Ann Arbor, 1962.

____ and Wagner, R. *The Consequences of Mr. Keynes*. London, 1978.

Carey, L. W. (ed.). *Freedom and Virtue. The Conservative/Libertarian Debate*. Lanham, 1984.

Cipolla, C. M. (ed.). *Economic History of Europe. Contemporary Economies*. Glasgow, 1976.

Coase, R. "The Lighthouse in Economics." *Journal of Law and Economics*, 1974.

Coase, R. "The Problem of Social Cost." *Journal of Law and Economics*, 1960.

Demsetz, H. "Toward a Theory of Property Rights." *American Economic Review*, 1967.

____. "The Exchange and Enforcement of Property Rights." *Journal of Law and Economics*, 1964.

Dicey, A. V. *Lectures on the Relation Between Law and Public Opinion in England During the Nineteenth Century*. London, 1974.

Dingler, H. *Die Ergreifung des Wirklichen*. Muenchen, 1955.

Dworkin, R. "Is Wealth a Value?" *Journal of Legal Studies*, 1980.

Erhard, L. *The Economics of Success*. London, 1968.

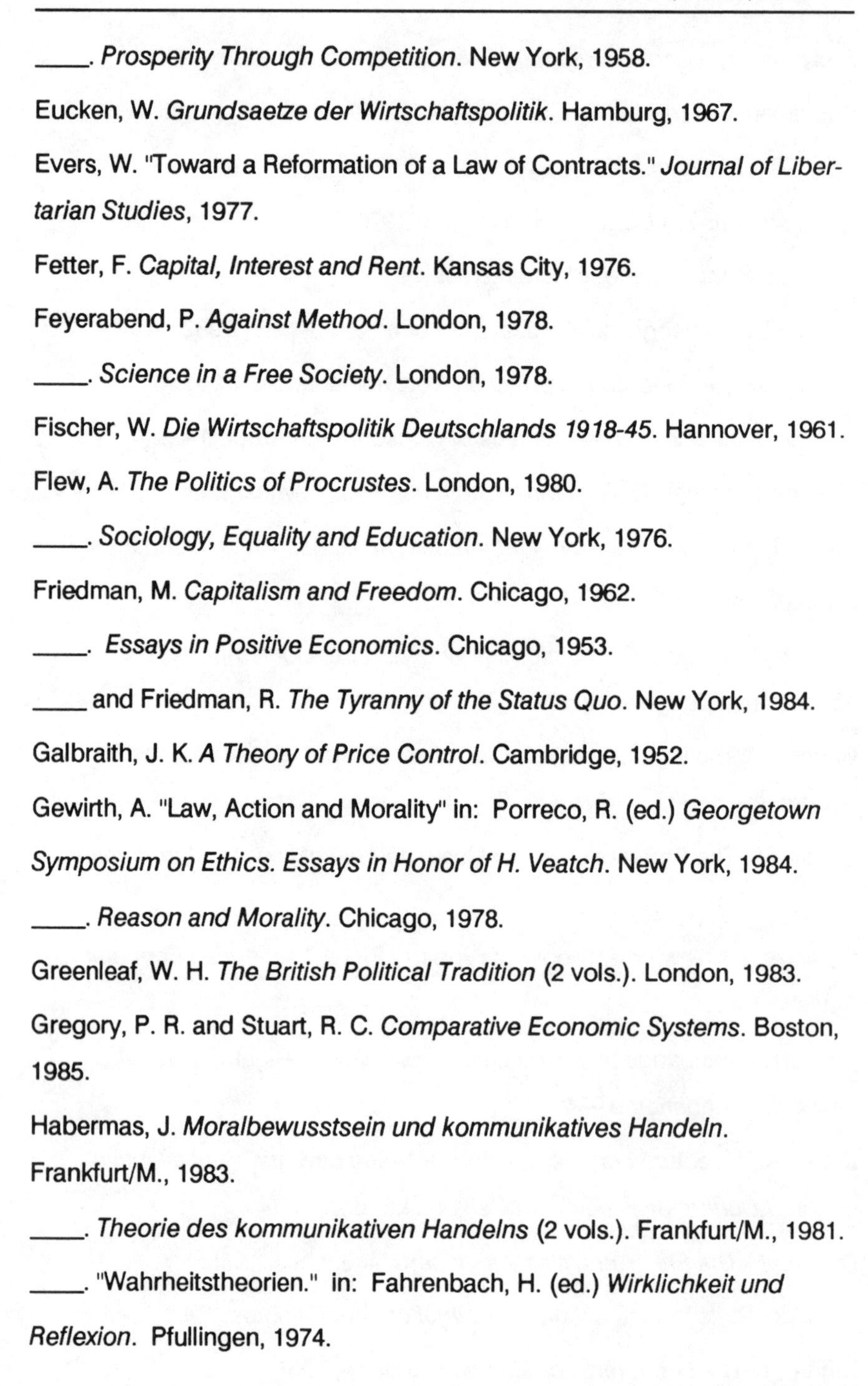

____. *Prosperity Through Competition*. New York, 1958.

Eucken, W. *Grundsaetze der Wirtschaftspolitik*. Hamburg, 1967.

Evers, W. "Toward a Reformation of a Law of Contracts." *Journal of Libertarian Studies*, 1977.

Fetter, F. *Capital, Interest and Rent*. Kansas City, 1976.

Feyerabend, P. *Against Method*. London, 1978.

____. *Science in a Free Society*. London, 1978.

Fischer, W. *Die Wirtschaftspolitik Deutschlands 1918-45*. Hannover, 1961.

Flew, A. *The Politics of Procrustes*. London, 1980.

____. *Sociology, Equality and Education*. New York, 1976.

Friedman, M. *Capitalism and Freedom*. Chicago, 1962.

____. *Essays in Positive Economics*. Chicago, 1953.

____ and Friedman, R. *The Tyranny of the Status Quo*. New York, 1984.

Galbraith, J. K. *A Theory of Price Control*. Cambridge, 1952.

Gewirth, A. "Law, Action and Morality" in: Porreco, R. (ed.) *Georgetown Symposium on Ethics. Essays in Honor of H. Veatch*. New York, 1984.

____. *Reason and Morality*. Chicago, 1978.

Greenleaf, W. H. *The British Political Tradition* (2 vols.). London, 1983.

Gregory, P. R. and Stuart, R. C. *Comparative Economic Systems*. Boston, 1985.

Habermas, J. *Moralbewusstsein und kommunikatives Handeln*. Frankfurt/M., 1983.

____. *Theorie des kommunikativen Handelns* (2 vols.). Frankfurt/M., 1981.

____. "Wahrheitstheorien." in: Fahrenbach, H. (ed.) *Wirklichkeit und Reflexion*. Pfullingen, 1974.

____. *Knowledge and Human Interest*. Boston, 1971.

Hamel, H. v. (ed.). *BRD-DDR. Die Wirtschaftssysteme*. Muenchen, 1983.

Harman, G. *The Nature of Morality*. New York, 1977.

Harris, M. *Cannibals and Kings*. New York, 1978.

Hayek, F. A. *Law, Legislation and Liberty* (3 vols.). Chicago, 1973-79.

____ (ed.). *Capitalism and the Historians*. Chicago, 1963.

____. *The Constitution of Liberty*. Chicago, 1960.

____. *The Road to Serfdom*. Chicago, 1956.

____. *Individualism and Economic Order*. Chicago, 1948.

____ (ed.). *Collectivist Economic Planning*. London, 1935.

____, et. al. *Rent Control. A Popular Paradox*. Vancouver, 1975.

Herbert, A. *The Right and Wrong of Compulsion by the State*. Indianapolis, 1981.

Hilton, R. (ed.). *The Transition from Feudalism to Capitalism*. London, 1978.

Hock, W. *Deutscher Antikapitalismus*. Frankfurt/M., 1960.

Hohmann, H. H., Kaser, M., and Thalheim, K. (eds.). *The New Economic Systems of Eastern Europe*. London, 1975.

Hollis, M. and Nell, E. *Rational Economic Man*. Cambridge, 1975.

Hoppe, H. H. *Eigentum, Anarchie und Staat*. Opladen, 1987.

____. "Is Research Based on Causal Scientific Principles Possible in the Social Sciences." *Ratio*, 1983.

____. *Kritik der kausalwissenschaftlichen Sozialforschung*. Opladen, 1983.

____. *Handeln und Erkennen*. Bern, 1976.

Hospers, J. *Libertarianism*. Los Angeles, 1971.

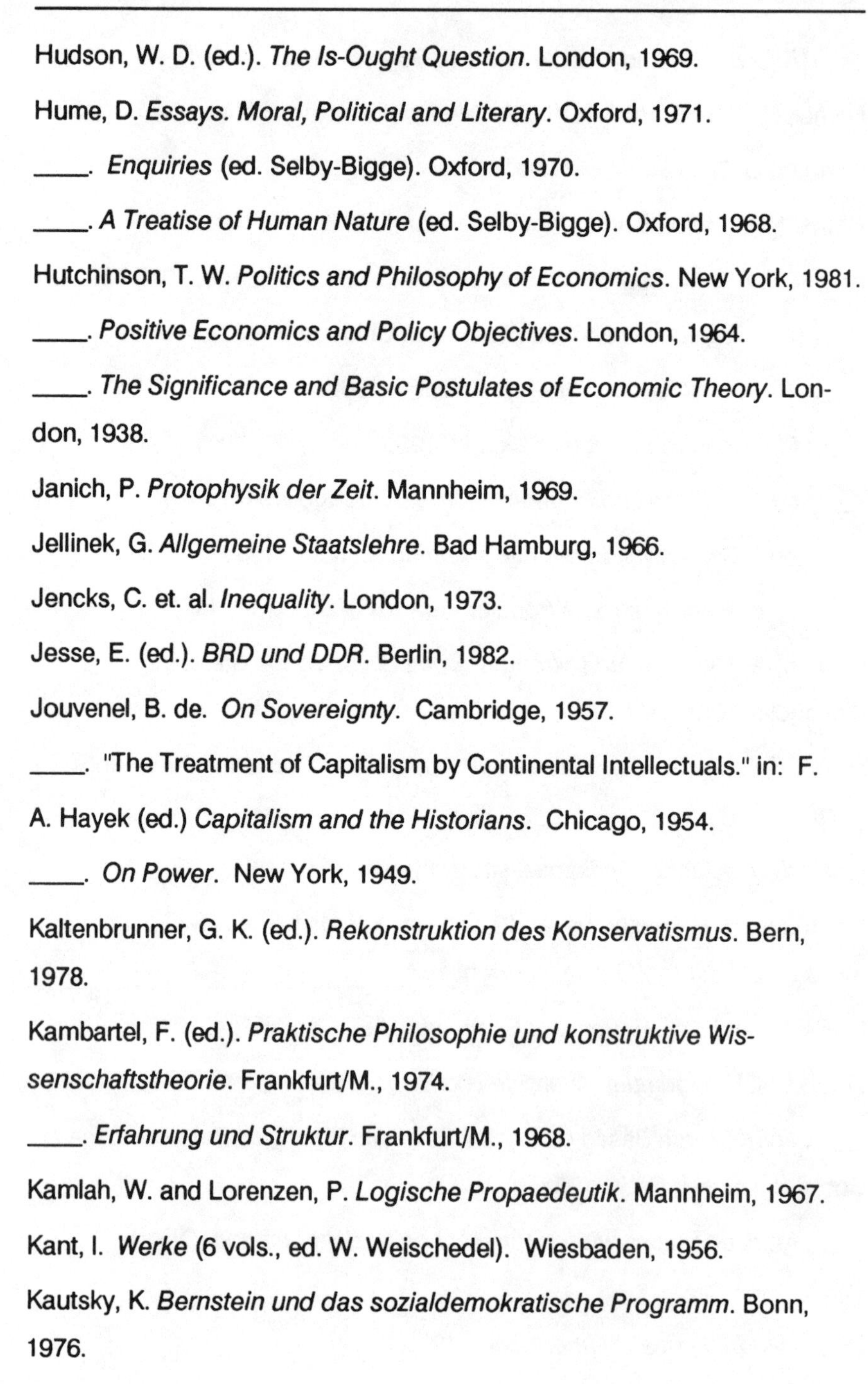

Hudson, W. D. (ed.). *The Is-Ought Question*. London, 1969.

Hume, D. *Essays. Moral, Political and Literary*. Oxford, 1971.

____. *Enquiries* (ed. Selby-Bigge). Oxford, 1970.

____. *A Treatise of Human Nature* (ed. Selby-Bigge). Oxford, 1968.

Hutchinson, T. W. *Politics and Philosophy of Economics*. New York, 1981.

____. *Positive Economics and Policy Objectives*. London, 1964.

____. *The Significance and Basic Postulates of Economic Theory*. London, 1938.

Janich, P. *Protophysik der Zeit*. Mannheim, 1969.

Jellinek, G. *Allgemeine Staatslehre*. Bad Hamburg, 1966.

Jencks, C. et. al. *Inequality*. London, 1973.

Jesse, E. (ed.). *BRD und DDR*. Berlin, 1982.

Jouvenel, B. de. *On Sovereignty*. Cambridge, 1957.

____. "The Treatment of Capitalism by Continental Intellectuals." in: F. A. Hayek (ed.) *Capitalism and the Historians*. Chicago, 1954.

____. *On Power*. New York, 1949.

Kaltenbrunner, G. K. (ed.). *Rekonstruktion des Konservatismus*. Bern, 1978.

Kambartel, F. (ed.). *Praktische Philosophie und konstruktive Wissenschaftstheorie*. Frankfurt/M., 1974.

____. *Erfahrung und Struktur*. Frankfurt/M., 1968.

Kamlah, W. and Lorenzen, P. *Logische Propaedeutik*. Mannheim, 1967.

Kant, I. *Werke* (6 vols., ed. W. Weischedel). Wiesbaden, 1956.

Kautsky, K. *Bernstein und das sozialdemokratische Programm*. Bonn, 1976.

Kelsen, H. *Reine Rechtslehre*. Wien, 1976.

Keynes, J. M. *The End of Laissez Faire* (*Collected Writings*, Vol. IX). London, 1972.

Kirzner, I. *Competition and Entrepreneurship*. Chicago, 1973.

Kolakowski, L. *Main Currents of Marxism* (3 vols.). Oxford, 1978.

Kolko, G. *The Triumph of Conservatism*. Chicago, 1967.

____. *Railroads and Regulation*. Princeton, 1965.

Kuhn, T. S. *The Structure of Scientific Revolutions*. Chicago, 1964.

Lakatos, I. "Falsification and the Methodology of Scientific Research Programmes" in :Lakatos/Musgrave (ed.) *Criticism and the Growth of Knowledge*. Cambridge, 1970.

Lange, O. "On the Economic Theory of Socialism" in: Goldman, M. I. (ed.) *Comparative Economic Systems*. New York, 1971.

Leonhard, W. *Sovietideologie. Die politischen Lehren*. Frankfurt/M., 1963.

Leoni, B. *Freedom and the Law*. Princeton, 1961.

Locke, J. *Two Treatises of Government* (ed. P. Laslett). Cambridge, 1960.

Lorenzen, P. *Normative Logic and Ethics*. Mannheim, 1969.

____. *Methodisches Denken*. Frankurt/M., 1968.

Luehrs, G. (ed.). *Kritischer Rationalismus und Sozialdemokratie* (2 vols.). Bonn, 1975-76.

Lukes, S. "Socialism and Equality" in: Kolakowski/Hampshire (eds.) *The Socialist Idea*. New York, 1974.

Machan, T. *Human Rights and Human Liberties*. Chicago, 1975.

Machiavelli, N. *The Prince*. Harmondsworth, 1961.

MacIntyre, A. *After Virtue*. Notre Dame, 1981.

Main, J. *The Anti-Federalists: Critics of the Constitution*. Chapel Hill, 1961.

Marx, K. *Critique of the Gotha Programme*. (*Selected Works*, Vol. 2). London, 1942.

McGuire, J. W. *Business and Society*. New York, 1963.

Melsen, A. v. *Philosophy of Nature*. Pittsburgh, 1953.

Mencken, H. A. *Notes on Democracy*. New York, 1926.

Merklein, R. *Die Deutschen werden aermer*. Hamburg, 1982.

____. *Griff in die eigene Tasche*. Hamburg, 1980.

Meyer, T. (ed.). *Demokratischer Sozialismus*. Muenchen, 1980.

Michels, R. *Zur Soziologie des Parteiwesens in der modernen Demokratie*. Stuttgart, 1957.

Miller, M. *Rise of the Russian Consumer*. London, 1965.

Mises, L. v. *The Anti-Capitalist Mentality*. San Francisco, 1983.

____. *Epistemological Problems of Economics*. New York, 1981.

____. *Socialism*. Indianapolis, 1981.

____. *The Ultimate Foundation of Economic Science*. Kansas City, 1978.

____. *A Critique of Interventionism*. New Rochelle, 1977.

____. *Planning for Freedom*. South Holland, 1974.

____. *Theory of Money and Credit*. Irvington, 1971.

____. *Human Action*. Chicago, 1966.

____. *Bureaucracy*. New Haven, 1944.

____. *Omnipotent Government*. New Haven, 1944.

____. *Liberalismus*. Jena, 1929.

Mittelstaedt, P. *Philosophische Probleme der modernen Physik*. Mannheim, 1966.

Molinari, G. de. "The Production of Security." Center for Libertarian Studies, Occasional Paper No. 2. New York, 1977.

Morgenstern, O. *National Income Statistics: A Critique of Macroeconomic Aggregation*. San Francisco, 1979.

Mosca, G. *The Ruling Class*. New York, 1939.

Murck, M. *Soziologie der oeffentlichen Sicherheit*. Frankfurt/M., 1980.

Nisbet, R. "Conservatism" in: Nisbet/Bottomore (eds.), *History of Sociological Analysis*. New York, 1978.

Nock, A. J. *Our Enemy: The State*. Delevan, 1983.

Nove, A. *Economic History of the USSR*. Harmondsworth, 1969.

Nozick, R. *Anarchy, State and Utopia*. New York, 1974.

Olson, M. *The Logic of Collective Action*. Cambridge, 1965.

Oppenheimer. *System der Soziologie. Vol. II Der Staat*. Stuttgart, 1964.

Osterfeld, D. "The Natural Rights Debate." *Journal of Libertarian Studies*, 1983.

Pap, A. *Semantics and Necessary Truth*. New Haven, 1958.

Parkin, F. *Class Inequality and Political Order*. New York, 1971.

Paul, R. and Lehrman, L. *The Case for Gold*. San Francisco, 1983.

Peden, J. "Property Rights in Celtic Irish Law." *Journal of Libertarian Studies*, 1977.

Pejovich, S. *Life in the Soviet Union*. Dallas, 1979.

Pirenne, H. *Medieval Cities. Their Origins and the Revival of Trade*. Princeton, 1978.

Polanyi, K. *The Great Transformation*. New York, 1944.

Popper, K. R. *Objective Knowledge*. Oxford, 1973.

____. *Conjectures and Refutations*. London, 1969.

____. *Logic of Scientific Discovery*. London, 1959.

____. *The Poverty of Historicism*. London, 1957.

Posner, R. *Economic Analysis of Law*. Boston, 1977.

Radosh, R. and Rothbard, M. N. (eds.). *A New History of Leviathan*. New York, 1972.

Rakowska-Harmstone, T. (ed.). *Communism in Eastern Europe*. Bloomington, 1984.

Rawls, J. *A Theory of Justice*. Cambridge, 1971.

Reisman, G. *Government Against the Economy*. New York, 1979.

Robbins, L. "Economics and Political Economy." *American Economic Review*, 1981.

____. *Political Economy: Past and Present*. London, 1977.

____. *Nature and Significance of Economic Science*. London, 1935.

Roepke, W. *Economics of a Free Society*. Chicago, 1963.

____. *A Humane Economy*. Chicago, 1960.

Rothbard, M. N. *The Ethics of Liberty*. Atlantic Highlands, 1982.

____. "Law, Property Rights and Pollution." *Cato Journal*, 1982.

____. "The Myth of Neutral Taxation." *Cato Journal*, 1981.

____. "The Myth of Efficiency" in: M. Rizzo (ed.) *Time, Uncertainty and Disequilibrium*. Lexington, 1979.

____. *For a New Liberty*. New York, 1978.

____. "Freedom, Inequality, Primitivism and the Division of Labor" in: K. S. Templeton (ed.) *The Politicalization of Society*. Indianapolis, 1977.

____. *Power and Market*. Kansas City, 1977.

____. "Toward a Reconstruction of Utility and Welfare Economics." Center for Libertarian Studies, Occasional Paper No. 3. New York, 1977.

____. "Ludwig von Mises and Economic Calculation Under Socialism" in: L. Moss (ed.). *The Economics of Ludwig von Mises*. Kansas City, 1976.

____. *Conceived in Liberty* (4 vols.), New Rochelle, 1975-79.

____. *Egalitarianism as a Revolt Against Nature and Other Essays*. Washington, 1974.

____. *What Has Government Done to Our Money?* Novato, 1973.

____. *Man, Economy and State* (2 vols.). Los Angeles, 1970.

Rousseau, J. *The Social Contract and Discourses* (ed. G. Cole). New York, 1950.

Rubner, A. *The Three Sacred Cows of Economics*. New York, 1970.

Samuelson, P. *Economics*. New York, 1976.

____. "The Pure Theory of Public Expenditure." *Review of Economics and Statistics*, 1954.

Schoeck, H. *Ist Leistung unanstaendig?* Osnabrueck, 1971.

____. *Envy*. New York, 1966.

Schumpeter, J. *Capitalism, Socialism and Democracy*. New York, 1942.

Schwan, G. *Sozialismus in der Demokratie. Theorie einer konsequent sozialdemokratischen Politik*. Stuttgart, 1982.

____. (ed.). *Demokratischer Sozialismus fuer Industriegesellschaften*. Frankfurt/M., 1979.

Senghaas, D. (ed.). *Imperialismus und strukturelle Gewalt*. Frankfurt/M., 1972.

Singer, M. *Generalization in Ethics*. London, 1963.

Skinner, Q. *The Foundations of Modern Political Thought*. Cambridge, 1978.

Smith, H. *The Russians*. New York, 1983.

Sombart, W. *Deutscher Sozialismus*. Berlin, 1934.

Spencer, H. *Social Statics*. London, 1851.

Spooner, L. *No Treason. The Constitution of No Authority*. Colorado Springs, 1973.

Statistisches Jahrbuch fuer die BRD. 1960.

Sterba, J. *The Demands of Justice*. Notre Dame, 1980.

Stevenson, C. L. *Facts and Values*. New Haven, 1963.

____. *Ethics and Language*. London, 1945.

Stigler, G. *The Citizen and the State. Essays on Regulation*. Chicago, 1975.

Strauss, L. *Natural Right and History*. Chicago, 1970.

Szalai, A. and Andrews, F. (eds.). *The Quality of Life*. London, 1980.

Tannehill, M. and Tannehill, L. *The Market for Liberty*. New York, 1984.

Templeton, K. S. (ed.). *The Politicalization of Society*. Indianapolis, 1977.

Thalheim, K. *Die wirtschaftliche Entwicklung der beiden Staaten in Deutschland*. Opladen, 1978.

Tigar, M. and Levy, M. *Law and the Rise of Capitalism*. New York, 1977.

Toulmin, S. *The Place of Reason in Ethics*. Cambridge, 1970.

Treue, W. *Wirtschaftsgeschichte der Neuzeit*. Stuttgart, 1973.

Trivanovitch, V. *Economic Development of Germany Under National Socialism*. New York, 1937.

Tullock, G. *Private Wants, Public Means*. New York, 1970.

Veatch, H. *Human Rights. Fact or Fancy*? Baton Rouge, 1985.

____. *For an Ontology of Morals. A Critique of Contemporary Ethical Theory*. Evanston, 1968.

____. *Rational Man. A Modern Interpretation of Aristotelian Ethics*. Bloomington, 1962.

Vonnegut, K. *Welcome to the Monkey House*. New York, 1970.

Weber, M. *Gesammelte Aufsaetze zur Wissenschaftslehre*. Tuebingen, 1922.

Weinstein, J. *The Corporate Ideal in the Liberal State*. Boston, 1968.

Wellisz, S. *The Economies of the Soviet Bloc*. New York, 1964.

Wicksell, K. *Finanztheoretische Untersuchungen*. Jena, 1896.

Wild, J. *Plato's Modern Enemies and the Theory of Natural Law*. Chicago, 1953.

Williams, B. "The Idea of Equality" in: Laslett/Runciman (eds.), *Philosophy, Politics and Society* (2nd series). Oxford, 1962.

Willis, D. K. *Klass. How Russians Really Live*. New York, 1985

Windmoeller, E. and Hoepker, T. *Leben in der DDR*. Hamburg, 1976.

Wooldridge, W. C. *Uncle Sam the Monopoly Man*. New Rochelle, 1970.

Wright, D. Mc. C. *Capitalism*. New York, 1951.

____. *Democracy and Progress*. New York, 1948.

Zapf, W. (ed.). *Lebensbedingungen in der Bundesrepublik*. Frankfurt/M., 1978.

Index

Note: A figure in parentheses following a page number indicates the number of a reference note on that page.